Sydmonton Strottons Fa. Edmond strop Summerhurst Gr. Ho. Lane Inhurst Gr. Bowling Green Beggars Gr. Pamber Forest

Pitchorn Fa. Hall Fa. Pithouse Puddinghill Axmans Ford Ham 23

Itchingswell Stanton Fa. Knowle Frith Fa. Frith Com. Baughurst Tadley Lit. Lon

Frobury Fa. Elmsgrove Sandford Town End Ho. Browning Hill Baughurst Street Comb Ho. Wyford Neville

KINGSCLERE 55 Kingsclere Delf Wootverton Str Woolverton Folse Cot Red Lion Charter Alley Pamber

Nuthanger Monks

Aqualate Sydmonton Park Woolserton Fa. Ewhurst Ramsdell Sherborne Gr. Sherborne

Cannons Lo. Stubington Ramsdell Farm Monks Sherborne

Warren Fa. Lo. Hannington Balsdon Elsworth Westgarston Up. Woolton Woolton Sher St.

Down Fa. 6 Tidgrove Nth. Oakley Tangier S. Laurence Woolton

Pool hampton Whit Lane Malshanger Manydown Worting Hou. Winkleb

Road Frosthill Somerdown Oakley Dell Worting BASINGSTO

Wellesleys Warren Ash Warren Clerken Gr. 3 Newfoundland Wst. Ham

Wetmell New Barn Harrow Way Dean 5 Hill Pla Church Oakley Battle Do. Fa. Buckskin F.

Goldings Quid hampton Poolhampton Ash 6 Dean Gate Inn Breach F. Basings Down

Norington Overton 7 Ash Pa Bills Bushes Sth. Wood Hatch Warren F.

Travellers 8 Ash Pa Steventon 3 Kempshot Ho.

Ho. Freefolk Delland Sopley Litchfield Hatch Gate Nth. Waltham Sun Inn Dummer Beechen Bury

Folly Hill Sth. Litchfield Folly 3 Nutley

Pot Bottom F. Cobley Bramley Copse 6 Popham Dummer Grange Nutley

Laverstock Wd. Popham Beacon Popham La. 6 Popham Wd.

Freefolk Wd. 9 8 Popham F. 7 Popham Breach F. Axford

Stratton Wd. Bradley Fa. B

Weston Down 10 Warren F. 8 Woodmancote Copse

Beckett's

of the environs of Basingstoke, by John Cary, ca. 1800, reproduced courtesy of Mr Philip Shewen

THE BASINGSTOKE ADMIRAL

The Basingstoke Admiral

A Life of Sir James Lancaster
(c. 1554 – 1618)

Michael Franks

with a foreword by
Andrew Lambert
Laughton Professor of Naval History, King's College, London

First published in the United Kingdom in 2006
by The Hobnob Press, PO Box 1838, East Knoyle, Salisbury SP3 6FA

British Library Cataloguing in Publication Data
A catalogue record for this book is available from the British Library.

The author and publisher acknowledge with thanks the financial contributions towards the cost of publishing this book made by Hampshire County Council and Basingstoke & Deane Borough Council.

ISBN 10 0-946418-59-4
ISBN 13 (from Jan 2007) 978-0-946418-59-6

Typeset in 11/12.5 pt Scala
Typesetting and origination by John Chandler
Printed in Great Britain by Salisbury Printing Company Ltd, Salisbury

Contents

Foreword

by Andrew Lambert
Laughton Professor of Naval History, King's College, London

In September 2004 I passed through Lancaster Sound, high in the Canadian Arctic, on board a Russian icebreaker. While my voyage was part of a research project concerned with a nineteenth century explorer I was struck the prominent place given to one of his Elizabethan precursors. Shortly after that Michael Franks contacted me, asking if I knew anything about James Lancaster. All I could offer was a little local knowledge, and a few photographs. After reading his chapters it beame clear that Lancaster had missed his chance in history, through accident or oversight, and fully deserved to be re-instated among the Tudor seafarers. His armed commercial voyages did more to build the British maritime empire than all of Drake's more spectacular raids. Lancaster's legacy was a system of oceanic commerce and an Indian Empire, Drake's little more than a heroic memory. James Lancaster richly deserves his biography, and by following his career from Hampshire through the City of London to the wider world Michael Franks has provided a lively portrait of a dynamic and ambitious businessman who was prepared to risk everything, including his life, in pursuit of wealth and knowledge. For over two hundred years navigators doubted the existence of Lancaster Sound, much as historians forgot the men whose name it carried. Now his place on the map has been reinforced by a full record of his remarkable life.

Acknowledgements

I first wish to thank Andrew Lambert, Laughton Professor of Naval History at King's College, London for his generosity over nearly three years in supervising my research and writing, and for contributing the Foreword. Professor Lambert saved me from many errors and the slipshod phraseology to which amateur historians are prone – however any inaccuracies and misjudgements which remain are down to me. He also contributed the fine photograph of Lancaster Sound (on the back cover) taken when he was on one of his naval expeditions around the globe.

In the course of research I received generous guidance and advice from the Hampshire Record Office (particularly Mr David Rymill); the Skinners' Company (particularly the Beadle, Mr Edward Hall); The College of Arms; the Instituto dos Arquivos Nacionais Torre da Tombo, Lisbon; the Reference Library at Basingstoke Public Library; the National Maritime Museum (particularly Mr. Roger Quarm, Mr Bryan Thynne and Mr David Taylor); the Guildhall Library; the British Library (both the East India Collection and the Map Room); Mr Nick Millea, Map Curator at the Bodleian Library); the National Portrait Gallery (Mr Paul Cox), the National Gallery (Dr Susan Foister) and Professor James Carley (regarding the 1596 portrait); Mrs Anne Hawker (on property ownership in Basingstoke) and Mr Denis Paravicini (on the prevalence of the Lancaster name and its variants in Portugal and Brazil).

I wish to thank the Publisher, Mr John Chandler of Hobnob Press, Salisbury, for his energy and ingenuity and to acknowledge his commitment to quality, unaffected by the tightness of our budget.

Finally, I would like to thank Mr Robert Peberdy, of the Victoria County History for Oxfordshire, both for introducing me to John Chandler and for his many ideas and suggestions about writing and publishing over several years.

Michael Franks

Introduction

James Lancaster found himself famous and a national figure when he returned to London aged 41 in 1595 after his triumphant Raid on Recife, a port in the extreme north east of Brazil. A pamphlet in extravagant language celebrating his victory was sold in the streets of London and news of the Raid spread through the capitals of Europe. A City of London syndicate had financed his tiny privateering force – which Lancaster more than tripled in size by forging alliances with other English, French and Dutch adventurers whom he met by chance in or on his way to Brazil – and he proceeded to capture and occupy Recife for a full month and return with 15 ships full of plunder worth some £ 50,000 (around £ 6 million in to-day's money).

The overall concept and bold and confident execution of the Raid displays the stamp of Drake: Lancaster had served under him as a captain of armed merchant ships in the Cadiz Raid in 1587 and in the Armada Campaign in 1588. At the same time Lancaster exhibited on his own account marked leadership qualities and commercial and entrepreneurial skill – he was an established London merchant, trained in Portugal, Spain and the Levant – as he persuaded new acquaintances to join his expedition, managing the resulting international force harmoniously, and sharing out the duties and the spoils to the satisfaction of all the participants.

This unique combination of military/naval skills, commercial flair and leadership qualities made Lancaster the obvious choice as commander[1] of the First Fleet of the East India Company five years later, in 1600. This first EIC voyage generated only modest profits but it immediately set the pattern for future voyages, established an English presence in the East Indies (the 'factories') and laid the foundations for the long, profitable life of the EIC – and thus, in due course, of the British Empire in the Eastern Hemisphere. On his return, in 1603, Lancaster was knighted by James I and 'came ashore' (at the age of 49), devoting the rest of his career to managing the EIC in London and promoting efforts to establish a 'short cut' to the East via a North West Passage.

How did such an outstanding man fall into comparative obscurity in the centuries which followed ? There are a number of possible explanations (which are considered later) but, in any case, this book seeks to restore Lancaster to his rightful position as one of the pioneers of English international trade. While the Dutch quickly overtook the English in the East Indies area itself and established a virtual monopoly there in the procurement of the spices (for which Europe had developed an insatiable appetite), their success was from the start based on force of arms and military occupation. By contrast, English international business (like all long-term successful business) was built on fair dealing and mutual advantage, and Lancaster may claim to have led the way, participating (as one of the first directors of the EIC) in laying down the rules governing how business was to be conducted and then seeing that the rules were followed on the ground.

To assess Lancaster's place in history we will describe his life and career as fully as the somewhat scanty material permits. In truth, it is an interesting story in its own right.

Lancaster lived at an exciting time for England: the country, and London in particular, was moving from being an exporter of wool and woollen cloth to engaging more generally in international trade; politically, following the failure of the Spanish/Portuguese Armada, England suddenly found itself a player in the major league – and Lancaster had a role in both these developments. On the social front, Lancaster's career showed that humble beginnings were no bar to advancement based on character and determination, and his career touched on many aspects of Elizabethan life at home and abroad – a school organized by the Basingstoke Fraternity of the Holy Ghost; the City of London in a period of dynamic expansion, with the livelier members of the Livery Companies switching from domestic business into international commerce and investment; the upsurge in interest in the wider world based on exploration and trade; government directly encouraging both international business and merchant shipping; the labyrinth of Puritanism ('the godly mafia'); the trend (still alive and well) for successful English entrepreneurs to become landed gentlemen, and so on. It is sad that Lancaster did not marry and found a dynasty, and that, while knighted as the commander of the first EIC voyage, he failed to win election as an alderman in the City of London to which he had given long and faithful service.[2]

Apart from his three main voyages (i) to the East Indies in 1591-4 (ii) the Recife Raid 1594-5 and (iii) the First Voyage of the EIC 1601-3, which are described in considerable detail by Hakluyt and Purchas, the published sources are short on hard facts about Lancaster's life. The patchy nature of the evidence – the marked imbalance between the day by day accounts of Hakluyt and Purchas covering 5-6 years and the comparatively empty other years – may well also have discouraged study of his life.

Apart from Hakluyt and Purchas, the main traditional sources for Lancaster's life and career are the article in the ODNB[3] and the valuable biographical note by Sir William Foster in his introduction to the account of the voyages published by the Hakluyt Society in 1940.[4]

Research for the preparation of this book has turned up some additional new material which throws light on Lancaster's family in North Hampshire; his schooling in Basingstoke; his launch into international trade by the London Skinners' Company; the timing of his stay in Portugal; his involvement in the Earl of Cumberland's 12th. privateering venture (in which Porto Rico was captured from the Spanish), and his involvement in five voyages in the ongoing search for a North West Passage in the early 1600s Some of this new material comes from unpublished sources[5] and some from further study of already published matter[6]

Details of the sources relied on (and the abbreviations used to refer to them in the Notes) are set out on page 204-5.

The published sources on Lancaster (referred to above) tell us that he was a native of Basingstoke; he was born probably in 1554; he probably attended the school attached to the Fraternity of the Holy Ghost in Basingstoke and that he was by birth of gentility; his father probably also being named James. Some further information is deduced from Lancaster's will, written 64 years later in 1618.

This meagre account of his beginnings may indeed be another of the reasons for the neglect from which Lancaster has suffered, since it is it hardly a firm base on which to build a biography, particularly when hard facts about the subject later in life are also in short supply.

However, we are now able to present a much fuller picture of Lancaster's origins, from new unpublished material and a re-working of the published records.[7]

From the wealth of new detail about the Lancasters generated in this way[8] we can now confidently describe several important features about Lancaster's family which, taken together, form a credible 'launching pad' for his career. Prior to this development James' life seemed something of a mystery, perhaps even a conjuring trick. According to the traditional accounts, there is his birth in Basingstoke, followed by a vague connection with Portugal. Then, suddenly he appears, aged around 34, as a fully-fledged naval captain, commanding an armed merchantman under Drake in the Armada campaign.

Now, however, we have a more complete, convincing progression leading to James' recognition as a national figure after his triumph at Recife in 1594-5.

Picture Credits

Permission to reproduce illustrations charts &c was kindly given as follows:

Front cover, Lancaster 1596 portrait, The National Maritime Museum; back cover, Lancaster Sound photograph, Professor Lambert; inside front cover, Carey's environs of Basingstoke, Mr Philip Shewen; inside back cover, London map, from Picard's Elizabeth's London, Weidenfeld & Nicholson, an imprint of Orion Publishing; p.29 Portuguese trade map and p.44.Mediterranean trading map, Mr Richard Natkiel; p.49. Photographs of race built galleon model, The Science Museum; p.84 Chart showing Recife and Pernambuco, The British Library; p.136, Map showing Frog Lane Farm, The Hampshire Record Office: p.144 NW Passage voyages after 1610 and p.147. Maps of John Davies' voyages, The Hakluyt Society; p.179. Engraving of the Basingstoke Moot Hall, Mr Robert Brown; and the extracts from facsimile charts of Linschoten on pp. 16, 70, 72, 73, 75, 110, 119, The Bodleian Library.

Part One
The Making of the Man

1

Family, Home and Education

James Lancaster's paternal forebears, the Lancasters, had arrived in Basingstoke and North Hampshire as young men some 50 years before, around 1500.[1] They were almost certainly economic migrants from the North West of England (tracing their origin to Lancaster in North Lancashire), part of a movement traceable over centuries. Like migrants everywhere, in every age, they probably had a drive to succeed in their new surroundings. They certainly did succeed, weaving cloth and acquiring houses and agricultural land. They married their daughters into some of the prominent Basingstoke families. Lancaster's father, also James (one of the 'second generation' of Lancasters in Hampshire) himself married well; his bride was Elizabeth Seagrave, whose father is variously described as a mercer, a merchant, and a fishmonger and with some connection with the bakery trade – obviously a prosperous member of the Basingstoke community. The Lancasters themselves had large families (Lancaster himself had three brothers and three sisters) and their houses were in the centre of Basingstoke, indicating prosperity and a degree of comfort. The decision of Lancaster's father in due course to apprentice both James and his brother Peter (but not the eldest brother John or the other brother, Richard, about whom we know virtually nothing) to members of the Skinners' Company in London was in line with the practice of ambitious middle-class families across England, and may, at the same time, echo the drive to succeed so often associated with migration. The same motivation may, in turn, underlie Lancaster's own rise to wealth and prominence. His whole career exemplifies single-minded commitment, careful planning and tenacity – but at the same time a marked sensitivity to the feelings of those around him and a capacity for easy relationships with all, whether peers, subordinates or superiors – an unusual and valuable trait in an age when 'rank' was an important fact of life. It seems reasonable to attribute these last two characteristics to his secure and comfortable early life within an extended family. While his family background and early life thus formed his character – which would have ensured his success in any walk of life – his choice of career (switching at around the age of 18-20 from the domestic business of making and selling furs into international commerce) seems to have resulted from a decision taken at that time by Lancaster and his father, probably following suggestions from within the Skinners' Company, based on his performance to date and the opportunities available.

Having described the Lancaster family in Basingstoke in general terms, it is convenient at this point to dispose of the attribution to James Lancaster of 'gentle birth'. This is simply incorrect, apparently resulting from the enthusiasm of the pamphleteer Henry Roberts who celebrated Lancaster's success in the Recife Raid in 1594-5 in high-flown prose and verse within weeks of his return to London in 1595. Lancaster's father was a weaver of woollen cloth (a 'draper') and a small farmer. When Lancaster was apprenticed to the Skinners' Company at around the age of 17 in 1571, his father described himself as 'husbandman' i. e. something less than a yeoman, and well below the rank of gentleman.

We started with a dearth of relations but with the material contained in the family wills unearthed from the Hampshire archives we now have a surfeit. An overall view can be obtained from studying the outline 'family trees' in Appendix II and more details about those not in Lancaster's immediate family are to be found in Appendix I. Beyond them there were more distant connections – kinsmen and 'cousins' (including relations by marriage) shading away into friends and acquaintances. It is often impossible to know where one category ends and the next begins. Most of these individuals are of limited relevance to Lancaster's life and career, but they were remembered in his will, so some description of them can be found in Appendix XII, where the legacies left by Lancaster to individuals are listed and his relationships with them considered. Where they are of greater importance to Lancaster's life, however, for example the Puritan father and son, Thomas and Samuel Crooke, and Mrs Thomasine Owfield, the rich widow who appears as part of Lancaster's household towards the end of his life, they will figure in the text later in the book.[2]

It is perhaps appropriate here to consider briefly the varying meanings for 'cousin' at this period. It seems not to mean first cousin (or cousin german): in Lancaster's will when he is referring to his first cousins he calls them 'the children of my uncle William' or 'the children of my aunt Izzard'. Again, it can describe any collateral relation, and especially a niece or nephew. Finally, like to-day's 'kinsman' or 'in-law', it can also describe more distant relations or persons related only by marriage.

Lancaster was almost certainly born in 1554.[3] Lancaster's father, also James, inherited a house in Basingstoke from his own father, Hugh Lancaster: probably it was Hugh's property known as Donte's and Heyron's, around the bottom of Wote Street, in the region of the present Bus Station and the previous Canal Dock.[4] Given the location the house probably bordered the Loddon stream. As Lancaster was one of seven children (and his father was one of six) it may be assumed that the house was of reasonable size; we know that his father combined cloth-

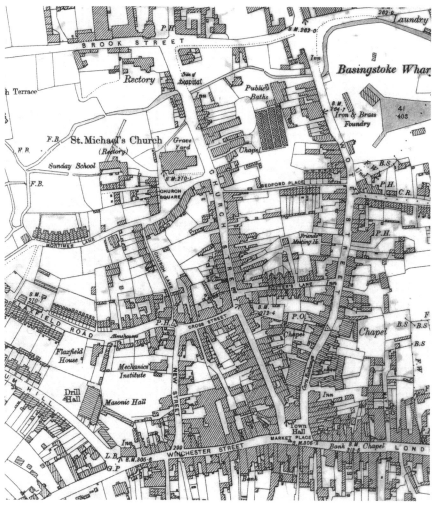

Basingstoke: the centre of the town from a 19th-century Ordnance survey map

making with farming; so it is likely that Lancaster enjoyed a comfortable start in life.

At that time there was no infant school in Basingstoke – Lancaster himself was to found a 'petty school' by his will in 1618 – so it looks as though he commenced his schooling at around the age of seven. It has always been assumed that Lancaster attended the boys' school attached to the Guild and Chapel of the Holy Ghost in Basingstoke, since by his will he left money to it. This assumption is strengthened by the donations to the Holy Ghost Guild/Chapel[5] made by Lancaster's great uncle Richard, his father and his uncle William, and by the fact that in the 1560s the Aldermen and Wardens of the Guild included men related by marriage to the Lancasters. The school was sited in the buildings of the Holy Ghost Chapel, the ruins of which still stand on the small hill to the north of Basingstoke railway station.

Ruins of the Holy Ghost Chapel and School

The original Holy Ghost Chapel was built at the end of the 1208-14 'Interdict' (the dispute between the Papacy and the English Crown over the appointment of the Archbishop of Canterbury) during which the dead of Basingstoke were buried in unconsecrated ground: it was known as the Liten. Certainly the Chapel in the burial ground had been completed by 1244. The Chapel was enlarged around 1520 by Lord Sandys, a local magnate who owned the Vyne estate three miles to the north of Basingstoke, by the addition of a Chapel of the Holy Trinity, in which in due course he was buried in 1542. The Guild or Fraternity of the Holy Ghost had become attached to the Chapel before 1525, since in 1524 Henry VIII granted a charter to 'A Guild or Fraternity in honour of the Holy Ghost', with an Alderman and two Wardens. Such guilds or fraternities were common all over England from mediaeval times. Some were trade guilds, organizing and monitoring particular trades (in London they were the precursors of the Livery Companies). Others, like the Holy Ghost guild in Basingstoke were more in the nature of friendly societies, organizing Christian worship, mutual support, social activities (including an annual 'feast') and education.

Because of their religious nature such guilds were affected by the Reformation. The property of the Holy Ghost Guild was accordingly acquired by Edward VI in 1550 but, following a petition in 1556, a new charter of incorporation was granted in 1557 by Philip and Mary which revived the Guild and restored its property. The Guild was to provide a priest 'not only for the celebration of Divine Service within the said Chapel, but also for the education and instruction of young men and boys within the said town'. For a short time – until the death of Queen Mary in 1558 – it appears from the nature of expenditure recorded in the Wardens' accounts that the Chapel maintained pre-Reformation images and rituals. Thereafter, the religious side of the Guild faded and the educational side was emphasized. Basingstoke seems to have accepted without fuss the 'middle way' religious policy followed by Queen Elizabeth, although Lancaster's Puritan friends, when intriguing over securing a Puritan to occupy the Lectureship established at Basingstoke by Lancaster and his cousin Sir James Deane around 1609, played up (probably without any justification) the irreligious character and Romish tendencies of the townsfolk.[6] The Accounts of the Wardens have survived[7] from the re-establishment of the Guild of the Holy Ghost in 1557 until 1658 and provide corroboration of the Lancaster family's connection with the school. Obtaining the new charter (granted by Philip and Mary) cost £25 15s. 4d. (much of it spent on lawyers and on procuring the application of the Great Seal by the Lord Chancellor). The townsfolk were invited to subscribe – and £14 16s. 4d. was raised. There were some 94 subscribers. Five subscribed 20/- each and others varying, lower amounts, down to 1d. Lancaster's father gave 4d. and his uncle William 12d. Other well-known Basingstoke names appear in the subscription list – Holloway, Stocker, Massam, Deane, Hall (Richard Hall was the first warden of the re-established Guild), and Blunden. In addition to the fees paid for tuition (until the school became free in 1609) the Guild could look to income from rent from its properties, which included a mill and various parcels of land in and around the town, together with 100 acres of arable land in the 'open fields'; fees for burials in the Chapel; and the organization of 'ales' (drinking parties for which the Guild brewed the beer or ale and sold it to the guests). Together with the Wardens' Accounts are listings of the Aldermen and Wardens for the 1557-1658 period. While no Lancaster figures here, it is interesting to find families with which the Lancasters were connected – the Deanes, Yeates and Massams. The schoolmaster in the 1570s was Richard Deane who appears to have been the brother of Sir James Deane,[8] and thus a kinsman of the Lancasters. The schoolmaster was paid £10-12 per year, but when – as quite often happened – the teaching duties were undertaken by the rector of Basingstoke the stipend dropped to £4-5 per year. This circumstantial evidence for Lancaster's attendance at the Holy Ghost School suggests equally that his brothers – John, Peter and Richard – were also pupils there.

We have no other direct evidence of this stage of Lancaster's life. No doubt he helped in the drapers' workshop and on his father's land after school and at harvest-time. When he completed his schooling, perhaps aged 14 or 15, Lancaster may have worked full-time on the land, or perhaps in the family weaving business, during the two years before he set off to commence his apprenticeship in London. We can safely assume that his schooling, and that of his younger brother Peter, was satisfactory, since apprentices needed to display competence in reading, writing and figuring.[9]

Lancaster was apprenticed to a member of the Skinners' Company in 1571 when he was around 17 years old: while many of the London apprentices came from middle-class families all over England, and Scotland, we have no explanation as to how James' father chose the Skinners. Since their cousin Sir James Deane was a Draper, apprenticeship to the Drapers' Company might have been expected.

2

The London Apprentice[1]

When Lancaster arrived in London in the 1570s the City was in a period of high activity and rapid growth. Throughout the century the population had increased, from under 50,000 around 1500 to about 85,000 in 1565 and the increase was to accelerate to around 140,000 in 1600 within the City proper, plus another 40,000 in the 'suburbs'. (There is a slight complication here, since 'the City' included some land outside the walls – particularly on the south bank of the Thames: Southwark was also known as the ward of 'Bridge Without'). The City was crowded, smelly and unhealthy – there was no drainage system and every few years there were outbreaks of the plague – and there was a permanent lack of accommodation. Deaths consistently outnumbered births so the population increase required constant immigration, estimated at 5,000 souls per year, mostly young men coming to seek their fortune. They came from all over England, and also from Scotland.

With its central position in the country, and a large, safe, tidal harbour in the Thames virtually facing Europe, London was predominant in England both in manufacturing and in trade – domestic and overseas – the latter being mainly with Europe in the earlier part of the 16th century. London, it was said, 'devoured' the business of many English provincial towns. What we now call 'financial services' – and associate immediately with the City of London – developed slowly in the course of the 16th century: in banking, trade financing, insurance &c. England was still well behind Europe. The orientation of overseas trade changed markedly around 1570, when Antwerp, which had been the main entrepot centre for Northern Europe, became unavailable. In addition to goods, the Low Countries exported to London Protestant ideas ahead of the Reformation and the City accepted the religious changes when they came, apparently quite content with the 'middle way' in religion pursued by Queen

Elizabeth. Indeed, the nationalization of church property was probably particularly welcome in the City, where, within the walls, the priests were regarded as parasitical and, without, the landscape was dominated by Bishops' palaces (known as 'Inns') along the north bank of the Thames and by church agricultural estates surrounding the City in all directions. When the expropriated buildings and land were immediately sold off a property boom erupted, particularly within the City. Religious buildings were turned into workshops, warehouses, stables and so on, and grand residences were constructed. (Lancaster later in life lived in a large house in St. Mary Axe which was built on the site of a redundant church, St Augustine Papeye – a previous occupant had been Sir Thomas Walsingham)[2] Amid the turmoil of property development special arrangements were made to preserve St. Bartholomew's and St. Thomas' Hospitals; and the Bethlehem Hospital (Bedlam) combined with Bridewell (prison/workhouse) and Christ's Hospital school and orphanage (ex Greyfriars).

The Reformation caused the closure of some schools connected with religious houses but new schools were started so that there was a strong net gain. During Elizabeth's reign 136 grammar schools were endowed and by 1600 70% of Londoners were literate. This in turn stimulated printing and the publication of pamphlets, ballads, almanacks, prints, popular stories and so on.[3]

The bulk of London's population lived within the walls, and as it increased, there was a movement of the heavier industries towards the east end of the City, and of the 'up-market' activities like tailoring, gold- and silver-smithing, silk retailing, together with private houses, towards the west end – and even outside the walls, attracted by the magnet of the Royal Court at Westminster. In Elizabethan times 'the Court' consisted of around 1500 individuals whom we might now describe, in marketing terms, as being of 'high net worth'.[4] In general the practitioners of particular trades had their shops, workshops (and homes) in the same street or neighbourhood within the City. In the compressed area of the City (which then, as now, can easily be covered on foot) and just outside it – there were many interests and attractions for the leisure hours of a hard-working business community. There were around 100 City parishes with their own churches for Sundays and other holy days; playhouses, mainly on the periphery outside the City's jurisdiction, to the north and on the south bank of the Thames (the first, 'The Theatre', was erected in 1576 in Shoreditch, and, subsequently, dismantled, moved and re-erected south of the River)); innumerable taverns and ale house; public executions; bull- and bear-baiting south of the river; brothels (also mainly over the water); the Inns of Court – primarily a training ground for the

English Bar, but also an effective third university (after Oxford and Cambridge), a finishing school for young men-about-town and a nucleus of literary and intellectual life; the social and ceremonial activities of the Livery Companies and the City's civic government; and, for those with social ambitions, the Royal Court itself.

The City was organized and managed by two intertwined organizations – the Livery Companies and the Civic Government. The Livery Companies (of which there were about 65 by 1600) were authorized by the Crown to oversee every industry or trade. Derived from the mediaeval guilds they were responsible for promoting the trade; admitting new members and supervising their training; regulating the trade and exercising quality control; settling disputes; preventing non-members from exercising the trade; dispensing charity to members and their dependants and supporting the Lord Mayor and the City as a whole. The Livery Companies were managed by a Master or Warden and assistant Wardens (elected annually) supported by a 'Court' consisting of past-masters and promising younger members on their way up the ladder. Below the Court were the members, originally one homogeneous body, but by the 16th century sub-divided into the 'livery' i. e. those entitled to wear the distinctive uniform of the company, who were elected to that rank, and the ordinary members, sometimes described as 'the yeomanry'. Membership of a Company was obtainable by (i) Patrimony i. e. presentation of a son by his father (ii) Redemption, by payment of an entrance fee, or (iii) Apprenticeship (or 'servitude'), the most usual method. As we will see Lancaster, and his brother Peter, entered the Skinners' Company by apprenticeship. A new member was thus presented with a cursus honorum which he might aspire to climb.

Traditionally there were (and are) 12 'Great Companies' of which the Skinners' Company ranks 6th or 7th (their position alternating each year with the Merchant Taylors – this being the Solomonic solution imposed by the City authorities to settle a dispute over precedence).[5] By the 16th century the Mercers and Grocers were dominant in the City, reflecting their commercial importance. The richer Companies acquired (and retain) extensive premises in the City, including magnificent Halls and possessions. They endowed, and still manage, substantial charities, particularly schools, for example, Merchant Taylors, Oundle, Tonbridge, Gresham's and Haberdashers' Askes, and they organized extensive social and ceremonial activities both within their premises and elsewhere in the City.

Viewed from the outside the Livery Companies appear somewhat forbidding, monolithic, even feudal. In practice, however, while there were some short cuts and preferences for a privileged few, they proved successful.[6] While all members were looking to advance themselves the overall objective – the prosperity of the Company – ensured that in general members rose by merit. With a pyramid structure it is obvious that not all can reach the top and, at every level, while there are duties there are also privileges. Further, belonging to a strong community offers security, social attractions and the reassurance that support will be forthcoming if one falls on hard times.

It is interesting to note that already by the 16th century some members joined Livery Companies not to learn and practice the trade of the Company but to use their apprenticeship and membership as a commercial education and a stepping-stone to some other trade or calling, in particular international trade, and to obtain the freedom of the City of London.[7] It is impossible to generalize as to whether this trend was the cause or the effect of the traditional activity of the Livery Companies declining or disappearing altogether. In the case of the Skinners, as examined below, it certainly seems to have resulted from the fall-off in the fur trade. This trend has continued down to the present day, when most (though not all) of the old Companies have no connection with any trade or industry (and their officers are no longer the 'movers and shakers' in international business) but function as social or dining clubs with priceless premises in the City of London in which they manage their charitable activities and enjoy their social and ceremonial events. James and Peter Lancaster appear not to have been following this trend initially, when they were originally apprenticed, but to have joined it when they were 'turned over', that is were transferred to work under different members of the Skinners' Company who were not working furriers but international merchants.

Complementary to the Livery Companies was the Civic Government of the City of London. Here we see the members of the Livery Companies as citizens of London. (By the second half of the 16th century about 75% of the male inhabitants of London were qualified as citizens). Here there is another pyramid structure and a parallel cursus honorum to climb. At the top is the Lord Mayor (elected annually), supported by an executive body – the Court of Aldermen (elected for life by the 26 'wards': these were and are civic districts of the City each containing several parishes). Below is the Court of Common Council of some 200 members, elected annually from the wards. Below again is the Common Hall, the general body of the citizens, which met only occasionally. The focus of authority is with the Aldermen who formed, literally, a self-perpetuating oligarchy. Despite the pejorative implications of that description, the system worked well in practice, for the same reasons noted above in relation to the Livery Companies. While there was considerable inter-marrying between the aldermanic families, no long-term dynasties developed (like the juntas in some European cities): promoting the general interests of the City and the need to bring on the next generation of able and dynamic men ensured that the pool of aldermen was constantly replenished. At a lower level were the local jurisdictions of the wards and parishes.

It is convenient at this point to describe a third group of organizations which appeared around the middle of the 16th century – the chartered Trading Companies. They are the precursors of our modern joint stock companies, in that the members came together to pursue a stated commercial objective. The Trading Companies were formed (by Royal Charter) to conduct, as a monopoly, international trade to a particular destination or within a specified geographical area. Since international trade has foreign policy implications, they represent an interesting Tudor government experiment in encouraging such trade while retaining some government control – at no cost to the government. (A further advantage was that the Queen and her friends and statesmen could invest in the trading companies and take profits if they were successful; while if they got into international political scrapes their activities could be curbed on a deniable basis) Since such charters were granted in the Queen's name, by the Privy Council, there was scope for courtiers to lobby on behalf of the promoters in return for ' a share of the action' – not always popular with the City merchants. The trading companies chartered by 1600 included:

> 1555 Russia or Muscovy Company
> 1577 Spanish/Portuguese Company (there had been an earlier charter in 1530)
> 1579 Eastland Company (Norway, Sweden, Lithuania, Prussia and the Baltic Sea)
> 1581 Turkey/Levant Company
> 1583 Venice Company
> 1585 Barbary Company (North Africa)
> 1588 Africa Company (Senegal and Gambia)
> 1592 2nd Levant Company (incorporating the Venice Company)
> 1600 East India Company (East Indies)

It was in these Trading Companies – specifically the Spanish/Portuguese Company, the Turkey/Levant Company and the East India Company – that Lancaster was to make his career. The main promoters of the Trading Companies were a small number of outstanding City merchants – these were to be Lancaster's patrons at the outset and, later, his colleagues.[8] As with all new commercial ventures, success depends on (i) the promoter with the idea or vision (ii) the necessary financial resources and (iii) the key 'managers' – leaders, ship captains, pilots/ navigators, merchants, pursers and so on – who can convert the promoter's vision into a profitable business. Lancaster in the formative years of his career fell into the third category – he was one of the men 'who made it happen'.[9]

Apprenticeship was the usual path for entry to a Livery Company. A formal apprenticeship deed was entered into between the apprentice and his master. A premium or fee was payable by the apprentice's father. The apprentice 'bound himself' to serve and obey the master and the master undertook to instruct him in the trade or 'mystery', provide board and lodging and sometimes also clothing.[10] In general the form and contents of these deeds, and the conduct of apprenticeships were supervised and monitored by the Livery Company in question. The deeds themselves rarely survive, but the Companies maintained registers recording the execution of the deeds and of the apprentice's entry as a member of the Company on successful completion of the apprenticeship – this step was described as 'becoming free of the Company'. Apprentices had to start before they were 21. The normal starting age was 14-16, though there were a few at an earlier age, and some at a later. The length of the apprenticeship was typically in the range 6-8 years, but the Statute of Artificers 1563 laid down a minimum of seven years: though it appears that this was not always observed in practice. It was usual for the apprentice to live with the master's family, which was normally 'over the shop' at the working premises, and help with household tasks as well as the business. The master and his wife were responsible for the general welfare and behaviour of the apprentice, including his attendance at church, learning his catechism and so on. It appears that London apprentices were normally dressed in blue – as a result this was not a popular colour with fashion-conscious Londoners.[11] Masters of apprentices had to be of a certain age, usually at least 25, and there were limits on how many apprentices they might take on. Girls were occasionally apprenticed to members of Livery Companies, for example to become pinmakers. Female 'masters' were very rare.

Apprentices were sometimes 'turned over': this means that a new master was substituted for the original one. This could happen in two types of case. First, as a result of circumstances, for example, if the original master died or retired or there was a falling-out between master and apprentice. Secondly, a 'turn over' might be arranged as a kind of career move if the apprentice (or more probably his father) reckoned that the apprentice should switch to a different trade or even to a different Livery Company. Both Lancaster and his brother Peter were turned over – with a view, it would seem, to their abandoning the Skinners' trade and becoming involved in trading with Portugal or Spain.

The romantic image of the apprentice marrying the master's daughter and succeeding to the master's business is based on reality. This seems to have happened in as many as 25% of apprenticeships.

Lancaster was apprenticed in 1571 (aged around 17) to one Blasse (or Blaise) Freeman, a member of the Skinners' Company in the City of London.[12] The apprenticeship was to last for 10 years – in fact Lancaster finished and became free of the Company after 8 years in 1579 i. e. when he was around 25.[13] It was at that time very common for provincial middle class families all over England, and also in Scotland, to enter their sons in London apprenticeships (and also for gentry, usually for younger sons). They would, at the least, learn a trade and gain employment and there were good opportunities for further financial and social advancement. The ultimate ambition was to gain a fortune and buy land. We do not know why Lancaster's father picked the Skinners' Company. There is no record of any earlier connection and the Lancasters' cousin Sir Richard Deane was a Draper, so an introduction to that Company might have been more likely.

The Skinners' Company was chartered by Edward III in 1327, bringing together several guilds or fraternities which had existed from an earlier date. The trade on which these guilds and the company were based was that of furriers – the manufacture and sale of furs for use in lining and decorating the garments of persons of rank. The Company was thus one of the oldest and counted royalty and aristocrats among is members. However, by the middle of the 16th century the use of fur had declined. Many reasons are suggested, for example – Houses had become more comfortable; England was simply following a European trend; the population of fur-producing animals was decreasing; the influence of the sumptuary laws – but the overriding one appears to have been a change of fashion – 'furs ceased altogether to be the favourite vehicle for the display of great wealth',[14] and velvets and silks took over. This sharp decline was reflected in the composition of the Company: in the mid 16th century (Lancaster was apprenticed in 1571 and his brother Peter in 1576) none of the prominent members was a skinner by trade, and by 1606 hardly a quarter of the 'Court' (the governing body of the Company) were working skinners.[15] It seems highly likely, therefore that the 'turnover' of James and Peter Lancaster to new masters (who were international traders rather than furriers) followed 'talent-spotting' among the new apprentices joining the Company.

The Skinners' Company had and has extensive premises on Dowgate Hill in the City of London, including a magnificent hall built after the Great Fire to replace the mediaeval hall. In addition to other

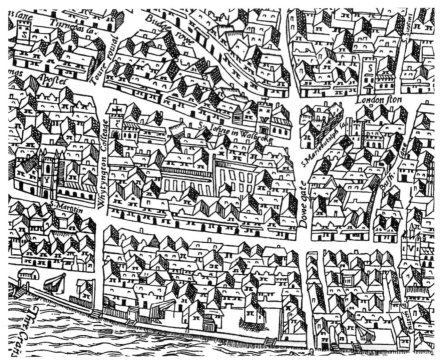

Dowgate Street, Budge Row and Walbrook – the Skinners' heartland

valuable and interesting possessions the Company has a fine portrait of Lancaster – apparently copied from the original which is now in the National Maritime Museum.[16] Until the Great Fire in 1666 the Company had a close association with the church of St. John the Baptist upon Walbrook, but the church was not rebuilt after the Fire.

In the 16th century the Skinners had their workshops and homes in two areas of the City, reflecting the two (or more) earlier guilds which were combined in the Company (i) near St. Mary Axe (the church was sometimes called St. Mary Pellipar – 'Pellipar' or 'pelliparius' is the mediaeval latin description of a furrier or skinner) and St. Andrew Undershaft (ii) near the Company's premises on Dowgate Hill, in Walbrook and Budge Row ('Budge' is the trade description of a superior lamb skin, derived from the name of a small Moorish kingdom, Bougie, in North Africa)[17] An early ordinance of the Company did in fact require all freemen of the trade 'to dwell in Walbrook, Cornhill or Budge Row'. The Walbrook stream was important to the Skinners, since 'tawing', the preparation of skins, required water.[18]

While we have no direct evidence it does therefore seem likely that Blaise Freeman lived and worked in the Walbrook/Budge Row area, and that Lancaster lived there with him.[19] It seems likely, too, that Freeman was a working Skinner, since a member of the Company named Freeman gave evidence to the Court of the Company in 1582 when it was adjudicating on a dispute concerning the quality of some skins.[20]

As already noted, Lancaster was 'turned over' in the course of his apprenticeship. We do not know at what date, but his new master was another Skinner, Robert Walkeden. Robert's father, Geoffrey Walkeden was also a Skinner and had been Master of the Company in 1576-7 and again in 1582 (apparently in the place of a Master who died in office): he was also an assistant (i. e. a director) of the Russia or Muscovy Company, and he died in around 1587. The new master was thus a prominent member of the Company, and he had international interests which give a pointer to Lancaster's future career. He was a founder member of the Spanish/Portuguese Company in 1577 and of the Barbary Company in 1585, and had some commercial connections with Brazil.[21] In view of these interests, and the fact that Lancaster's turnover took place, we may assume that Robert Walkeden (unlike Blaise Freeman) was not in the domestic Skinners' trade.

Lancaster claimed later in his life (in words attributed to him by Hakluyt) that he 'lived in Portugal as a merchant', but no other direct evidence of this has yet come to light;[22] so the connection with Robert Walkeden provides some corroboration, particularly as this connection resulted from a 'turn over' i. e. a planned change of direction. It is reasonable to assume, therefore, that the 'turnover' was arranged by Lancaster, or more likely his father, with the intention that he should enter the Portuguese trade. This 'turnover' to a prominent Skinner also suggests that Lancaster's performance to date recommended him for this career move away from London furrier business into international trade.

Apart from this, we have no direct knowledge of Lancaster's time as an apprentice, but it looks as though, in Hogarth's classic definition, he might be classified as an 'industrious prentice' rather than an 'idle' one, resisting the temptations close to hand of the masters' daughters and maidservants, taverns, theatres, brothels, cock-fighting, bull- and bear-baiting, and the general yobbish lifestyle to which London apprentices appear regularly to have succumbed (football, in particular, then as now, seems to have often degenerated into fighting, especially on the Shrove Tuesday holiday). Apprentices were not allowed to wear swords, but they seem to have carried cudgels or clubs: if an apprentice became involved in trouble – which seems to have occurred quite often – a cry of 'Clubs' was the signal for other apprentices to come to his assistance.

We have already noted that masters of apprentices (and their wives) were responsible for the general behaviour of the young men. Lancaster no doubt attended church regularly, and there were many churches close at hand to pick from. At some time in his life Lancaster formed close associations with some prominent Puritan churchmen, in particular with the father and son Thomas and Samuel Crooke. We will explore these connections later in this book,[23] but it seems possible that Lancaster first came under this influence as a young man, soon after the completion of his apprenticeship. Thomas Crooke was appointed Preacher to Grays' Inn in 1581 (and held this appointment until his death in 1598).[24] At that time non-members were admitted to services in Grays' Inn Chapel, so it may be that Lancaster's link with the 'godly preachers' originated at this time. We described above the glamour and intellectual attractions associated with the Inns of Court, so that may also have been a factor to draw him towards Gray's Inn, at that time the largest and most fashionable Inn.[25]

While not directly relevant to Lancaster's development the experience of his brother Peter as a Skinner does throw some light on his career. We can assume that Peter was approximately five years younger,

Grays' Inn Chapel and Hall, rebuilt after WWII

since he was apprenticed in 1576, some five years after James.[26] His first master was a Skinner (and Merchant Adventurer) named Roger Jenkins. The reference to Peter's completion of his apprenticeship raises some questions, as he appears to have been admitted as a member of the Company only in 1597 i. e. some 21 years after being apprenticed.[27] In the meantime he had been 'turned over' to a new master Sir Richard Saltonstall – we do not know exactly when. It was not invariably the case that an apprentice, immediately on completing his time, became free of his company; and a number of apprentices fell out without completing their time. A common reason was inability to pay the appropriate fee to the company: that may be the case here, or there may be some other reason, for example ill-health or absence abroad. We simply do not know – though in the light of subsequent events shortage of cash may have been a factor.

What is interesting is the standing of Peter's new master. Sir Richard Saltonstall. He was one of the leading merchants of his day, being Governor of the Merchant Adventurers, an original director of the Spain /Portugal Company in 1577 and a grantee of the (second) Levant Company in 1592. He also assisted the Government in raising money. He was Master of the Skinners' Company (four times), elected an Alderman in 1588 and Lord Mayor in 1597. Peter's turnover to him suggests a plan for him, like James, to enter the Spanish/Portuguese trade. Again, since Saltonstall was Lord Mayor in the year in which Peter was (eventually) admitted to freedom of the Skinners' Company the long delay cannot have reflected adversely on Peter.

Whatever Peter did, once admitted to freedom, he must have made some progress and remained 'in good standing' with the Skinners' Company, since in 1605 (when he was around 45) he was elected a Warden of the 'Yeomanry'.[28] However, disaster struck. He had been appointed a Warden in September 1605. In December the same year Peter found himself unable to pay his share (£4) of a Royal loan which had been levied on the City by the King and passed on by the Lord Mayor to all the Livery Companies. On demonstrating to the Court of the Skinners' Company that his net worth was less than £100 Peter was relieved of his obligation to subscribe to the loan – but also of his office as Warden of the Yeomanry.[29] We have no more information about Peter Lancaster except that he appears never to have married, and that he survived James, being appointed an overseer of his will and receiving a legacy of £200 plus a lease of property when James died in 1618.

With Lancaster established by turnover as an apprentice to Robert Walkeden our next task is to consider the circumstances in which he entered the Portuguese trade: but before doing that we will divert to give a brief overview of the Oriental Spice Trade down to the 1590s. The trade in spices formed the background to the move into international trade by England (and other European countries) and, more specifically, to the businesses of the Spain/Portugal, Turkey/Levant and East India Companies in which Lancaster was to become engaged.

Part Two
Beyond the Seas

3
The Oriental Spice Trade to the 1590s[1]

'Close sailing from Bengala, or the Iles/ Of Ternate and Tidore,
whence merchants bring/ Thir spicie drugs'
Milton, *Paradise Lost* (1638) II. 638

The Spice Trade formed the background to the whole of James'
commercial career, once he had switched from the Skinners' furriers
business to international trade, so that a brief description of it will make
it easier to follow his involvement in Portugal, Spain, the Levant trade
and the voyages to the Indies.[2]

In this context we are looking principally at pepper (the most
important commodity by volume), cloves, nutmeg and mace, cinnamon
and ginger. A detailed description of these spices is set out in Appendix
III.

Spices have been used from time immemorial for flavouring food
and drinks and also for medicinal purposes. Because it is easy to keep
them fresh and in view of their extremely high value in relation to their
weight and bulk, spices have been traded since the earliest times over
enormous distances. By the time that they reached Northern Europe,
possibly in the 12th century, they had an added attraction. Prior to modern
agricultural developments it was impossible to over-winter stock on any
scale, so that during most of the year meat from domestic stock was far
from fresh: nutmeg could both slow the process of deterioration and
improve the flavour. English interest in oriental spices may have been
roused by the First Crusade: their use was well known by Chaucer's time.

This traditional view – that oriental spices enabled Northern
Europeans to stomach meat that was old or bad or both – has been
challenged by Professor John Munro of Toronto University.[3] An economic
historian, Professor Munro, on both historical and culinary grounds,

maintains that (i) spices were a luxury (not a necessity), used to enhance the taste of meat and fish and also sauces, soups, vegetables, pies, cakes, jams, jellies and drinks (ii) if meat needed to be preserved there were cheaper and more efficient ways of doing this, for example, salting, pickling or smoking (iii) the demand for oriental spices in Northern Europe fell away towards the end of the 17th century, long before refrigeration was available. Professor Munro's arguments are persuasive and it must be admitted that contemporary recipes and accounts of feasts on special occasions (two are given below) suggest that spices were indeed employed to improve fresh meat and fish and the other dishes mentioned above.

Whichever explanation is correct there is no doubt that spices were extremely popular in England by the 16th century, even if their price meant that the rich used them frequently and the less well off only on special occasions.

By the 16th century in England, too, physicians and apothecaries were prescribing various concoctions based on spices to cure or prevent the Plague, which broke out in England, particularly London, every few years. It is not thought that these medicines were in any way effective, but in the desperate state of medical ignorance they were snapped up by those rich enough to afford them. Cloves were also claimed to be effective as an aphrodisiac.

The Clown in 'The Winter's Tale' (1611) asks 'What am I to buy for our sheep-shearing feast ?' and continues 'Three pound of sugar, five pound of currants, rice, what will this sister of mine do with rice ?. . I must have saffron, to colour the warden pies; mace, dates – none of that's out of my note, nutmegs seven, a race or two of ginger – but that I may beg; four pound of prunes and as many of raisins o' the sun'. A feast indeed.

A similar account comes from closer to home. The Guild which managed James Lancaster's school in Basingstoke (the Fraternity of the Holy Ghost), like many other guilds across England, held an annual feast or dinner.[4] The accounts of the Guild for the 1558 feast tell the story:

> (i) Payments for meat – two loins of mutton, three sheep and a calf, totalling £1 2s. 4d.
> (ii) For other provisions – 2 ½ lbs of butter, a gallon of cream and eggs, totalling 2s. 3d.
> (iii) Miscellaneous items – three dozen spoons, two salts, four dozen of trenchers, faggots for baking the pies and boiling the meat, a man to tend the fire, totalling 5s. 6d.

(iv) Nails to make our booth (the temporary building in which the feast was held) 2d.

(v) Finally the spices and 'treats'. (The price per pound calculation on the right has been added to indicate comparative costs):-

	£	s	d	Price per Pound £	s	d
¾ pound pepper			23		2	7
6 pounds prunes			9			1½
½ oz mace			5		13	4
2 oz cloves			10		6	8
4 lbs currants			20			5
12 lbs great raisins		2	0			2
3 lbs sugar		2	3			9
Saffron			3			
			3			
Total		**10**	**1**			

The grand total cost of the feast was £ 2 0s. 4d. It looks as though drinks were paid for on the spot as there is an item 'receyved at the diner' £2 19s. 0d.[5] Received separately, by way of contributions to the feast, was £1 3s. 8d. , part in cash, part in kind; so the Guild's finances seem to have been in good shape.

Another slightly different angle on the consumption of spices is stressed by Beaumont & Fletcher in *The Knight of the Burning Pestle* (1613):

'Nose, nose, jolly red nose
And who gave thee that jolly red nose ?
Nutmegs and ginger, cinnamon and cloves
And they gave me this jolly red nose'

The most concentrated source of pepper, cloves and nutmeg was found in the Molucca Islands (often called simply The Spice Islands), a small group of tiny islands (including Ternate, Tidore, Amboina, Banda and Rum) in the extreme east of the Indonesian Archipelago (see map overleaf). The combination of volcanic soil and tropical climate appears to be responsible.

These and the other spices were also found in other eastern countries, for example in Java (pepper, nutmeg, cloves), Nicobar (cloves), Borneo (pepper), Sichuan, in China, (cloves, ginger, cinnamon), the Malabar Coast (pepper, cinnamon, ginger), Gujarat (pepper, ginger), Ceylon (cinnamon) and so on.

It seems that originally the spices were collected from the plants growing wild, and indeed this was still often the case in the 16th century.

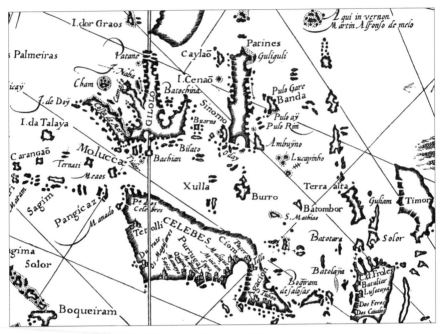

The Spice Islands (Moluccas)

The next step, over many years, was to cultivate the plants in the same countries. Later again, by trial and error, transplantation took place to other countries found to be suitable, for example Zanzibar for cloves and in more modern times, Grenada for nutmeg and mace. The Chinese were particularly skilled at this aspect of husbandry and may have led the way.

Until the 15th century the trade in oriental spices was in the hands of Chinese and Arab (particularly Omani) merchants, with the additional involvement of Gujaratis and other communities of the Indian peninsular (not Hindus, since embarking themselves or their produce on board ship raised religious problems). The international wholesale trade was mainly conducted by sea and was on a very large scale. Using the convenient two-way pattern of the monsoons, spices were carried from their sources to all the seaports from China and Japan in the east to Sofala on the south east coast of Africa – this was the southern extremity of the monsoon system. Along this extensive trading route large entrepot seaports developed, where stocks of spices were held for sale, together with all the other products which were traded around the Indian Ocean region – Chinese porcelain and silk, Venetian glass, Arabian horses, Indian cloth, Gujerati leather, pearls, precious stones and so on. The main entrepot ports were Malacca, Calicut, Hormus, Aden, Malindi and Sofala.

A comparatively small offshoot of the Indian Ocean trade supplied spices to the Mediterranean, at least from Roman times. The relative scale is illustrated by an observation made by Marco Polo in around 1280, when visiting the Chinese port of Zaiton (on the mainland opposite Taiwan: now known as Qanxhou) 'And I assure you that for one spice ship that goes to Alexandria or elsewhere to pick up pepper for export to Christendom, Zaiton is visited by a hundred. For you must know that it is one of the two ports in the world with the biggest flow of merchandise.'[6]

There were three routes to the European market. The first was by sea up the Red Sea, where the cargoes were either transferred into smaller vessels to travel by canal to the Nile and thence to Alexandria or carried overland to the Levant ports. The second was by sea to the Persian Gulf and then overland (perhaps with some river travel on the Tigris and Euphrates) to the Aleppo/Tripolis area. The third route was an extension of the Chinese Silk Route, ending by ship along the Black Sea to Constantinople.

From the Eastern Mediterranean the spices were shipped, almost exclusively, by Venetians to Venice and from there overland to Antwerp, the centre of the Northern European trade.

It will be apparent that a newcomer to the trade could, in principle, buy spices anywhere in the Mediterranean and Indian Ocean regions. It was not necessary to go to their source, though the higher costs and risks of doing so might be more than offset by lower purchase prices.[7] Cheapest of all would be to steal spices already on the high seas. However, these considerations and developments still lay in the future.

The dominant traders and shippers in the Indian Ocean were the Chinese. The challenging work of Gavin Menzies (published in 2002) '1421 – The year the Chinese discovered the World' suggests that, by the early 1400s, the Chinese Imperial 'Treasure Ship Fleets' not only were the largest traders across the vast Indian Ocean region but also exercised considerable political influence. Menzies contends that the final, and largest treasure ship fleet (or more accurately five separate fleets), launched in 1421, went on beyond the limit of the monsoon pattern to round the Cape of Good Hope, and visited West Africa, the east and west coasts of America (both north and south) – passing through the Magellan Strait just under 100 years before Magellan arrived to name it – approached the North and South Poles, and sailed back home across the Pacific, across the Southern Ocean – visiting Australia and New Zealand – and by the North East Passage above the Asian land mass.

The trading activities of the final Chinese treasure fleets, according to Menzies, in the event fell short of what had been planned since they could find little worth buying until they returned to their traditional Indian

Ocean region, but this disappointment was more than offset by their staggering achievements in other fields, which Menzies describes: in astronomy and navigation – they established the star Canopus as the southern navigational aid to match the North Star, and a system of measuring longitude, based on the observation of lunar eclipses, over 300 years before Harrison's chronometer; in cartography – charts based on Chinese observations smoothed the path for Portuguese and Spanish voyages of 'discovery'; useful plants and animals were transplanted both to and from China; colonies were established; and minerals were prospected, worked and brought back to China.

The claims by Menzies that the 1421 Treasure Fleets (i) sailed on beyond the Cape of Good Hope (ii) produced charts and navigational information which, incorporated in early western charts, enabled the European 'explorers' to have in advance a good idea of what they were looking for, have been hotly contested by professional historians and the debate seems set to continue. Clearly there is a wealth of evidence connecting many countries with China and Chinese flora and fauna, artifacts, DNA and so on (and the boldness of Menzies' claims has attracted an army of volunteer researchers around the globe who are adding to and evaluating the evidence) but it may be that the evidence so far available does not support the Menzies' hypothesis in its present form.

In 1421 and the following 15 years three major events disrupted the trading patterns for spices described above. First, the Chinese in 1435 (under a different emperor) totally withdrew from and prohibited international trading, shipping and foreign travel: the main reason, according to Menzies, seems to have been that the enormous cost of the treasure ship voyages had critically weakened the Empire. This embargo lasted for over 100 years. Commercial navigation was limited to China's rivers and the Grand Canal. Despite the impressive achievements of the treasure ship voyages the Chinese attempted to obliterate all record of them (and almost succeeded). The colonies in North and South America and Australia were abandoned: but Chinese characteristics – appearance, style of dress, silk, porcelain, building methods, social customs and so on – survived to be noted by the first European explorers in those areas, and their settlements can still be identified by DNA analysis of their descendants.

Secondly, in 1421, the Ottomans surrounded and cut off Constantinople, thus interrupting the Silk Road traffic. Thirdly, in the same year 1421, a regime change in Egypt brought about the nationalization of the spice trade.

This disruption of the trade – and particularly the withdrawal of the Chinese traders and shippers – presented an opportunity, which was,

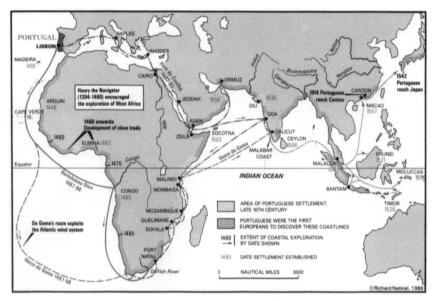

Portuguese eastern trade

in due course, seized by the Portuguese. On the basis of charts produced in Europe from 1428 onwards, which showed in detail parts of the world then still unknown to Europeans, Menzies argues that these were based on information obtained by the Chinese treasure ship voyages, and suggests that the link was an unusual Venetian, Nicolo da Conti. He travelled from Venice to Alexandria in 1414, married and converted to Islam, reached India in 1420 and was present at Calicut in 1421 when the last treasure ship fleet arrived there from China. It appears that da Conti visited the ships and may have taken passage with them.[8] da Conti returned to Italy in 1424, made his peace with the Church (over his conversion to Islam) and, according to Menzies, was de-briefed on his travels by Dom Pedro, the eldest son of Joao II of Portugal and by Paolo Toscanelli, an Italian cartographer. One of Dom Pedro's younger brothers was Prince Henry, known as 'the Navigator', who in 1419, with his father's support, had established his School of Navigation on the cliffs of Cape St. Vincent, teaching ship design and construction, seamanship and navigation, and launched the 'Voyages of Discovery', starting with the opening up of Morocco, discovering and settling Madeira and the Azores, and moving progressively down the West African coast.

Menzies maintains that Dom Pedro brought back with him from Italy at least two of the critical charts and these were held, in the utmost secrecy, by the Portuguese Crown. It is suggested that these charts, or copies, or the information which they contained, were made available (i) to Bartolomeo Diaz's expedition which rounded the Cape of Good Hope in 1487 (ii) to Vasco da Gama, ten years later, on his first voyage to Calicut on the west coast of India, and (iii) to Pedro Alvarez Cabral who, in the course of his voyage to the East, discovered Brazil in 1500 and named it Vera Cruz.

In 1502-3 Vasco da Gama's second expedition occupied Sofala and Mozambique, and reached Calicut (which he bombarded in revenge for his treatment on his first visit). In 1511 the Portuguese occupied Malacca and in the same year reached the Spice Islands themselves. Cargoes of oriental spices began to arrive in Lisbon.

We may now return to the Italian cartographer Paolo Toscanelli, who joined in the de-briefing of Nicolo da Conti. According to Menzies [1421 p. 352-3] he wrote and sent a chart, passing on the 'westabout to the East' navigational information, to Christopher Columbus, and in this way it reached the Spanish Crown. Columbus reached the Bahamas on his first voyage in 1492. In 1518 Charles V dispatched the Portuguese Magellan to sail round the world westabout: he, too, had received the secret charts and/or sailing directions. (Magellan had gained extensive experience of the Orient while in Portuguese service in the period 1505-12 but had fallen out of Portuguese favour) Magellan was thus aware of the latitude at which he might enter the strait which was, thereafter, to bear his name, and so avoid the perils of Cape Horn. Magellan was killed at the Philippine Islands in 1521, after a non-stop voyage across the Pacific

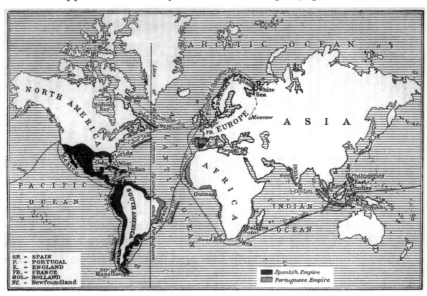

The Treaty of Tordesillas 1494 – the world divided between Spain and Portugal

Ocean, but his fleet called at the Spice Islands, received a friendly reception and loaded a full cargo of spices which was brought safely back to Cadiz. Despite this success, in 1529 Charles V was persuaded to relinquish any claim which Spain might have to the Spice Islands by a Portuguese payment of 350,000 gold ducats.

The Treaty of Tordesillas was concluded between Spain and Portugal in 1494. The treaty divided the world beyond Europe and the Mediterranean between these two countries by drawing a North-South line of longitude some 370 leagues west of the Cape Verde Islands. This had the effect of allocating to Portugal Brazil, all of Africa and the entire Orient, and to Spain North and South America (the latter excluding Brazil). Each country was permitted to travel through the 'territory' of the other. This ambitious plan had the backing of the Papacy and was indeed founded on a Papal Bull of 1493 (Inter Caetera).[9]

Professor Boxer has analysed the earlier background to the Treaty, particularly three Papal Bulls in 1452, 1455 (Romanus Pontifex: the 'Charter of Portuguese imperialism') and 1456; a verbal presentation to the Pope made by Portugal's representative in 1485, and a letter to the Papacy in 1499 from the Portuguese King. There are some interesting points (i) the narrative introduction to the 1455 Bull gives an extensive account of Portuguese exploration down the west coast of Africa to date – obviously drafted for the Pope by the Portuguese (ii) a clear Portuguese statement of their intention to circumnavigate Africa in the near future is spelled out – as noted above Bartolomeo Dias did not in fact round the Cape until 1487 (iii) the presentation of 1485 indicates a Portuguese intention to sail to India very shortly – as noted above Vasco da Gama reached Calicut only in 1497 (iv) the Portuguese King in the 1499 letter claims sovereignty over the navigation and conquest of Ethiopia, Arabia, Persia and India some years before his subjects arrived there (v) the Bull of 1455 makes it clear that all countries other than Spain and Portugal were excluded, under Papal authority, from the allocated territories – the Bull was formally read in Lisbon Cathedral in October 1455 in the presence of specially invited representatives of Castile, Galicia, the Basques, England and France.

We have already noted that the rehabilitation of Nicolo da Conti on his return from the Orient and Islam was organized by the Papacy, and that the secret navigational information (derived, according to Menzies' assertion, from the Chinese treasure ship voyages) was originally passed only to Portugal and Spain. Later it was more widely disseminated, for example in 1513 the Ottoman Admiral Piri Reis published a map known by his name, incorporating some of the earlier information, and, eventually, even England benefited: Captain Cook was provided by the

Admiralty before he set off in around 1770 with accurate charts of Eastern Australia.[10]

There seems little doubt that we are looking at a friendly 'carve–up' between the Papacy, Portugal and Spain, with the shared vision of a long-term development plan, combining colonial expansion with the spread of Christianity. It is tempting to go a little further and assert that it was the possession of the shared secret navigational information that encouraged the parties to announce so confidently what was going to happen some years later (as explained above). In any event, Spain and Portugal – though they were not able always to enforce the monopolies which they claimed by grant from the Pope – got a head start, which gave them a virtually clear run for some 170 years.

Throughout the 16th century Portugal worked vigorously to build and maintain its monopoly position, establishing the headquarters of their eastern empire at Goa and armed forts throughout the Indian Ocean region from Macao to Sofala, together with a network of unarmed trading factories. The Portuguese were always ready to use force of arms, and this accelerated their progress in a part of the world where there was no naval power after the withdrawal of the Chinese.

Following the annexation of Portugal by Spain in 1580-81, and the entry to the oriental spice trade of England and the Netherlands, the importance of Portugal declined. Considering the tiny population of Portugal (1-1 ½ million), their perennial shortage of ships and sailors and the immense spread of their operations – from Brazil to Macao – their achievements in the 16th century are remarkable.

There is no doubt that the political and religious weight behind the Treaty of Tordesillas was recognized, though with the Reformation its authority declined in importance for Protestant countries. In England the enthusiasm for entering the spice trade further upstream was certainly

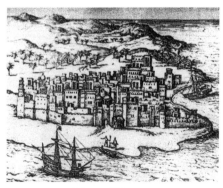

View of Hormus

affected, with efforts being made to work round the prohibitions. There were numerous attempts to establish North East and North West Passage routes – all sadly unsuccessful, though one result was the Muscovy Company, chartered in 1555, which successfully for a time imported oriental commodities along the cumbersome, overland route via Persia.[11] The commercial vision of Sir Edward Osborne and Richard

Staper (the leading merchants of their day and the effective founders of the Turkey/Levant Company in 1581) focused initially on extending their involvement along the overland/river stretch from Hormus and the Persian Gulf to the Levant; and it may be that the deliberately camouflaged objectives of Drake's circumnavigation in 1577-80 owed something to Tordesillas.

The navigational and financial success of Drake's voyage marked a turning point. He arrived from across the Pacific (with rich pickings from the Spanish on the west coast of America) to a friendly reception from the King of Ternate, a treaty for all Englishmen to come there to buy spices – and a cargo of pepper: it is not surprising that this stimulated enthusiasm at home. Several follow-up schemes for direct voyages to the Orient were quickly mooted in the 1580s, but all fell through, or failed to reach the Orient: apart from bad luck, a contributory factor may have been that they were organised by mercurial buccaneers without the involvement of the steady, experienced merchants of the City of London.

A different stimulus for England appeared in 1581. The Spanish annexation of Portugal did not, surprisingly, put an end to Anglo-Portuguese trade as such, but one of the main attractions disappeared when Portuguese spice

Eoum nobis heìc dat Lynscotius Orbem,
Lynscotum, artifici sculpta tabella manu.

Jan Huygen van Linschoten

imports were diverted from Lisbon to Cadiz. The 1586-8 circumnavigation by Thomas Cavendish again underlined the feasibility and financial attractions of direct voyages. In the event, the first English direct voyage to the East took place only in 1591, under Captain George Raymond, with Lancaster third in command.[12]

To complete the picture we may describe the entry to the spice trade of the Dutch. They came a little later than the English but, once started, were extremely active. They had been watching English developments and were presented with a remarkable commercial traveller's guide to doing business in the Orient. In the early 1590s Jan Huygen van Linschoten returned to the Netherlands after five years as Secretary to the Bishop of Goa. While working at the heart of the

Portuguese Eastern Empire – which claimed a trading monopoly over the whole Indian Ocean region – Linschoten had put together a detailed corpus of trading information, accompanied by accurate charts – a remarkable commercial coup.[13] In 1594 a company was formed by Amsterdam merchants to send two fleets to the east. The first set out in 1595 and despite weak leadership and the loss of one of its four ships, brought home a small cargo of pepper in 1597 which covered the costs and showed a small profit. As a result, in 1598, five other companies sent out 22 ships (one sailed westabout and completed the first Dutch circumnavigation). The second fleet of the first Amsterdam company sailed in 1598 and returned in 1599 (a very speedy voyage) with a full cargo of spices which realized a 400% profit. In 1601 14 fleets totaling 65 ships sailed for the East. Faced with this explosive growth the Netherlands government stepped in to rationalize the trade. A national East India Company was formed, usually known as the V. O. C. , and this absorbed most of the previous private adventurers (but not all, since some of the merchants were not comfortable with the powers to wage war and build forts set out in the VOC charter). The VOC was based on its constituent companies in Amsterdam, Enkhuisen, Groningen, Hoorn, Middleburg and Rotterdam, and six 'chambers' representing these towns remained a permanent feature of the organization. Its large capital base and its broad national representation provided the power. When ruthless commercial drive, outstanding seamanship and a readiness to use armed force and establish fortified settlements were added, the VOC became a formidable competitor and it sought and established a monopoly position in the Indonesian archipelago.

4

The Portuguese Experience

Our only direct evidence to date for Lancaster's time in Portugal are some remarks which he made (according to Hakluyt) in 1595 in the course of the Recife Raid. This was a highly successful privateering expedition, in 1594-5, led by Lancaster and backed by a City of London syndicate, which we will describe in detail later.[1] Recife is in the extreme north east of Brazil and was the port for a town called Pernambuco, a prosperous Portuguese settlement, re-named by them Olinda.

Lancaster's force had stormed, captured and fortified Recife and was organizing the loading of the considerable booty which they had found, when a deputation of the leading local Portuguese sought a meeting with him. He put them off and avoided a meeting. When this reaction was questioned by his men Lancaster – as was his custom, somewhat different from the normal practice of commanders at that time – explained his conduct to them. He said:-

'Sirs, I have been brought up among this people: I have lived among them as a gentleman, served with them as a souldier, and lived with them as a merchant, so that I should have some understanding of their demeanors and nature; and I know when they cannot prevaile with the sword by force, then they deal with their deceiveable tongues; for faith and trueth they have none, neither will use any, unless it be to their own advantage. And I give you warning, that if you give them parle, they will betray us; and for my part, of all the nations in the world, it would grieve me most to be overtaken by this nation and the Spaniards: and I am glad it was my fortune to pay them with one of their owne fetches, for I warrant you that they understand me better than you thinke they do. And with this I pray you be satisfied; I hope it is all for your goods: for what shall we gaine by parle, when (by the help of God) we have gotten already that we came for, should we venture that we have gotten with our swords, to see if they can take it from us by words and policy? there were no wisdom in so doing'.

Lancaster went on to instruct his men that if any further approaches are made the individuals are to be warned that thereafter anyone coming over will 'hanged out of hand'.

First, should we believe this story of Lncaster's time in Portugal as a young man? In view of its particularity it is suggested that we should: he could easily have explained his actions without going into this long and interesting reminiscence of what had happened some 20 years earlier. It is possible that, in the excitement of the moment – having just achieved a stunning victory – he may have exaggerated his achievements as a young man, but it is suggested that it should certainly be accepted as an indication that he did indeed spend time in Portugal.

Next, since the evidence is scanty we must look closely at Lancaster's statements.

'I have been brought up among this people'

This suggests that Lancaster was in Portugal before he was grown up, or perhaps before he was grown up and independent. This would be consistent with our hypothesis, developed below, that he went to Portugal either as part of his apprenticeship or as a trainee merchant.

'I have lived among them as a gentleman'

For us 'as a gentleman' implies independent means. In principal, this might have come about through successful trading, the purchase of a viable estate or by marriage to a rich woman (the last possibility is unlikely, since by the time that Lancaster reached Portugal the Catholic/Protestant divide was pronounced).[2] Alternatively, Lancaster may merely be saying that he was accepted by the Portuguese as a young Englishman 'of rank' who happened to be engaged in trade (younger sons of gentry were often so employed). His name 'Lancaster' may have helped in this, and can certainly have been no handicap. The Portuguese Royal House of Avis stemmed from the marriage of Joao I and Philippa Lancaster (the daughter of John of Gaunt, Duke of Lancaster) in the 14th century, and the Portuguese may not have appreciated the nice distinctions between an English surname and an English title of honour, both derived from a geographical part of England.[3]

'served with them as a souldier'

This statement is usually explained by assuming that Lancaster sided and fought with the forces of Dom Antonio when Philip II of Spain annexed Portugal in 1580-1, and indeed this seems to be the only feasible explanation. In view of what happened to Lancaster later, and the deductions which various writers have drawn from his conduct, it is necessary to give a brief description of these events.

Spain had since the end of the 15th century nursed the ambition of unifying the Iberian peninsular. An opportunity arose when the young King Sebastian of Portugal (he was a nephew of Philip II of Spain) in 1578 led a rash and ill-prepared crusade to fight the 'moors' in Morocco and was decisively defeated. Sebastian was killed as were many of the Portuguese nobility. Sebastian was succeeded by his elderly great uncle Cardinal Henry. Here was the opening, and the rich revenues from the Indies, underpinning Spain's fragile domestic finances, gave Philip the freedom of manoeuvre to switch to an expansionist policy. Philip commenced a propaganda programme, backed by bribery, to persuade Henry himself and the Portuguese nobility to accept him as the successor to Henry, in preference to the rival claimant Dom Antonio, the Prior of Crato, who was Henry's (illegitimate) nephew. Henry died in January 1580, having publicly accepted Philip as his successor, but the bulk of the Portuguese, including the lower clergy, favoured Dom Antonio (this preference had been expressed in the Cortes on 9th January); so the Regency Council was unable to declare Philip as the new King. Philip therefore switched from diplomacy to force of arms and the Duke of Alba led an army into Portugal in June 1580. (In defiance at this move Dom Antonio was crowned King on 19th June) Meeting up with the Spanish admiral Santa Cruz at Setubal and making an amphibious landing at Cascais, the Spanish army crushed Dom Antonio's forces in a battle near Lisbon in August. Dom Antonio fled to the north of the country and in the following year, 1581, into France. England, not surprisingly, (and also France) had been backing the claims of Dom Antonio but at this stage seems to have taken no steps to help his cause.

The victorious Philip acted with considerable restraint. He delayed his entry to Lisbon until 1581 and, once there, undertook to stay for a period (as Philip I). He promised to uphold Portuguese laws and privileges and to maintain native-born Portuguese in their positions. He abolished customs duties between the two countries. The overseas empire was undisturbed. Philip issued a general pardon to those who had fought against the Spanish – except for Dom Antonio himself and 50 named men. The Portuguese fleet was, however, absorbed into the Spanish and their best ships provided the nucleus of the Armada fleet in 1588. Surprisingly, too, trade between Portugal and England was not directly interfered with, nor were the English merchants resident in Portugal expelled (this did not happen until 1589), though a heavy blow to them was the diversion of Portuguese oriental imports from Lisbon to Cadiz.

If Lancaster did indeed fight on the losing side in the fight against Spanish annexation, it is possible that this made his continued presence in Portugal impossible.[4] An alternative, and more likely, explanation is that Lancaster, like other English expatriate merchants (who had sensibly kept their heads down during the war), drifted away as soon as it became clear that they could no longer buy oriental spices in Lisbon. They transferred their attentions (as we will suggest that Lancaster did too) to the Levant trade, where the same spices (carried by a different route) could be bought in the Eastern Mediterranean.

'I lived with them as a merchant'

Between Portugal and England from early times there had been both friendship (The Treaty of Windsor with 'our oldest ally' was concluded in 1386 and Philippa of Lancaster married Joao I in the following year) and active trading, both direct and via the entrepots of Middleburg and Antwerp.[5] Further, before 1500 a 'factory' of resident English merchants was established in Lisbon, with extensive privileges granted by the Portuguese Crown. While 'factory' elsewhere could mean a building where expatriate merchants lived and stored their goods, in Lisbon it meant merely an association of merchants (or 'factors'), with no dedicated building. England exported basic commodities, mainly woollen cloth but

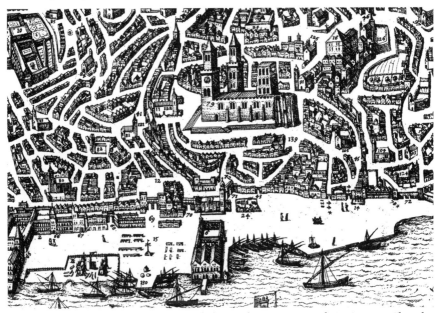

The Lisbon waterfront, 1593. The English merchants supported St George's Church, immediately to the north-east of the Cathedral.

also grain, lead and tin. In return Portugal supplied chiefly luxury goods – wine, sugar and spices; the last-named being the most important and the largest single product being pepper. These were the commodities in which Lancaster received his early training and experience. In 1530 Henry VIII granted a charter to English merchants trading to Spain and Andalusia, but this did not extend to Portugal. After years of negotiation (mainly over the eligibility of merchants who had entered the trade more recently) a new Spanish/Portuguese Trading Company was established by Queen Elizabeth in 1577. It was in what became the standard form of granting monopoly trading rights to the members, and – for present purposes – it included two interesting facts. First, the list of English merchants included Robert Walkeden, Lancaster's new master after his 'turnover' from Blaise Freeman, and, secondly, it listed 28 English merchants already resident in Spain and Portugal. As we have already noted, since this 'turnover' was deliberately arranged by Lancaster and/ or his father, in collaboration with the Skinners' Company, it is reasonable to assume that there was a plan to introduce him to the Portugal trade. We thus have some corroborating evidence that Lancaster became a merchant in Portugal.

While the 1577 Charter included Portugal it was still predominantly directed to trade with Spain, and in particular to the 'Brotherhood of St. George' – the expatriate English merchant community long established in Andalusia under the patronage of the Duke of Medina Sidonia.[6] Of the 28 merchants listed in the Charter as already resident in Spain and Portugal it might therefore be reasonable to estimate that no more than, say, 5-10 were living in Portugal. At that time Lisbon was predominant (The port trade through Oporto came later), so all or most of them would have been located there.

When and how did Lancaster become a Portuguese merchant?

The tradition in the Skinners' Company is that Lancaster definitely was a merchant in Portugal but that this occurred only after he had completed his apprenticeship. This occurred on 10th March 1579 when he was around 25 years old. Examination of the timing involved, however, suggests that Lancaster probably went to Portugal while still an apprentice. We attempted, above, to analyse his achievements in Portugal as a merchant, a gentleman and a soldier – from a standing start as a raw expatriate trainee he could hardly have managed all this in less than five years. If Lancaster had only gone to Portugal as soon as he completed his apprenticeship in 1579 and (as we have deduced) left Portugal in 1580 or 1581, there just would not have been enough time. Further, if he did not reach Portugal until he was 25 (and out of his apprenticeship) it would be inappropriate for him to say that 'I have been brought up among this people'. It is thus difficult to accept the tradition that Lancaster completed his apprenticeship before going to Portugal.

The following scenario may therefore be suggested. Lancaster was 'turned over' from Blaise Freeman to Robert Walkeden at around the age of 18-19 with a view to becoming involved in the Portuguese trade. Walkeden started him in the Portuguese trade, initially in London, and then sent him, at around the age of 20 (say in 1574) to Lisbon. He was probably put under the resident merchant with whom Walkeden arranged his business. In due course Lancaster developed trade on his own account, but saw this business evaporate when the oriental spice trade was diverted to Cadiz. It is possible that Lancaster went to Portugal a little earlier i. e. before he was 20. It was quite normal for bright young men in their late teens to be sent overseas as trainees.[7]

A Lifelong Grudge against the Portuguese?

Modern writers about Lancaster, starting (it seems) with John Knox Laughton[8] have asserted, on the basis of his famous remarks during the Recife Raid, quoted above, that he harboured a lifelong grudge against the Portuguese because they had deprived him of the fruits of his labour in their country. Later writers have followed this line.[9] It is suggested that this assertion needs careful consideration.

In the first place, Lancaster, in his Recife speech, does not accuse the Portuguese of wronging him in any way: he simply describes their behaviour in certain circumstances, explaining that he has had plenty of experience in their country to observe it. He is certainly not polite – still less politically correct – but he only describes what he has seen them try to do when defeated by force, and how they do it. The charge against the Portuguese – that they in some way had wronged Lancaster 15 years earlier – can only be deduced, and it is hardly an obvious deduction either from what actually happened or from what Lancaster actually said to his men. Secondly, the remark about repaying the Portuguese with one of their own 'fetches' simply means that he sees through their attempt to talk him out of his winnings and parries it by making himself unavailable – a response that they will understand very well. If Lancaster left or had to leave Portugal because of his involvement in what was effectively a civil war, it is suggested that any loss or misfortune he suffered was entirely his own fault. Making all allowance for youthful, quixotic enthusiasm, it is axiomatic that expatriate businessmen, while wooing men of influence, keep out of local politics and certainly keep out of civil wars. Even if one emerges on the winning side, the other half of the local population will have been alienated. Again, at the next election or when civil war breaks out again, the position may be reversed. So he could hardly blame the Portuguese.

If, as we suggest is more likely, Lancaster left Portugal because the spice trade dried up, then, again, he could hardly blame the Portuguese – if anyone, it would be the Spanish, who had caused the trade to be diverted to Cadiz. It should be noted that, in his remarks, he links the Spanish with the Portuguese. Most English merchant adventurers of the day – including those who, like Lancaster, were conventionally religious and principled – were quite single-minded about Portugal: once she had joined Spain (albeit under compulsion) she had joined the Queen's enemies and they regarded her citizens and their possessions as fair game. The Admiralty Court, in granting letters of reprisal under the policy laid down by the Privy Council, took the same view

This is not the only time that Lancaster, on the basis of his observations and experience, describes people in various parts of the world as treacherous, thieves &c., and adapts his conduct (and that of his men) accordingly. Examples can be drawn from the Comoros Islands; ('very treacherous') Nicobar; ('wholly given to deceit') Javans at Bantam; ('the greatest pickers and theeves of the world') Indians in Indonesia ('their bodies and soules be wholly treason'). Lancaster was not alone in this ruthlessly practical attitude: the indexes to Hakluyt and Purchas have entries under 'Treachery of Spanish/ Portuguese/ Indians'.[10]

Finally, it is worth noting an incident which occurred about three weeks before his Recife speech. At Maio in the Cape Verde Islands. Lancaster and the other commanders decided that this was a safe place for them to build the galley-frigate (the frames for which they had brought pre-fabricated from England) 'of purpose to land men in the country of Brazil'.[11] Lancaster, as ever, was punctilious about security, 'not without great care of the capitaine for the safety of them all, by keeping good watch'. However 'one negligent fellow, which had no knowledge of the country, straying from his company, was by the Portugals taken, and very kindly used, and brought again unto us: for which good the general rewarded them well with gifts very acceptable, which they took as kindly'. The commander personally thanked and rewarded the rescuers – hardly consistent with lifelong resentment against the 'Portugals'.

It is therefore suggested that the 'lifelong grudge' theory cannot be sustained.

After Portugal

We have suggested that Lancaster left Portugal in 1580 or 1581, probably because the trade in which he was engaged had dried up. In 1581 and in April 1582 he was in Seville, apparently trading in cloth.[12] We have no explanation for this, but it may be that he was trying to follow the trade diverted from Lisbon to Cadiz/Seville and to establish himself in the Brotherhood of St. George, the long-established community of English expatriate merchants in that area.[13] There is no indication that he was acting covertly as someone who had been blacklisted or expelled or had been compelled to flee from Portugal by the Spanish because he had supported Dom Antonio.

In the next chapter we look at the period from 1581-2 until 1586-7 during which. Lancaster transformed himself from a merchant to a naval commander. We will work from what we know for certain, through what can be deduced, to arrive at a satisfactory working hypothesis.

5
Merchant to Navigator 1581-7

We last sighted Lancaster trading woollen cloth in Seville in April 1582. This was some months after the Portuguese imports of oriental goods, above all of spices, had been diverted by the Spanish from Lisbon to Cadiz, thus destroying the activity in which he had been engaged for the last seven years. He had started as an apprentice for Robert Walkeden, under the umbrella of the Spanish/Portuguese Company (chartered in 1577) On completing his apprenticeship in 1579 Lancaster may well have continued as factor for Walkeden (and perhaps for other London merchants) but in any event he was by then becoming established as a successful merchant in his own right. His progress would have been observed by the directors and members of the Company. Many of these men were also officers or members of the Skinners' Company, so they would have been following his career since 1571 when he was first apprenticed.[1] By a fortunate coincidence, a new door was opening as the Portuguese door was closed – a new Trading Company, the Turkey/Levant Company, was chartered and commenced trading to the eastern Mediterranean in 1581.[2] Since the same spices, carried from the Orient by a different route, were now available in the Eastern Mediterranean, many English merchants, and their factors, agents and servants, switched their efforts to this new quarter. It seems very probable that Lancaster was among their number.

Looking forward to 1585, 1586 and 1587 we can find corroboration for this supposition.

In 1585 Lancaster was back in Seville acting as factor for Sir Thomas Starkey, a leading merchant, a prominent Skinner and an original director of the Spanish/Portuguese Company, confirming that Lancaster's talents as a merchant had indeed been noticed.[3] In 1585 or 1586 Lancaster was described by the leading chronicler and analyst of English exploration

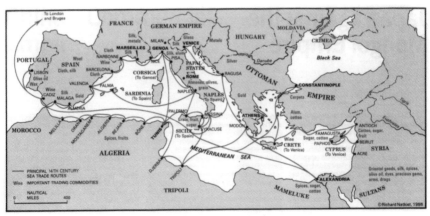

Mediterranean Trade

and marine activity, Richard Hakluyt, as 'James Lancaster, the navigator':
this is the first reference to him as a naval commander.[4] In 1587 Lancaster
was involved in a commercial dispute which was referred by the other
party to the Privy Council, and the record refers to him as 'one James
Lancaster of London, Merchaunte' : the description suggests that, by that
date, he was indeed a merchant in his own right, based in London.[5]

In the four years from 1587 Lancaster was commanding armed
merchant ships – the Susan in the Cadiz Raid in 1587 under Drake, the
Edward Bonaventure in the Armada campaign in 1588 again under Drake,
the Salomon in the Coruna/Lisbon Expedition in 1589 and the Edward
Bonaventure in a privateering expedition in 1590.[6] These ships were all
engaged in the trade organized by the recently formed Turkey/Levant
Company. At this stage the Company was a 'joint stock company', that is,
all its activities were organized and carried out by the Company, not by
individual members.[7] When armed merchant ships were contracted to
serve with the Royal Navy[8] they of course came under naval operational
command but it is difficult to imagine the Turkey/Levant Company
offering any ship without having 'their own man' in charge.[9]

Based on the foregoing, we can, with some confidence, suggest
that Lancaster was recruited as a merchant by the Turkey/Levant
Company, probably in 1581 or 1582; that he undertook one or more
trading voyages to the Levant (the round trip was 6000 miles and took
up to 9-12 months); that as an energetic and intelligent young man
(around 27/28) with some military experience (and probably recognized
as enjoying the patronage of senior members of the Company), he was
encouraged to become involved in working the ship and, when
necessary, defending it against pirates, Spanish galleys and so on; that
from basic seamanship he progressed to pilotage, navigation and

command; and in this way added the skill of naval command to his proven qualifications as a merchant.

While the details and timing of this scenario are necessarily speculative, it seems that something of this sort must have happened in the years between 1581-2 and 1586-7. Having introduced Lancaster to the Levant trade we can now describe it more fully. The main export from England in the early 16th century to the Levant (as indeed to all destinations at that time) was woollen cloth, with some skins and occasionally tin and lead. The main imports were silk, malmsey, muscatel and other wines, cotton wool, turkey carpets, currants, spices and indigo. The goods were carried partly by English ships but also in those of other nationalities. The main ports were Sicily, Crete, Chios, Cyprus and Tripolis. The dominant shippers from Turkish ports were the Venetians and Genoese and the Venetians effectively monopolised the movement of oriental spices from Constantinople, the Levant ports and Alexandria, carrying them to Venice, whence they moved overland to Antwerp to supply Northern Europe.

While quite active in the early years of the century, English trade in the Mediterranean fell off in the second quarter of the 16th century, probably due to the activity of 'Barbary' i. e. North African, pirates, combined with the convenience of the Antwerp market. As Antwerp declined around 1560 the trade revived. In 1563 English merchants procured a charter for the Venice Company, mainly to import currants. In 1575 two leading London merchants Sir Edward Osborne and Richard Staper at their own expense sent agents overland to Constantinople.[10] After months of negotiation they secured Turkish trading rights for another factor employed by their principals, William Harborne. Harborne therefore went to Constantinople in 1578 and obtained rights for English merchants generally to trade with the Turkish Empire, following the pattern of the capitulations already granted to the Venetians, Genoese and French. After the English negotiators had left Constantinople, these rights were overturned by the efforts of the French and Venetians but were eventually re-confirmed in 1583.

The efforts being made by Sir Edward Osborne and Richard Staper were known to and supported by the Queen (who paid for Harborne's first trip) and the Privy Council. Following lengthy consideration, Queen Elizabeth in September 1581 granted a charter to the Turkey/Levant Company, led by Sir Edward Osborne, Richard Staper, Sir Thomas Smythe and William Garrett, granting exclusive rights for English trade with the Turkish Empire, initially for seven years.[11]

There were some interesting clauses in the charter. Sir Edward Osborne was to be the Governor of the Company. The trade must generate

Sir Edward Osborne (above), and Sir Thomas Smythe (right)

at least £ 500 per annum in English customs duties. The ships might display the red cross of England on their sails. Voyages were to be notified to the Admiralty and the Master of the Ordinance who might inspect the ships and their ordinance at the start and end of each voyage.

Further light on the Government's thinking is available from the Privy Council memoranda which preceded the grant of the charter. The trade proposed was to be encouraged since it would substitute English for foreign merchants; and because an enlarged merchant fleet and additional seamen would provide underpinning for the Royal Navy. The political problems with the French and Venetians would be handled by appointing an English ambassador to Constantinople. The risk of attack by pirates, or the French or Venetians, would be countered by having the merchants sail in convoy and in the winter months when hostile galleys tended to stay in harbour.

William Harborne was appointed to the dual role of ambassador and representative of the merchants – but the Queen insisted that the Company should pay him, another typical Tudor touch. He proved a success, being most energetic on behalf of both the Queen and the merchants.[12] Arriving en poste in 1583 he quickly appointed a network of consuls covering the following:- Cairo, Alexandria, Egypt and other parts adjacent; Aleppo, Damascus, Aman, Tripolis, Jerusalem and all other parts whatsoever in the provinces of Syria, Palestina and Jurie; and Algiers, Tunis and Patras. These appointments indicate the wide range of the target markets.

Official backing was followed by investment support (the Queen herself lent Sir Edward Osborne £ 10,000 in silver), and the trade proved profitable from the start. In 1592 a second charter was granted for a new Levant Company which absorbed the Venice Company whose charter had also expired. Sir Edward Osborne was again appointed Governor, although he was in ill health and died a few months later.[13] In support of the application for the new charter it was stated that by 1590 i. e. after about eight years of trading under the original charter, 19 ships were employed, 27 voyages had been made, 787 men were employed and English customs duties of £ 11,259 had been paid.

Another important feature of the 1592 charter should be mentioned. We have already described how the vision of Sir Edward Osborne and Richard Staper led to the formation of the first Turkey/Levant Company in 1581, thus moving further 'upstream' in the flow of oriental spices and 'leapfrogging' Venice. They continued to look forward and in 1583 – again at their own expense – sent four 'agents' – Ralph Fitch, John Newbery (both merchants), William Leedes (a jeweller) and James Story (a painter) on a reconnaissance further east. Travelling by sea to Tripolis and Aleppo in the 'Tiger' [This particular voyage took only 50 days and was described as a 'very good passage': see further below p. 51] the four set out overland (with some other English merchants) to the Euphrates. Here they bought a boat and floated downstream to Babylon, and from there by boat on the Tigris to Basra. From Basra they boarded a ship (with sewn planks in the Arab manner) for Hormus, already a very large trading city. Here the four encountered their first setback – but the eventual outcome was to prove favourable. The Portuguese were by this time in control of Hormus and the captain of their castle (Don Mathias de Albequerque) arrested the four, on the basis that they were challenging the trading monopoly claimed by the Portuguese, and sent them in his own ship (with 124 horses – there was an active trade in Arab horses) to the Viceroy in Goa, the headquarters of the Portuguese Eastern Empire.

Again they were imprisoned and investigated as 'spies', but were eventually released against sureties. Story became a Jesuit – but subsequently recanted. The other three escaped and eventually reached the court of the Great Mogul Akbar at Fatepore, near Agra. Here Leedes took service with Akbar and Newbery set off, aiming to return to England via Persia. Ralph Fitch however continued travelling over the next seven years, sailing down the Jumena and Ganges rivers, visiting Burma, Siam and Malacca, and returning via Ceylon, India and the Euphrates valley. He arrived in England in 1591 to a hero's welcome, having been presumed dead. His account of his travels was as fascinating as it was commercially valuable. It ends with a listing of the products 'which India and the countrey farther Eastward do bring forth'.[14]

The achievements of the reconnaissance party and the vision of their principals were reflected in the 1592 charter. The extent of the Company's monopoly was expanded to include 'by land, through the countries of the said grand signior into and from the East India lately discovered by John Newbery, Ralph Fitch, William Leech and James Storie'. The restless urge among the leaders of the Levant Company to enter the Oriental spice trade further 'upstream' also inspired the first English voyage to the Indies in 1591, in which, as we will see,[15] Lancaster served initially as third in command. The concept of the Company (and its ships and men) acting as a naval reserve was formally confirmed in the 1592 Levant Company charter: it empowered the Crown to commandeer the ships and crews in time of need.

At the start until around 1589 the Turkey/Levant Company operated on 'a joint stock basis', that is to say, everything was done by the Company, not the members – ownership of the ships and the merchandise, conduct of the trade, handling cash, employing the seamen and factors. Thus Lancaster would have become an employee of the Company, not of a particular merchant or shipowner. The investing members of the Company took their profit share by way of dividend.

As noted above, it is clear that the Privy Council saw the Company as a Royal Navy reserve force – paid for by someone else. The ships which were acquired, built or chartered by the Company did not disappoint in terms of quality – they appear to have conformed to the new ideas which Sir John Hawkins (as Treasurer of the Royal Navy 1578-88) had been struggling to introduce into the Queen's ships: hulls designed for speed, manoeuvrability and ability to point to windward. The new designs incorporated hull length at least three times the beam; an enlarged

Sir John Hawkins, moderniser of the Royal Navy ships

A model race-built Galleon, based on actual ship dimensions

'beak' or cutwater on the bows; a lower forecastle (foc's'le), set back from the bows (the previous higher foc's'le set right forward had caused the ship's head to 'fall off' under pressure from the wind), giving a smooth, rising 'sheer' line from bow to stern; and a 'tall ship' rig of sails for speed, with fore and aft rig on the mizzen mast(s) to assist sailing into the wind.[16] These 'modern' ships were known as 'race – built galleons'.[17] The ordnance also followed 'modern' English practice. Longer-barrelled, longer-range guns were preferred: they were intended to damage and cripple enemy ships (and kill their crews) from a distance, abandoning the traditional 'close, grapple and board' land-style battle tactics. The preferred guns were known as culverins or semi-culverins, the heavier ones as cannons or ship-smashers.

The Levant Company ship with which Lancaster was most closely connected was the Edward Bonaventure.[18] She was built in about 1574, displaced 250-300 tons and carried up to 70 crew, depending on the nature of the service. She had 14 cannon on each side, some of which were of brass, rather than cast iron.[19] Further, lighter cannon were installed in the bows and stern. She followed the description of a race-built galleon given above. The Edward Bonaventure's principal owner was Thomas Cordell, a prominent merchant, who was a Mercer and Alderman.[20]

Some of the armed merchant ships which were engaged in the trade of the Turkey/Levant Company are listed in Appendix V. The six or so which were repeatedly employed were recognized as equal, in sailing and fighting qualities, to Royal Navy vessels of the same size.

The 1590 statistics quoted above suggest an average of three voyages per year. If several ships sailed in convoy – as recommended by the Privy Council – this would of course distort the figures; though from the accounts of voyages it looks as though convoys were not the norm. However, there is an account of a famous voyage in 1586 ('the Worthy Fight' Hakluyt calls it) of five Company ships in convoy (including the Edward Bonaventure which Lancaster was to command later, and the Merchant Royal which was larger and appears to have been regarded as the Company flagship). They sailed together to Sicily, then parted company to proceed to their various destinations, setting a rendez-vous at Zante (off the north west coast of the Peloponese) to which they all repaired after completing their trading. They then had a major battle with a fleet of 13 Maltese galleys (employed by Spain) which they beat off after five hours of heavy fighting. Taking refuge in Algiers, they heard that a separate fleet of Spanish galleys was waiting for them at the Straits of Gibraltar, but determined to take their chance. Fortune favoured the brave, as dense fog and a stiff easterly breeze allowed them to slip past the Spanish before they were spotted, and they return safely to England with their cargoes.

The 'Worthy Fight' established, and the Cadiz Raid was to confirm, that galleys were no match for galleon type ships, unless they had an overwhelming numerical superiority. A similar engagement (dubbed 'the Valiant Fight' by Hakluyt) took place in 1590 when ten merchant ships[21] fought off 12 Spanish galleys in the Straits of Gibraltar in an engagement which lasted six hours. There were, miraculously, no Englishmen killed, only some damage to the rigging of the Saloman.[22] An even more courageous action was (in Hakluyt's description) 'The Centurion's Valiant Fight' in the next year 1591, again off Gibraltar. Centurion was sailing in company from Marseilles with several smaller ships at their request (when battle was joined they 'lay aloofe'). Becalmed off Gibraltar the Centurion was set upon by five galleys. She was badly damaged and suffered casualties, but the Spanish disengaged after 5 ½ hours.[23]

The typical size of crew for the armed merchantmen was 40-50 per ship. The majority of these would have been employed to work (and if needed fight) the ship, with two or three 'factors' i. e. merchants, to manage and sell the outward cargo and buy up the return cargo at the destination ports. Where ships were employed on privateering expeditions (these did not occur in the Mediterranean) a larger crew was engaged to support the aggressive strategy, to supplement losses from disease and action and to man the expected prizes back to England. The approximate distances involved in the Levant trade were three stages of approximately 1000 miles each (i) Southern England to Gibraltar (ii) Gibraltar to Central Mediterranean e. g. Malta, Sicily, Tunis and (iii) Central to Eastern

Mediterranean. From the records of voyages it looks as though the round trip of about 6000 miles usually took 9-12 months, which of course allowed for contrary winds, stops for trading and so on. A non-stop voyage from Falmouth to Tripolis in Syria in 1583 took 50 days and was described as 'a very good passage': though this gives an average achieved speed of only 2 ½ knots. With a strong stern or quarter winds the speed of a 'race-built galleon' might be 5-6 knots or even more.

In 1585 another trading monopoly was granted, to the Barbary Company, which covered trade with North Africa, both within and outside the Mediterranean. It is interesting to find among its original members the ubiquitous Richard Staper and also Lancaster's (second) master Robert Walkeden, who had been one of the original members of the Spanish/ Portuguese Company in 1577.

We turn now to describe in greater detail the sightings of Lancaster in 1585, 1586 and 1587 already mentioned. An undated entry in the 1586 CSP(Domestic) states that Mr. Hakluyt 'the bearer and author' will present to Mr. Secretary twenty chapters from a book of Walter Raleigh's voyage to the West Indies 'probably in the hand of James Lancaster, the navigator'. The entry comments that no one else has read them except the Queen. Sir William Foster investigated the original document[24] and felt that the attribution to Lancaster, on the basis of handwriting, could not be sustained. He also dated the document to 1585, not 1586. We have no reason to question Sir William's conclusions, but it is suggested this does not invalidate the relevance of the entry to Lancaster's career. 'Mr. Hakluyt' appears to have been the famous Richard Hakluyt, scholar, divine, tireless collector and publisher of accounts of voyages of discovery, trading, colonization, privateering and so on, and 'Mr. Secretary' was presumably Sir Francis Walsingham, the Secretary of State. If, as seems to be the case, the attribution to Lancaster was made by Hakluyt, the interest is not whether this attribution was correct but the fact he felt able to describe Lancaster as 'the navigator'. Richard Hakluyt was expert in all maritime matters and made it his business to meet all the important people involved. He was roughly the same age as Lancaster (32 in 1586) and it is reasonable to assume that they had met by this time,[25] We thus have confirmation, from an impeccable authority, of Lancaster's progression from merchant to naval commander by 1585 or 1586.

In 1585 Lancaster was back in the Iberian peninsular, at Seville, acting from the beginning of that year as factor for Sir Thomas Starkey, Master of the Skinners' Company and Alderman, and an original director of the Spain/Portugal Company (from 1577) – he would thus have followed Lancaster's career. In May 1585 Lancaster also visited Lisbon to meet with Sir Thomas' factor there, one John Dorrington . Unlike the earlier trips to Seville in 1581 and 1582.[26] this was definitely expatriate residential employment – although it was cut short within a few months by the action of the Spanish authorities. These facts emerge from a deposition sworn by Lancaster in proceedings in the Court of Admiralty in which Sir Thomas was seeking letters of reprisal to compensate him for losses incurred around the middle of 1585 when the Spanish seized English ships and goods and imprisoned Englishmen – some were handed over to the Inquisition.[27] Lancaster was lucky to escape. The dating of the deposition fixes him back in London by the middle of 1586.

At a meeting of the Privy Council at Greenwich on 16th February 1587 a complaint against Lancaster (referred to as 'one James Lancaster of London, merchaunte') by a merchant named John Chilton was considered. The Council had been informed that 'there dependeth certain accomptes and reckonings' between them, and 'it should appere that there is a good rounde somme of monie due to Chilton'. The Council therefore wrote a letter to Richard Staper, William Saunderson, John Archer and John Watts (all high powered merchants of the time), stating that they were themselves too busy 'by reason of her Majesties other services and affaires' to investigate, and requiring them 'or anie three or two of you' to sort the matter out. It seems likely that the dispute arose over trading in Spain, since there was a Leonard Chilton resident in Cadiz as part of the community of English merchants in Andalusia, and he had a brother John. It is possible that he was the same John Chilton who made an extensive journey through the Spanish colonies in the Caribbean and Central and South America, which is recorded by Hakluyt.[28] Leaving England in 1561 this John Chilton passed seven years in Spain and then spent no less than 17 or 18 years travelling in the Spanish colonies in the Western hemisphere. He then returned to Spain and was back in London in July 1586. The transactions in question may have occurred during Lancaster's time in Spain in 1585.[29] The selection of arbitrators by the Privy Council provides some support for a Spanish connection. Richard Stapers had interests in every overseas market (including the Iberian peninsular – he was an assistant i. e director, of the Spanish/Portuguese Company). John Watts was also an assistant of the Spanish/Portuguese Company. He was prominent in trade with Spain, the Canaries and the Azores in the 1570s and 1580s (and later was the leading merchant backer of privateering ventures – with letters of reprisal based on the losses he had suffered from Spanish confiscations in 1585). John Archer was a merchant in spices who acted as an appraiser for the Court of Admiralty. William Saunderson (sometimes Sanderson) was a prominent merchant in northern Europe, who had been trained by Thomas Allen, who was engaged in purchasing for the Royal Navy. He was also a backer of John

Davis, the famous explorer of the North West Passage, and of Sir Walter Ralegh with whom, eventually, he had a disastrous quarrel.

Lancaster seems always to have been a man of high principles but this did not prevent him from fighting his corner. As we shall see[30] he stood his ground against the East India Company over his entitlement to his profit share on the first EIC voyage and the dispute rumbled on from his return to England in 1603 to 1609. Since the dispute with John Chilton was not referred back to the Privy Council, we may assume that Lancaster, on his side, had answers to the case raised against him and that the matter was settled by the arbitrators, without any damage to his reputation. Certainly Richard Staper, through his connections (particularly the Levant Company and the EIC of which he, like Lancaster, was one of the first directors) continued to support him. Sir John Watts (as he became) was a partner with Lancaster in the Cadiz Raid syndicate in the same year 1587 [see below] and an investor in Lancaster's Recife Raid in 1594 (he sent his son to serve under Lancaster on that voyage).

A few weeks later, on the 18th March 1587, Lancaster, with 18 other London merchants, negotiated the deal with Sir Francis Drake under which 10 armed 'merchaunte ships and pinnaces' would join forces with four Royal Navy ships and two pinnaces, under Drake's command, to undertake the Cadiz Raid.[31] Among the London merchants were some leading City men, including Thomas Cordell, William Garraway, Simon Boreman, and John Watts. Lancaster and Robert Flycke (a Draper, who commanded ships in both the Cadiz Raid and the Armada campaign) appear to have been the only individuals who were both merchants and naval commanders. This seems to be the first occasion on which Lancaster was admitted to the City of London 'top table': he was around 33 years old. It may also have been his first meeting with Drake. The deal provided that all booty to be taken 'shall be equally divided according to their propocions (that is to say) man for man and tonne for tonne'. The formula produced the following entitlements:

> Her Majesty 40. 93%
> The Lord High Admiral 3. 8%
> Sir Francis Drake 15. 99%
> The Merchants 39. 28%

In due course this formula was applied to apportion the unprecedented treasure captured in the San Felipe in 1587.[32] 'Pillage' (that is booty taken above the main deck) was to be divided equally between the companies of the merchant ships and the companies of the Royal Navy ships. Men were to be stationed throughout the fleet to see that these arrangements were observed. The combined fleet under Drake sailed from Plymouth for Cadiz (the destination had been successfully kept secret) in April 1587. We will pick up the story in the next chapter.

6

Royal Navy Service 1587-9

The Armada Campaign in 1588 is too well known to require any detailed description. It lasted some 15 days, from 29th July when the Armada was reported off the Lizard (and Drake was playing bowls on Plymouth Hoe) to 12th August when the main English fleet broke off its pursuit of the Armada somewhere off the Firth of Forth. In between there had been skirmishes up the English Channel, particularly off Portland Bill and the Isle of Wight, a brief anchorage by both fleets off Calais, a fire-ship attack mounted by the English fleet the same night and a full-scale engagement all the next day off Gravelines, with the Armada saved from complete disaster on the Low Countries lee shore only by a last minute change of wind direction. Without command of the sea for even a short period – the same problem was faced by Napoleon and Hitler later – the main Spanish Army around Calais and Dunkirk was never able to embark for the invasion of England. The rigid instructions under which the Spanish Fleet operated ensured that their crescent formation was preserved all the way up the Channel to Calais – in itself a very considerable achievement – but it prevented any opportunistic landing on the south coast of England prior to the planned link-up with the army of the Duke of Parma.

While its fate was thus decided in only a few days the Armada had cast a long shadow before it. The actual preparation in Spain and Portugal took several years and the possibility of a Spanish attack, in some form, on England had been on the cards since around 1570 when the Pope excommunicated Queen Elizabeth. A 'cold war' had existed between England and Spain during these years, with diplomatic manoeuvering punctuated by provocative actions on both sides. The final trigger was probably the execution of Mary, Queen of Scots on 18th February 1587, a religious and political double blow which made turning back impossible.

With a Spanish sea-based attack in prospect the English naval 'modernists', led by Sir Francis Drake, advocated pre-emptive action, taking naval action to the coast and harbours of Spain and Portugal and maintaining fleets at sea; thus forestalling the later naval strategy based on the concept of 'the fleet in being'. Drake was recognised, not least by the Queen herself, as the outstanding naval commander of the day, but England – that is, the Queen – could not afford to keep ships fully commissioned, still less at sea, for more than short periods. Apart from

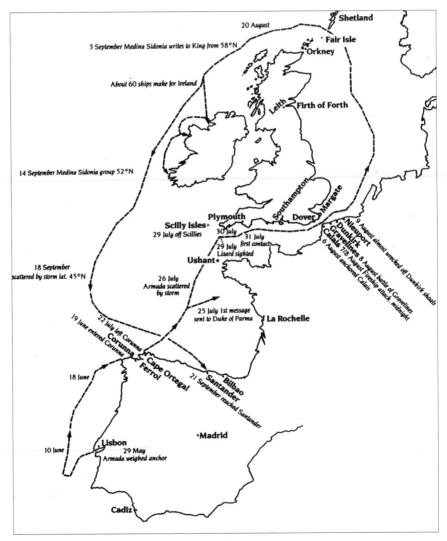

The Armada campaign

the cost, it was operationally very difficult. After a few weeks at sea the ships themselves had to be careened, that is, beached (or docked) and scraped down and re-painted. Standing and running rigging and sails needed repair and replacement. More seriously, the conditions on board at sea and the quality of the victuals, meant that, after a few weeks, the crews were weakened by malnutrition, bad water and epidemics and needed to be 'refreshed' by time ashore. Judged by the experience of the Spanish fleet in the Armada campaign, it may also be questioned whether the Royal Navy, even reinforced by merchantmen, actually had the capability to maintain an operational squadron nearly 1000 miles from home and at the same time to deploy additional ships to (i) replace the squadron on station after a few weeks (ii) supply additional stores, particularly the replacement of shot and powder and (iii) defend England and cover other naval responsibilities. A partial answer to this logistical problem was demonstrated by Drake in 1587, when he took and held Sagres as a forward base at which he could refresh both his ships and his men: but such daring, opportunistic measures could not survive for long in hostile territory.

Despite the financial constraints, however, in about March 1587 Drake was authorized to take a fleet to Spain and Portugal to 'impeach' i. e. hinder, the gathering of the constituent parts of the Armada at Lisbon and generally damage the enemy. His instructions allowed entry to enemy ports and landing on their coast, though this was cancelled by the Queen soon afterwards – but Drake had sailed immediately, probably expecting her 'second thoughts', and the change of instructions never caught up with him. There followed the bold, but highly successful, surprise attack on Cadiz – in which around 30 enemy ships were destroyed; without English loss.[1] Drake's operation included a landing at Lagos, which was immediately withdrawn on meeting opposition (It may have been a feint); the storming of Sagres Castle on the cliffs of Cape St. Vincent and occupation of the harbour of Sagres as a forward base for 'refreshing' the ships and the men, for destroying ships, fishing fleets and Armada stores[2] up and down the coast and cutting contact between the Spanish/ Portuguese Mediterranean and Atlantic fleets; an aggressive demonstration at the mouth of the Tagus; and, finally, a secret dash by Drake (without telling the rest of his force) to the Azores to attack and capture the San Felipe carrack on her way home from the Indies full of valuable cargo. When realized this prize gave over £40,000 to the Queen, a little less to the City of London merchants who had joined the expedition on a percentage basis (even though they took no part in the actual capture) and £17,000 to Drake personally. The total value of the prize of some £114,000 was unprecedented.[3]

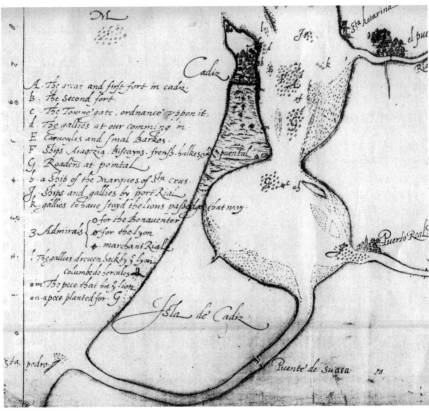

William Borrough's chart describing the Cadiz Raid

The Cadiz Raid had an important effect on morale – on both sides – and put back the Armada for a year, but Drake recognized that – in the context of Spanish resources – it was really only an irritant; ('Singeing the King of Spain's Beard') so he continued to urge the authorization of further pre-emptive strikes. King Philip drew similar conclusions 'The loss was not very great but the daring of the attempt was very great indeed'. However, the English fleet went back into mothballs, until early the following year, just before the Armada was due to sail. Drake was then again authorized to attack the enemy on his own coasts, but the expedition had to turn back when the winds turned southerly, lest the Armada slip past the English fleet and get between it and the South Coast of England. The main part of the English fleet returned to Plymouth to await the Armada.

Lancaster's Participation

In the Cadiz Raid Lancaster commanded the Susan (350 tons). He was part of the Levant Company Squadron which was under Robert Flicke, the Rear Admiral of the whole fleet in the Merchant Royal. The Squadron consisted of seven ships. Of these the Merchant Royal particularly distinguished herself, since Drake, transferring from his flagship (the Elizabeth Bonaventure) after the initial battle inside Cadiz harbour in order to enter the inner harbour, picked her to cover this move. They destroyed a 1200 ton carrack which was personally owned by the Marquess of Santa Cruz, the Spanish Admiral. In addition, according to Hakluyt,[4] Drake 'made particular mention in his private Letters directed to her Majestie' of the 'especiall good service' of 'certaine tall ships of the Citie of London'. As mentioned above the City merchants received nearly £40,000 from the San Felipe.

The service of the merchantmen was recognized when, in March next year (1588), preparations were made to re-commission the fleet to meet the Armada. Drake's Vice Admiral, Captain Thomas Fenner, listed 23 merchant ship commanders, rated by the Royal Navy as captains (and when serving paid as such). The list included Robert Flicke and Lancaster. Fenner wrote 'I have sent you the names . . . of such captains as are here and have had places heretofore . . . And as there are of them that are now, if the service goes forward, to proceed as captains, their experience and deserts deserving the same, so there are a great number of serviceable gentlemen and soldiers that are to step up into place; which is left undone, until perfect directions from your Honour . . . be known . . . ' Robert Flicke again commanded the Merchant Royal. Lancaster captained the Edward Bonaventure and both ships (with 32 other merchantmen) were 'appointed to serve westwards under the charge of Drake'. They thus started with Drake from Plymouth and seem to have accompanied Drake throughout the campaign.[5] We have no details of their service, except a report that the Merchant Royal on Tuesday 23rd. July, in company with five other English ships, became dangerously isolated and they were attacked by Spanish galleasses. After an hour and a half of spirited defence Royal Navy reinforcements drove off the Spanish. Three or four other Levant Company ships served in a separate squadron commanded by Nicholas Gorges in the Susan Parnell (a different ship from the Susan), which operated under the Lord High Admiral but started from the Eastern end of the Channel.

We should mention the comments of Royal Navy Captain Sir William Wynter, immediately after the Armada campaign, when he wrote to Sir Francis Walsingham on 8th August 1588, belittling the contribution of the merchant ships and coastal vessels, ' . . . if you had seen that which I have seen, of the simple service that hath been done by the merchant and coast ships, you would have said we had been little holpen by them, otherwise than that they did make a show. . . . ' This may, or may not, have been a fair comment with regard to the general involvement of merchantmen in the Armada campaign, but it seems to be completely inappropriate in relation to the larger Levant Company ships, like the Merchant Royal and the Edward Bonaventure, which were widely regarded as equal, in sailing and fighting qualities, to Royal Navy ships of the same size. It is also at variance with Drake's decision to pick those ships (i) for the Cadiz Raid and (ii) to serve under his immediate command in the Armada campaign, and with his chief of staff's approval of 23 merchant ship commanders as deserving rating as Royal Navy captains. At Cadiz, Drake, as already noted, designated the Merchant Royal Rear Admiral of the fleet, and picked her to cover his dash in smaller craft into the inner harbour to destroy Santa Cruz's galleon. It may be that Wynter, as a conventional Royal Navy man, felt entitled to run down the 'Volunteer Reserve'.

Post Armada

There is little doubt that the dispersal and discomfiture of the Armada fleet gave a great boost to English national morale and sent out a strong message around the world that Spain (combined with Portugal) was no longer the unchallenged European power. Informed naval opinion, however, was not at all complacent. While the superior sailing qualities of the English ships was recognized – well before the Armada campaign – other countries were already modifying their thinking and ship design. The failure of English gunnery to destroy the Armada ships in the running fight up the Channel at once stimulated re-thinking on design, use of powder and, above all, better training of the gun crews. Further, the part played in the Campaign by luck (or the intervention of the Almighty) did not go unnoticed. 'God breathed and they were scattered' was true but so was the last minute change of wind direction which saved the Armada from total disaster on the lee shore after Gravelines.

For present purposes we may note two developments which stemmed from the Armada victory. First was the attempt to build on the victory itself by sending the 1589 Expedition to Coruna and Lisbon, comprising over 100 ships and almost 20,000 soldiers under Drake and Sir John Norris. The expedition was a complete failure, with 8,000 men lost, and the planned alternative – an attack on the Azores – was abandoned. Drake's reputation suffered and he was not employed again until five years later in the attack on Panama, which was to be his last – he was buried at sea in January 1596. We know that Lancaster and his colleague Robert Flicke were employed in the 1589 Expedition to Portugal. Flicke commanded the Merchant Royal again and served in the fifth of the five squadrons into which the fleet was divided. Lancaster commanded a smaller Levant Company ship the Saloman (200 tons) in the third squadron.[6] We have no further details of their involvement in the Expedition. Secondly, the English victory 'cleared the air' by (i) dispelling the uncertainties which had distracted the London merchants from pursuing the direct route to the Spice Islands, and (ii) removed the total preoccupation of the Queen and the Privy Council with the Armada threat. The Dutch and the French, too, turned their thoughts in the same direction. The first English direct voyage to the Indies sailed in 1591, led by Captain George Raymond, who commanded the Elizabeth Bonaventure (600 tons) in the Armada campaign[7] and Raymond had long experience of privateering. Lancaster was to be third in command, but took overall command when the Admiral was lost with all hands off the Cape of Good Hope.

After the 1589 Portugal Expedition Lancaster did not serve again with the Royal Navy. He might have expected to be called up for the 1596 Raid on Cadiz (when the devastating attack led by The Lord High Admiral, the Earl of Essex and Sir Walter Raleigh probably made the Spaniards believe that Drake had returned). Certainly there were 12 London armed merchantmen involved and four of those were associated with the Levant Company. Perhaps by then Lancaster was regarded as 'too senior' simply to command a single ship.[8] Alternatively, he may have been too closely identified with Drake.

We turn therefore to the next stage in Lancaster's naval career – when peaceful trading and ruthless freebooting were closely combined.

7
Traffic or Purchase/ Trade or Privateering ?
1590-5[1]

In this chapter we describe three important events in James' life – a privateering venture in 1590, which got him into a scrape; his first major voyage to the Indies in 1591-4 and the successful Recife Raid in 1594-5.

Up to now Lancaster's naval experience has consisted of (i) serving in armed merchant ships engaged in the Levant Company's trade to the Eastern Mediterranean and, when necessary, defending them against attack (ii); and waging naval war against Spain (and Portugal) as a ship commander as part of the Royal Navy, with the leadership and example of Drake. Now he was to put his experience into practice, acting alone or with others. As we will see on some occasions the object is peaceful trading, in others licensed freebooting with ruthless aggression, in others again a mixture of the two. It is not always easy to decide which is the predominant objective – and the matter is often settled only by the last minute opportunistic decision of the commander.

First, however, to clear the ground, we may briefly outline the nature of privateering. This involved authorizing Englishmen to attack Spanish and Portuguese ships, men and goods in order to obtain compensation for damage which they had suffered from the Spanish or Portuguese. The authority was conferred under 'letters of reprisal' (similar to a court judgment), issued by the Judge of the Admiralty Court under the direction of the Lord High Admiral, who was himself empowered to do this by policy decisions of the Privy Council of which he was a member. As the war with Spain progressed it appears that the scrutiny by the Court of the damage which had been suffered became more perfunctory, and it has been authoritatively stated that there is no record of any application for letters of reprisal being refused.[2] Further, it is clear that much 'prize' i.e. booty seized, was siphoned off before it reached the jurisdiction of the Court.[3] The letters of reprisal imposed conditions on the privateer, and sureties for the due performance of these were required. Failure to observe the conditions could be investigated by the Court, as could unauthorized attacks, for example on 'neutrals' – which, strictly speaking, amounted to piracy. The system, which followed the customary law of the sea, may therefore be described as a combination of (i) self-help relief for the wronged individuals (ii) an inexpensive, additional way for England to wage war on the Spanish and their subjects. From the standpoint of shipowners, privateering was undertaken as a means of profitably employing English ships and crews for whom there might be no alternative work, for example where trade patterns had been disrupted by the war and there was no call for service with the Royal Navy. Economists have, in general, condemned privateering as being less beneficial to the national economy than trading.[4] While no doubt logically correct, it may be questioned whether investors really had a number of options available to them at any given time. Again, some writers have expressed disapproval of privateering on moral grounds, based either on their personal feelings or on the standards of a different age.[5] These criticisms, it is suggested, carry little weight if those involved at the time i.e. the Queen, the Privy Council and the privateers themselves, felt comfortable with the arrangements. Further, it seems certain that the general public thoroughly approved City magnates financing privateers to damage the Queen's enemies.[6] Perhaps the only valid and relevant question is, Was privateering a cost-effective additional way for the straitened Elizabeth to wage war against the wealthy Spanish?[7]

The 1590 privateering venture involved the two most active Levant Company ships – the Merchant Royal and the Edward Bonaventure, with Lancaster commanding the latter and Samuel Foxcroft the former: Foxcroft had commanded the Centurion (200 tons) in the Armada campaign and the Advice in the Coruna/Lisbon Expedition in 1589. So far as we know it was Lancaster's first privateering experience. The ships were sent out by George Raymond,[8] Henry Sackford, Thomas Cordell[9] and Riblum Sadler. The story is not altogether clear – the ships, like many privateers, made for the Azores, and in the period 20th – 27th.September 1590 were at Flores, Gratiosa, Faial and Pico in company with the Royal Navy fleet commanded by Sir John Hawkins, which was looking for a Spanish treasure fleet returning from the West Indies.[10] At some point – probably around 15th.September and before they joined up with the Royal Navy – the Merchant Royal and the Edward captured a small Dutch vessel named Hope, which had just picked up cargo (woad and sugar) and was still close to St..Michael (i.e. Sao Miguel) . She was from Middleburg in Walcheren and had been charted for a voyage from there to the Azores and back. The Captain was Spanish, which may have been significant. According to the evidence given subsequently by Dutch witnesses to the Admiralty Court.[11] Foxcroft physically maltreated the captain of the Hope and another crew member, who had been brought on board the Merchant Royal, and goods were taken out of the ship were only partly restored later. The Dutch complained through their ambassador in London and the case was heard by the Admiralty Court. The Judge, Master Dr. Julius Caesar, held that the complainants had been fully satisfied – as indeed they had acknowledged in the Court proceedings.[12] If it had been established that a neutral ship had been attacked and damaged it could have been a case of piracy. In the event no more seems to have been heard, and James seems to have emerged unscathed. From the garbled account it looks as though at least two, and perhaps more, other small prizes were taken, so the venture may overall have realized a profit.

The 1591-4 Voyage to the Spice Islands[13]

The expedition, consisting of the Penelope, as Admiral, commanded by George Raymond, the Merchant Royal, Vice-Admiral, commanded by Abraham Kendall[14] and the Edward Bonaventure, Rear-Admiral, commanded by Lancaster, sailed from Plymouth on 10th.April 1591.[15] The Merchant Royal was sent home from the Cape with the sick. The two other ships were lost, and only a handful of men (apart from the repatriated sick), including Lancaster himself, Edmund Barker (his lieutenant) and Henry May (the purser of the Edward Bonaventure), made it back to England in 1594, taking passage in other ships.

We have no specific information about the identity or motivation of the backers or about the preparation of the fleet – simply two account of the voyage by Hakluyt put into the mouths of Edmund Barker, lieutenant to Lancaster (who was third in command) and of Henry May (purser of the Edward Bonaventure). At the end of the main account ('by Barker') there is a 'testimonium' 'Witnesse; Master James Lancaster', presumably to make certain that, despite the editorial device of narration by Edmund Barker, the account carries full endorsement by Lancaster: we have already suggested that he and Richard Hakluyt were known to each other. Despite the lack of background information it is generally accepted that, since two of the three ships employed were Turkey/Levant Company ships, either that Company or perhaps several members of it were behind the 1591 voyage.[16] We have already noted that the moving spirits in the Company, over a long period, followed a consistent objective – to move their trading in oriental spices 'upstream' towards the source.

The Ships

We have no hard facts about the Admiral, the Penelope, except that she seems to have been owned by Captain Raymond.[17] However, since she was the Admiral and since the fleet was described by Hakluyt as 'of the three tall ships above-named' she is likely to have been of the modern 'race-built galleon' type[18] and probably larger and/or more heavily armed and/or more handy than the Merchant Royal, itself the pride of the Levant Company fleet. The same conclusion is also suggested by (i) her commander (who was also Admiral of the expedition) George Raymond. He was an experienced privateer captain[19] and had commanded the Elizabeth Bonaventure ('No ship of the time had such continuous and distinguished service') in the Armada Campaign in 1588[20] (ii) by the reallocation of the men remaining fit at the Cape, the Penelope had 101 and the Edward Bonaventure 97. We have already described the Edward Bonaventure.[21]

Manning

Since two men are recorded as dying on the way to the Cape and 50 sick were sent home, the original fleet complement was about 250, perhaps divided, as to the Penelope 100, the Merchant Royal 80 and the Edward Bonaventure 70. (After the re-allocation, as we have noted, the Penelope had 101 and the Edward 97). By way of comparison in the Armada campaign the Merchant Royal had a crew of 160, while the Edward had 120. On Fenner's voyage in 1582 the Edward's crew was around 80. A Levant Company record of 1592 shows the Merchant Royal with a crew of 70 and the Edward Bonaventure with 50. The comparatively higher manning levels on the 1591 voyage perhaps suggests more emphasis on fighting than on trading.[22]

We now turn to discuss four important aspects of the voyage; then give an abridged account of it, and, finally, attempt to draw some conclusions. First, was this voyage made for trade, or for plunder ? We have assumed that its purpose was to seek to trade for oriental spices closer to their source. The two earlier English successes in the East – the fleets of Drake and Cavendish – showed that the producers of spices were happy to trade with Englishmen.[23] It is therefore somewhat surprising to find that the 1591 voyage actually turned out, according to

Hakluyt's account, to be predominantly a privateering enterprise. [24] One merchant is recorded on board the Edward Bonaventure, one Rainold Golding, a man 'of great honestie and much discretion', who died at Penang in 1592. Probably there was also one (or perhaps more) in the Penelope, the Admiral – but she was lost with all hands soon after they entered the Indian Ocean. Some minor trading is reported, for example, for ambergris and rhino horn at Malacca and for hides in the West Indies, but for the most part trading effort was restricted to obtaining provisions and ship's stores, like pitch for recoating the hulls. Once the Edward Bonaventure was on her own all the navigational plans were directed (apart from stops for 'refreshing') to seeking out Portuguese ships to be attacked and captured. Again, there is no reference to trade goods or other saleable cargo, or coin, being embarked in the fleet at the outset, or to the possibility of buying spices or any other commodity. In general it was not unusual for the commanders of voyages primarily directed to trade to be given discretion to undertake privateering, [25] so this may have been the case here. Based on the circumstances – in particular the return home of the Merchant Royal and the total loss of the Admiral soon after the Cape – and our knowledge of Lancaster as a systematic planner and analyzer, it is suggested that the most likely explanation is that he, after cool consideration, decided that his best chance of 'making up the voyage' i.e. realising a profit, was to concentrate on privateering. With only one ship left; no factors or factory established in the area of the spice markets; any trade goods or cash which may have been embarked in London lost with the Admiral, and a disgruntled crew who eventually mutinied – this must have seemed the best bet, and it nearly succeeded. If the crew had not ransacked and refused to unload the 700 ton carrack belonging to the Captain of Malacca which Lancaster captured in December 1592, the voyage might, after all, have turned a profit. Two other incidents tend to support the view advanced above – that Lancaster deliberately chose 'purchase' as the most promising course in the circumstances in which he found himself. In December 1592 he took up position at Point de Galle at the south west of Ceylon – 'Here our capitaine meant to stay to make up our voyage' i.e. render it profitable, by capturing Portuguese ships rounding Ceylon. Mutiny forced James to abandon this plan. Lancaster's expressed desire to visit Pernambuco in north east Brazil on the way back to England could have been based on a desire to carry out reconnaissance for his Recife Raid in the following year or, perhaps more likely, represented a final effort to save the voyage's fortunes by picking up a prize as she left Pernambuco for Portugal or Spain. This, too, was prevented by the mutinous crew. Others have taken different views, however, and these must be reported. Sir William Monson had no doubt about the purposes of the 1591 Voyage: 'I cannot say our first voyages to the East Indies were by way of traffic, as out latter years have produced . . . their employment was to obstruct the trade of the Portuguese, and to seize their goods by way of letters of reprisal'.[26] It is not clear whether Monson is describing the original purpose of the voyage or the actual activities as they turned out: but, given the employment of at least one merchant, it seems an unfair judgment on the original intentions. Sir William Foster in 1940 took a somewhat different view.[27] 'The voyage was naturally to be mainly one of reconnaissance. No trading was in fact attempted, and the mention of soldiers as being on board seems to show that prize-taking was held in view from the first'. Keay's view (in 1991) was similar, 'Neither here [Penang and the Malay peninsular] nor anywhere else was any attempt made to open honest trade; it was easier to plunder Portuguese ships and easier still to waylay Burmese and Indian vessels which paid for, but rarely enjoyed, Portuguese protection. No doubt Lancaster was under pressure from his decimated and prize-hungry crew'. It is suggested that Foster's view is the more perceptive – 'no trading was in fact attempted', and 'prize-taking was held in view from the start', as it always was where letters of reprisal were held.

Secondly, we may consider the navigation and pilotage. The tentative explanation offered above for the emphasis on privateering is to some extent supported by considering this aspect of the voyage. Reading Hakluyt's account, and comparing it with the accounts of the Recife Raid and the 1601 First EIC Voyage, we see the Edward Bonaventure, both in eastern waters and, later, in the West Indies, sailing about somewhat aimlessly. Even after allowing for the uncertainties of the weather, it is difficult to feel impressed either by the knowledge shown of the channels, islands, anchorages, currents and winds or by the master's ability to get the vessel where the captain wants. There are two recorded instances where mistakes or errors of judgment in navigation prevented the Edward Bonaventure achieving its plans when crossing the Indian Ocean towards Ceylon – the criticism of the master is quite bad-tempered 'the obstinacitie of the master', 'through our master's default'. The original Master (William Mace) had already been killed at the Comoros Islands and his replacement was being referred to (John Hall – he was to die a few weeks later at Penang). It seems more than likely that the loss of the fleet pilot and the death of William Mace were serious blows to Lancaster, followed very soon by the loss of John Hall. The effect of losing his navigational experts is echoed in Lancaster's 'Hints' produced for the guidance of the Third Voyage of the EIC in 1607:[28] he describes how he was nearly wrecked on the Bassas da India[29] in the 1591 Voyage 'for I myselfe (having two very sufficient masters in my ship) was by the said currant much deceived'.

Thirdly, we must comment on the issues of leadership and discipline. Here, too, we can see a marked contrast with the Recife Raid in 1594 and the EIC First Voyage in 1601. Lancaster's concern for his men (both officers and crew), and his management style (in particular his readiness to explain to them what he was trying to achieve), normally ensured discipline and loyalty. A possible explanation here is that while Lancaster would, as third in command of the fleet, have had some influence on the picking of the Edward's original crew, the reallocation of men at the Cape may have started the trouble. While always solicitous about his men, Lancaster never forgot his 'owners' – the investors backing the voyage.[30] This would have been behind his decision, when left alone, to go for privateering, after careful weighing of the possibilities. When Lancaster arranged for a passage home for Henry May (the purser of the Edward Bonaventure), 'he requested the captaine of the French ship that he would give mee passage home with him, to certify the owners what had passed in all the voyage, as also the unruliness of the company' The purser was probably the nearest to an 'owners' representative' on board.

Fourthly, we should look at the implications of sending home the Merchant Royal, though it is not possible to provide firm answers to the questions raised. On the outward journey it took the fleet nearly four months to reach the Cape and they suffered severely from scurvy. Accordingly they 'thought good to seeke some place to refresh' the crews, and the fleet anchored in the Agoada de Saldanha, 15 leagues short of the Cape.[31] Initially, for 15 or 20 days, there were problems securing fresh victuals but eventually they succeeded in trading with the local population. There was then obviously a debate about the future. 'It was thought good rather to proceed with two ships wel manned then with three evill manned'. The conclusion was 'We left behind 50 men with the Roiall Marchant whereof there were many pretty well recovered; of which ship was master and governour Abraham Kendal, which for many reasons we thought good to send home'. The ravages of scurvy and dysentery on long ocean voyages were all too common and the standard response, as applied in this case, was to 'refresh' the crews ashore.[32] The Cape area, with its healthy climate and abundant food, was particularly effective in restoring sick men to good health quite quickly, perhaps in two weeks. The voyage would then continue: why was this course not followed in the 1591 Voyage ? We see that 'many' of the 50 were pretty well recovered, so perhaps half were fit to work the ship and half not yet recovered. Why not wait another week or two in hope that all, or most, would be fit ? If, for whatever reason, it was thought best to send one out of three ships home, why was the smallest, the Edward, with the junior ranking commander, Lancaster, not selected ? It is difficult to avoid the suspicion that there was some additional consideration ('which for many reasons we thought good to send home'), perhaps some friction or difference of opinion between the commanders. As things turned out, the safe return of the Merchant Royal with her crew of 50 represented the principal recovery from a disastrous investment, but one cannot imagine the backers of the voyage being overly pleased to see the Vice Admiral arrive back in England with an empty hold. However, Abraham Kendall served subsequently in a voyage to the West Indies in 1594-5 and again, with Drake and Hawkins, at Porto Bello in 1596 (where he died), so no blame appears to have attached to him. We have already suggested that these decisions, and the re-allocation of the sailors, may have been responsible for the unhappy state of the Edward's crew.

The 1591 Voyage – An Abridged Account[33]

1591

10/4 Sailed from Plymouth
23 to 29/4 At Canaries
2/5 Off Cape Blanco
8/5 Off Cape Verde
13/5 Within 8 degrees of the Line. Contrary winds. Took a caravel out of Lisbon for Brazil, with wine and a variety of provisions 'better to us than gold'
6/6 Crossed the Line. Wind ESE took us along the coast of Brazil. At 26 degrees south wind N, set course for the Cape of Good Hope
28/7 Sighted the Cape but winds contrary.
1/8 'We bare up with the land to the Northwest of the Cape' Anchored in Agoada de Saldanha, 15 leagues NW on hither side of the Cape to refresh.[34] Traded cheaply for bullocks, oxen and sheep. Decided to send 50 men (some sick) home in the Merchant Royal (with Abraham Kendall) and re-allocate sound men to Penelope (giving her 101) and Edward Bonaventure (97)
?September Penelope and Merchant Royal passed the Cape.
14/9 Penelope disappeared in a violent storm off Cape Dos Corrientos. 'We saw a great sea breake over our admiral, the Penelope' Edward waited at the designated rendezvous, the Comoros Islands.
18/9 Edward's mainmast shattered by lightning. Four men killed and all others injured, though they later recovered. Proceeded NE through the Mozambique Channel, narrowly avoiding the Bassas da India. Reached Quitangonha Island, 10 miles north of Mozambique. Captured

The Cape to Madagascar

3 or 4 'moorish' i.e.islamic or arab, pangaias [small sailing cargo boats] with foodstuffs and some blue Calicut cloth for Mozambique and one Portuguese boy, whom we retained to act as interpreter

?**October** Reached Comoros Islands, heavily populated by 'moors', 'very treacherous.and diligently to be taken care of'. Some foodstuffs and water were obtained but on a fourth visit for water, in the Edward's only boat, the Master (William Mace), two Mates and 14 men were killed

7/11 Set course for Zanzibar where we stayed, building a replacement boat. Captured another pangaia, with an important priest aboard, but released it against two months victuals. Attacked a Portuguese pangaia, but were beaten off. Zanzibar offered excellent anchorage and plentiful food and water and the 'moors' were friendly, warning us of the approach of the Portuguese Admiral responsible for Melinde to Mozambique in an 18 oar galley. 'This place . . .is carefully to be sought for by such of our ships as shall hereafter passe that way'

1592

15/2 Set sail for Cape Comorin, SW India, intending to lie off to intercept Portuguese vessels, but we were driven by currents and wind to the N, so decided to make for Socotra or the Red Sea for refreshment and booty. However the wind changed to NW and we set course for Cape Comorin.

May Passed Cape Comorin [and Ceylon] without sight of land after missing the Laccadive islands 'partly by the obstinacie of our master' [he was John Hall, replacement for William Mace]. Ran for the Nicobar Islands but after six days missed them 'through our master's default, for want of due observation of the south starre' .

1/6 Reached Gomes off Sumatra, two or three days becalmed. Anchored at Penang, remaining 'until the winter was overpast' at end-August. 26 men died, including John Hall (Master) and Rainold Golding 'a merchant of great honestie and much discretion'

end-August Set sail with 33 men and one boy (of whom but 22 were fit) and anchored near Malacca. Shot seafowl (called oxe birds) [A name used to describe shore-birds/waders, particularly dunlin: they shot some eight dozen with haile-shot 'being very tame'] and obtained victuals ashore. Saw three ships of 60-70 tons out of Martaban (near Moulmein): took one and loaded her cargo of pepper from Perak. Took another ship from Pegu [Burma] but released her. Early Sailed for Sembilan Islands to intercept Portuguese shipping. Took a September 250 ton Portuguese ship out of Negapatam [SE India] laden with rice. Took a pilot and four

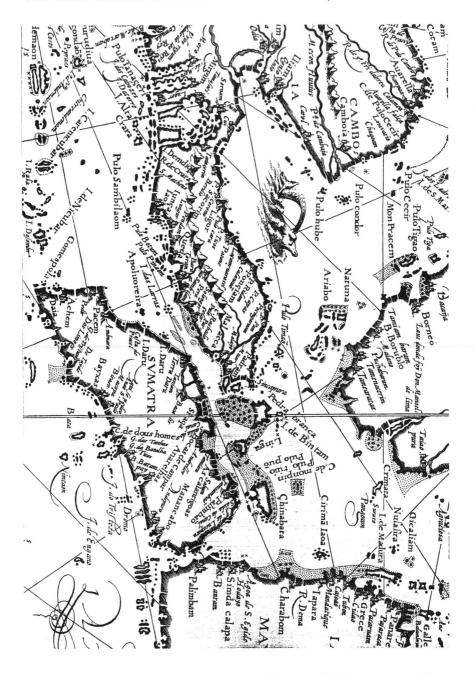

Malaysia, Sumatra and Java. Priaman (not shown on this chart) was 40 miles south of the Equator on the south-west coast of Sumatra.

moors from her. Attacked another 400 ton Portuguese ship out of St.Tome 'but our ship was so foule shee escaped us'

6/10 Attacked a 700 ton ship of the Captain of Malacca with 18 cannon and rich cargo: the crew fled ashore. The sailors pillaged her and refused to unload her. So we took the choicest things and set her adrift. Made for a bay near Junkceylon (Salang) to careen the ship. Obtained pitch ashore and bartered with the King for ambergris and rhino horn.

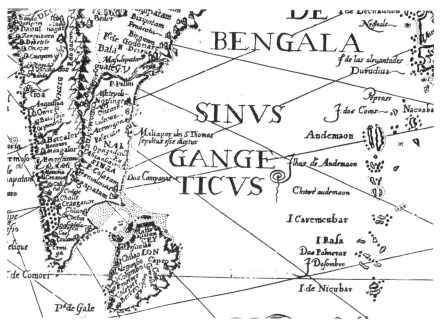

The Andaman and Nicobar Islands to Ceylon

?Late October Returned to Nicobar Islands. Obtained victuals. Traded Calicut cloth for rials of plate from two sunk Portuguese ships bound for China. 'This was the furthest place that we were at to the south east'

21/11 Set sail for Ceylon

3/12 Anchored on S side of Ceylon then moved to anchor off Point de Galle to await the Portuguese ships of which we had intelligence. 'Here our capitaine meant to stay to make up our voyage' [i.e. to capture sufficient booty to make the voyage profitable] The crew insisted that we should sail for home, 'our capitaine at that time lying very sicke, more like to die than to live'.

8/12 Set sail for the Cape, passing the Maldive islands and passing Madagascar to starboard. The captain recovered his health.

1593

February Made Africa landfall at Delgoa Bay

March With contrary winds took 4-5 weeks to round the Cape

3/4 Reached St.Helena and stayed 19 days. Good refreshment. Found John Segar left behind sick by the Merchant Royal: he died from the shock of seeing us after 18 [? 14] months alone. Once refreshed the crew demanded to sail direct for home. The captain who wished to go to Pernambuco agreed. [Perhaps Lancaster hoped to pick up a prize or merely intended to investigate the prospects of plunder for his Recife Raid the following year]

12/22 April Set course for Pernambuco but the crew demanded a direct course for England which we were forced to adopt. Spent six weeks with contrary winds and calms between the Line and 9 degrees N. Crew mutinous. Altered course for Trinidad for refreshment.

Early June Entered the Gulf of Paria, became embayed and took 8 days to claw out at the N end. ['The Dragon's Mouth'] After four days reached Mona Island [between Santo Domingo and Puerto Rico]; anchored for 18 days and obtained victuals from the Indians and also from a French ship from Caen (M. de Barbotiere). Watered and repaired a leak.

?July-August Intended to set course for Newfoundland but a N storm set us S of Santo Domingo where we were nearly wrecked on flats off Saona Island. Sailed westwards, doubled Cape Tiburon and passed the channel between Santo Domingo and Cuba for the Cape of Florida. Again met with M.de Barbotiere, purchased some hides but he could not spare more victuals.

September Passing the Cape of Florida and clearing the Bahamas Channel we set course for Newfoundland.

17/9 We were to the E of the Bahamas. Lay there 2/3 days, with variable winds 'contrarie to our expectation and all men's writings'

?October Wind shifted to N and increased to storm force, carried away our furled sails. Six feet of water in the hold. Wind slackened but increased again. Lost the foremast. When the wind eased it was contrary, so we made for Santo Domingo, but the wind again shifted and we sailed west to the Cloudy Islands [not identified], near Puerto Rico. After seven days refreshing we decided to return to Mona: at this five men deserted [They eventually got back to England] .

20/11 Returned to Mona. Lancaster and Edmund Barker with part of the crew went ashore seeking provisions. The crew left on board, five men and a boy, by night cut the cable and sailed away, leaving 19 men ashore. [The ship was wrecked and eventually captured by the Spanish]

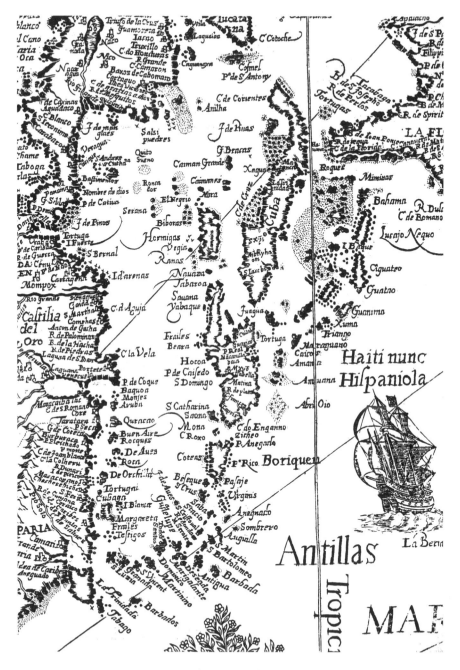

The West Indies

?**December** After 29 days ashore Lancaster and Barker went aboard a French ship and when a second French ship arrived the surviving crew members (less seven who went missing ashore) were allocated equally between the two, and sailed for the north coast of Santo Domingo, remaining there until April 1594. 'Spent some two monethes in traffike with the inhabitants, by permission, for hides and other merchandises of the countrey'

1594

7/4 Lancaster and Barker took passage in another French ship out of Dieppe (Captain was John Le Noyer or Lenoir), having arranged passage for the rest of the crew in other ships.
19/5 Lancaster and Barker arrived Dieppe.
24/5 Arrived Rye.
1/8 Henry May (purser of the Edward) reached Falmouth, after having been wrecked with Captain de Barbotiere at Bermuda.

By any standards the 1591 voyage was a failure. Apart from the Merchant Royal returning from the Cape with the sick, the total investment was lost and all but a handful of the men. It did mark the first direct voyage from England to the Far East (which actually got there)[35] though the feasibility of English ships sailing round south east Asia, and trading successfully with the local inhabitants, had been demonstrated some years earlier by Drake and Cavendish. However, the only real error was the late departure which meant that the fleet effectively missed a season on entering the Indian Ocean. This was probably due, not to any fault of the commanders, but to delay in equipping the ships. This is echoed in the rather wistful comment near the end of Hakluyt's account, 'having spent in this voyage three yeeres, six weekes and two dayes (which the Portugals performe in halfe the time) chiefly because wee lost our fit time and season to set foorth in the beginning of our voyage'. Over six months was completely wasted (at Zanzibar and Penang), with the Edward Bonaventure at anchor, waiting for the season and the winds to change.

Lancaster was to use citrus fruit to combat scurvy on the 1601 EIC First Voyage, but there was already some knowledge of this solution[36] and, perhaps, if he had been in overall command of the voyage at the outset it would have been adopted. The terrible weather encountered after passing the Cape (and, much later, in the West Indies) was plain bad luck. Deficiencies in pilotage and navigation seem to have stemmed from the loss of the Admiral, and with her the fleet pilot, charts and routers. We have suggested that the failure to carry out any substantial trading was due to Lancaster's measured decision, following the loss, with the Admiral, of the senior merchant or merchants and, perhaps, the supply of trade goods and/or cash to prime the trading pump. Where there were no expatriate factors and no 'factory' in the market being visited, successful trading required a sustained programme of careful selling and purchasing at sensible prices to fill the hold. Such a plan was hardly feasible with a mutinous crew. With privateering, on the other hand, one lucky prize could cover the costs and any further prizes then build up the profits (and, perhaps, restore the morale, if not the discipline, of the crew). The ship belonging to the Portuguese Captain at Malacca, which the sailors refused to unload, might have been enough. High risks may generate high rewards – this, sadly did not happen on the 1591 voyage.

Considerations of the kind discussed above probably explain that, while the voyage in commercial and human terms was a disaster, no blame was laid at Lancaster's' door and, if anything, his reputation appears to have been enhanced. We must conclude that the 1591 voyage backers were hard-headed merchant adventurers who understood the inherent risk/reward formula, and reckoned that Lancaster, having succeeded unexpectedly to the command, had done as well as was possible. Within a few months of his return a City of London syndicate dispatched Lancaster on the Recife Raid, when sound management and bold leadership generated good luck and spectacular rewards.

The Recife Raid 1594-5

Here, at least, there was no doubt – this was a voyage for purchase i.e. plunder.

To set the scene, it is interesting to note that Hakluyt, while describing the 1591 Voyage to the East Indies as 'A voyage....to the East Indies' introduces the Recife Raid as 'The well governed and prosperous voyage of Master James Lancaster....'.[37] It was indeed well managed and extremely successful, in both military and commercial terms. It made Lancaster famous and wealthy and confirmed him as a leading naval/military commander.[38] In its boldness, strong leadership, and adaptation to circumstances as they changed the expedition has all the hallmarks of Drake – demonstrating Lancaster's ability to learn fast and apply what he had learned. Additional characteristics contributed by him on his own account were a firm but flexible plan, meticulous attention to detail, paternal consideration for his men and a cooler, less tempestuous style. By bringing together and applying his skills and experience Lancaster made the Recife Raid a copybook amphibious operation.

Lancaster returned to England from the 1591 Voyage, landing at Rye, on 24th.May 1594. He sailed on the Recife Raid in September the same year, only four months later. We do not know for certain whether some such enterprise was already being planned – and Lancaster and his faithful Lieutenant Edmund Barker were invited to lead it – or whether a new plan was hastily put together and implemented, at James' instigation. In April 1593 Lancaster in the Edward Bonaventure (by then the only surviving ship in the 1591 Voyage) called at St.Helena to 'refresh' his crew. He announced his intention to set course for Pernambuco (the town in north east Brazil for which the port was Recife), but his mutinous crew would have none of it and demanded a direct course for England. It seem likely that Lancaster either felt that there was still a chance (even with a depleted and unhappy crew) of recovering the fortunes of the 1591voyage by picking up a valuable prize in that locality (the prospect of booty could do wonders for unhappy sailors), or alternatively, that he might usefully reconnoitre a port which could offer an opportunity for some future action. Obviously, if Lancaster thought that Pernambuco might be a promising target for privateering, others at home might be thinking the same.

Until James and Edmund Barker got home in May 1594 it seems likely that there had been no news of the voyage since the Merchant Royal reached England with the sick crewmen around the end of 1591 or early in 1592. The Edward Bonaventure seems to have kept away from the busier ports in the East from which word might have got back to England. Lancaster's return, even without any ships and with a handful of survivors, may have come as a surprise. So on balance it is reasonable to assume that having explained himself satisfactorily to the backers of the 1591 Voyage he immediately went on to sell the idea to a City of London syndicate of an attack on Recife, or on Portuguese ships using that port on their way to or from Portugal.

The real commercial success of the Recife Raid, in the event, turned on the happy coincidence of the rich cargo of a wrecked carrack on its way home having been unloaded at that port some time before Lancaster arrived: from the account in Hakluyt it seems as though intelligence of this only reached him when he was already on his way down the coast of West Africa. 'At this place [Cape Blank] he understood, of one of the pilots of those ships [which the Salomon had captured], that one of the caracks that came out of the East Indies was cast away in the rode of Fernambuc, and that all her goods were layd upon the Arracife [i.e. the port of Recife], which is the lower town. Of these newes we were all glad and rejoyced much; for our hopes were very good, seeing such a booty before us.' Leaving aside this windfall, it looks as though the attractions of Recife for a privateer were local produce – 'brazil wood',[39] cotton and sugar and the possibility of capturing visiting Portuguese ships, either outward bound from Portugal or on their way home from further south in Brazil or from the East Indies.

The Investing Syndicate

The backers of the Recife adventure included John Watts, Paul Banning, Master Sute Salter, Simon Boreman, Thomas Cordell, Roger Howe and John More – a high powered City group.[40] Sir John Watts was a member of the Clothworkers Company, was knighted in 1603 and became Lord Mayor in 1606-7. He owned the Margaret and John, a 200 ton armed merchantman. She served with distinction in the Cadiz Raid in 1587, in the Armada campaign (with Watts on board as a 'volunteer') and also in 'The Valiant Fight' in 1590 when a fleet of merchantmen, sailing in convoy, fought off an attack by Spanish galleys off Cadiz. She was listed as a Levant Company ship in 1592, but on that occasion she was probably chartered in from Sir John. His son served in the Recife Raid, being given command of the galley frigate which was built on frames brought from England at Maio in the Cape Verde Islands: he was described as 'an honest, skilfull mariner'. Sir John who died in 1616 'was certainly the greatest of the merchant promoters of privateering'.[41] Paul Banning (1588-1616) was a member of the Grocers' Company, an original grantee of the Venice Company in 1563 and a member of the Levant Company 1592. Nothing is known of Salter. Boreman in his youth was an expatriate merchant with the 'Brotherhood of St. George' in Andalusia. He married a Spanish wife and returned to England in 1576, becoming an original member of the Spain/Portugal Company in 1577. He is stated to have been the owner of the Salomon,[42] which was engaged on several occasions on Levant Company voyages, no doubt being chartered in for that purpose.[43] His son, Simon, also served in the Recife Raid and is described as 'a toward and likely youth'. Thomas Cordell was a Mercer and Alderman and was the principal owner of the Merchant Royal and the Edward Bonaventure – ships with which Lancaster had been closely connected. John More was a Master of the Skinners' Company and an alderman, and became a director of the EIC.

The Command Structure

The initial arrangement was:- Lancaster, as Admiral in the Consent; Edmund Barker (Lancaster's Lieutenant in the 1591 Voyage) Vice Admiral in the Salomon, and John Awdely (or Addey) (of Poplar) Rear-Admiral in the Virgin. Once the galley frigate was constructed its command was entrusted to John Watts, junior, the son of the chief investor Sir John Watts. On the way down the Channel the fleet was forced by heavy weather into Dartmouth to repair the mast of the Salomon. Here Lancaster fell in with Captain Randolph Cotton, an experienced commander who had served with Thomas Cavendish. Displaying his usual opportunistic bent and diplomatic skill, Lancaster persuaded Cotton to join the expedition as his Lieutenant, and also, it appears, to invest in the voyage. At Maio in the Cape Verde Islands the fleet met up with Captain John Venner of Plymouth. He was in his own ship, the Peregrine, with a Biscayne prize which he had taken at Cape Blanck, and with the Welcome of Plymouth and her pinnace. Here again Lancaster's courtesy and charm, and the explanation of what he was planning, led to Venner and his squadron joining forces with Lancaster's team. Venner's group would take 25% and Lancaster's 75%, and thereafter Venner became a trusted senior colleague. Sadly, Venner appears to have died in the course of the voyage, though the circumstances are not clear. Once at Recife, Lancaster found three large Dutch vessels. They had come from Spain 'sent by the owners...to bring those goodes home which was left, now two years since, by a carick which was cast away'. . After some initial suspicion the Dutch were persuaded to carry Lancaster's Brazil wood to Europe for freight payments, and thereafter the Dutch officers and crew fought and worked alongside the English 'as truly and as faithfully as our owne people did'. Finally, a few days later at Recife a French squadron arrived which included, coincidentally, the Captain Noyer (or Lenoir) who had rescued Lancaster the previous year when he had been abandoned on the island of Mona by his mutinous crew. They too were bent, not on trade but on booty, so Lancaster, after offering hospitality and kindnesses,[to 'both him and his whole companie; wherein showing himself a most brave and grateful gentleman'] promised to fill their three ships with Brazil wood, and he gave them one of the prize ships, again with a lading of Brazil wood. Lancaster also gave Captain Noyer the remainder of the commodities out of the carrack that the English ships could not load. The French and the Dutch did yeoman service manning the guard boats permanently moored in the river at Recife, to protect the anchored ships, and served alongside the English in the disastrous sally, where two of the French captains were killed.

Thus while Lancaster left England with three small ships he sailed out of Recife leading a fleet of fifteen ships all fully laden with the pick of the booty found in the town.

The Ships

The original fleet consisted of three ships, the Consent (240 tons), the Salomon (170 tons) and the Virgin (60 tons). In addition the fleet carried the pre-fabricated frames[44] for a galley frigate which would be assembled, planked and rigged on the way to Brazil: this ship, equipped with oars as well as sails, was designed as a 'landing craft' – 'of purpose to land men in the country of Brasil'. The Salomon had had a distinguished trading and fighting record with the Levant Company,[45] participating in the Cadiz expedition with Drake in 1587 and being engaged in The Valiant Fight in 1590.[46] She is stated as being owned by Master Boreman. Nothing is known of the Consent, but since she was much larger than the Salomon and was designated Lancaster's Admiral,[47] it is reasonable to assume that she was superior in all respects to the Salomon. No other information has been found concerning the Virgin. The plan for the galley frigate is interesting. It was quite usual for ships to carry prefabricated frames which would be built into a complete pinnace in the course of a voyage, but a special design based on combined sail and oar power – 14 oars on either side – (with 'in her prow a good sacar and two murdering pieces'), is unusual and suggests knowledge (or supposition) of special local conditions. In the event, this special design seems not to have been needed for the dash of a few hundred yards from the anchored ships to the shore., at which point she was smashed on the beach and sank. The actual landing, in the event, could have been effected by ordinary ships' boats, but the galley frigate was larger, being packed with some 80 armed men. Perhaps the sophisticated galley frigate design was decided upon for general purpose use in Brazil without detailed knowledge of the conditions at Recife. The total tonnage of Lancaster's original fleet (including the galley frigate of 60 tons) amounted to 530 tons. The total crew was 275, thus maintaining the conventional ratio of approximately one man to two tons.

The Target

We have already noted that Lancaster seems to 'have had his eye on' Pernambuco for some time.[48] There is no indication that he had been there (in fact his wish to do so in the course of the 1591 Voyage suggests that he had not) but had perhaps been tipped off by Drake or some other mariner, or perhaps by a merchant – Lancaster's (second) master, Robert Walkeden had commercial connections with Brazil. Olinda was some five miles up the River Bebearibe which seems not to have been navigable in 1595 for large vessels. This river has continued to silt up over the years.

Recife was the port for Olinda, at the mouth of four rivers, the Barretta, the Aeffogados, the Capibiribi and the Bebearibi. The flow from these four rivers has no doubt, over many years, formed the bar and the long, thin promontory on the eastern end of which stood Recife.[49] The neighbourhood was described in 1587 by Lopez Vaz, an experienced Portuguese traveller; 'Now to return to Fernambuck [a variant on Pernambuco] inhabited by a Portugall Captaine called Duarte Coelio, it is the greatest towne in all that coast, and hath above three thousand houses in it, with seventie Ingenios [mills] for sugar, and great store of Brassil-wood and abundance of cotton, yet are they in great want of victuals; for all their victuals come either from Portugal or from some other places upon the coast of Brasil.[50] The harbour of this towne is a barred harbour, and fit only for small barques: this place belongeth as yet unto the sonne of Duarte Coelio'[51] When the original grantee of the Pernambuco area arrived by sea soon after 1530 he exclaimed 'O que linda situacam !' – What a beautiful place ! It is said that his comment was abbreviated to form the name Olinda. It is difficult to know whether Lancaster had any charts or sailing instructions for Recife. There is no mention of a pilot with local knowledge. He certainly arrived there with a plan to capture the town using boats, so he is likely at least to have known about the tricky bar at the harbour mouth, which probably only allowed seagoing ships to enter and leave at high water with a favourable wind. We suggest below[52] that the fleet seemed to have arrived sooner than expected at Recife, perhaps by reason of a favourable W/SW current in the Atlantic which they had been unable to detect, having no means of measuring longitude.

Apart from attacking Recife there is no doubt that it was Lancaster's intention to capture any worthwhile Spanish or Portuguese ships. A number of prizes were indeed taken on the voyage out.

The Passage to Brazil

The fleet was victualled at Blackwall in September 1594 and set sail in October. Storms were encountered in the West Country and the Salomon lost her mast off Dartmouth, so the fleet put in there for shelter and repairs. Lancaster here recruited Captain Cotton to join the expedition as his Lieutenant. They sailed again at the end of November with a northerly gale. After only 50 leagues from Devon the Consent was separated from the Salomon and the Virgin in heavy weather, but pressed on to the first agreed rendezvous at the Canary Islands or Cape Blank. With no meeting there the Consent set course for Tenerife. Arriving there in calm conditions she spotted a ship being towed by her boats. She turned out to be Spanish and the crew tried to escape in their boats. They were captured together with their ship, which was laden with 80 tons of Canary wine 'which came not unto us before it was welcome'. Another Spanish ship was taken the next day, with 40 tons of wine, and her crew was set ashore in Tenerife. The Consent then set course for Cape Blank where she met up with the Virgin who reported that the Salomon had again lost her mast and returned to England. The crew became upset, feeling that the fleet which had been small at the outset was now so reduced as to be unable to carry out its purpose and urged Lancaster to make for the West Indies instead. He, however, as was his custom (and 'as not unacquainted with the variable pretenses of mariners') discussed the situation with them in a firm but friendly manner: 'Sirs, I made known to you all at my comming out of England what I pretended [i.e.intended], and that I meant to go for Fernambuck....I mean to go forward, not doubting but to meet her at the appointed places...for I am assured that Master Barker.. is so resolute to perform this voyage that his mast being repaired he will not fail to meet us, and it were no wisdom for us to divert our course, till we have sought him where our appointed meeting is; for the diverting of courses is the overthrow of most of our actions.' Lancaster talked them round – and at Cape Blank the Salomon duly appeared, having already captured 24 Spanish and Portuguese vessels. Lancaster retained four of the Salomon's prizes plus one of his own, 'for to serve us in the country, drawing little water, for divers purposes'.. It was at this point that Lancaster learned, from the pilot of one of the captured vessels, that a carrack returning from the East Indies had been wrecked off Pernambuco and her cargo had been landed at Recife. The prospect of this rich booty, following the reunion of the fleet, sent morale rocketing. The fleet made for Maio, one of the Cape Verde islands and Lancaster and the other commanders went ashore to seek a safe place to build the galley frigate. Work commenced and was completed in about three weeks. John Watts, junior 'an honest skilfull mariner' was given the command. It was during the ship building that a member of the crew wandered away, became lost and was rescued and brought back by the 'Portugalls', who were warmly thanked and rewarded by Lancaster in person – not (as we have already suggested) the actions of a man with a lifelong grudge against the Portuguese. While at Maio Captain John Venner and his Plymouth fleet came to anchor nearby and, after social exchanges and explanations of the planned operation, James and Venner negotiated a deal to work together – with 25% for the Plymouth team and 75% for the original fleet. Venner's fleet consisted of his own ship, the Peregrine; a Biscayen which he had captured at Cape Blank; the Welcome of Plymouth and her pinnace. With the galley frigate completed the fleet, now doubled in size,

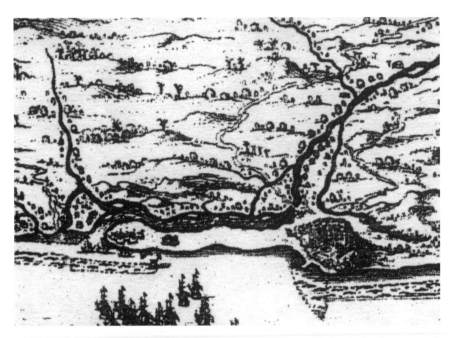

Recife and Pernambuco (Olinda) in NE Brazil. Recife stands at the harbour mouth on the extreme end of the sand spit and is the deep water port for Olinda, seen at the landward end of the spit. Note the bar across the harbour mouth.

sailed to Braya, another of the Cape Verde Islands, to water and then, without delay, set course for Pernambuco., and made its South American landfall south of Cape St. Augustine [The old name for the extreme NE tip of Brazil] 'From thence wee plied still to our desired port of Fernambuck'.

The Recife Raid – A Day by Day Abridged Account

[The account by Hakluyt does not permit exact allocation of the days]

Day 1 Lancaster's fleet arrived off Recife around midnight on Maundy Thursday, 17th.April 1595.[In 1595 Easter Day, according to Whittaker's Almanac, fell on 20th.April – see the reference to Good Friday below] It looks as though they made a quicker passage than had been expected – the original plan was probably to make a surprise attack at first light in the best Drake manner.[53] Since the entrance to the harbour was risky, with a bar to cross, it was decided to sail up and down the coast and enter in daylight. Throughout the night Lancaster went in his boat from ship to ship, urging each one to arm as many men as could be spared and embark them in their boats, with a view to an attack at first light. The ships were to remain outside until the fort and the lower town (Recife) had been taken

Day 2. Unfortunately the boats were set past the harbour to the north, added to which the tide turned adverse, so that it was 2pm. before the fleet of small boats was back opposite the entrance and able to enter.

In the meantime, around noon, a representative of the governor came on board Lancaster's ship 'to know what he would have, and wherefore he came'. The Admiral did not mince his words, answering 'that he wanted the carrack's goods; for them he came and them he would have and that that he should shortly see'.

Lancaster embarked in the galley (just built at the Cape Verde Islands) with 80 men from his ship the Content. In addition to the ships' boats there were the five small prizes (which had been taken off Cape Blank). Perhaps some 230 men in total.

Before the attack could commence there was another problem – which, in the event, proceeded to solve itself. As soon as it was light three large Dutch ships were seen to be anchored in the mouth of the harbour (one of 450 tons; one of 350 and one of 300) – in fact they had been employed to come to recover the carrack's cargo. Lancaster did not know how they would react, so he instructed the five prize vessels that, if the Dutch showed any sign of aggression, they should board them and set them on fire. The Dutch appear to have sized up the situation – the exchange of fire between the English ships and the fort and the landing party embarking in the ships' boats – and they warped their vessels away from the harbour mouth.

By now the Portuguese and their local supporters had rallied and sent a party of some 600 armed men[54] to man the fort at the tip of the long promontory and resist an English landing. Fire was exchanged between the fort and the ships. The latter were undamaged but the Consent's gunners[55] scored two direct hits on the fort.

Before leading in his flotilla Lancaster ordered that all the boats should be driven violently ashore under the fort and that no one should remain in the boats – he was determined that there would be no way back. (The brand new galley frigate broke her back and sank). With the flood tide under them the boats made for the fort, which opened fire. Fortunately, no important damage was suffered on the way in and as the galley and the boats hit the beach Lancaster leapt into the water and led his men up to the fort. Fortunately, again, the seven guns in the fort were too depressed and their salvo drove into the sand. One of the landing party lost his arm. 'Upon them, upon them' shouted Lancaster, 'all (by God's help) is ours', and they stormed the fort.[56] The defendants fled, leaving seven brass cannon undamaged.

The anonymous teller of the story commented on this splendid victory (it is tempting to attribute the words to Lancaster himself):- 'This day of our arrival was their Good-Friday, when by custome they usually whippe themselves : but God sent us for a generall scourge to them all, whereby that labour among them might be well spared'.

As soon as the fort was taken Lancaster signalled the ships to enter the harbour, and himself led his men towards the lower town (Recife), only about three hundred yards away, leaving a party to occupy the fort and re-position the cannon against a counter-attack from the upper town (Olinda). As Lancaster and his men entered Recife the inhabitants fled by boat. In the town of some 100 dwellings, they 'found... great store of merchandise of all sorts: as Brasil wood, sugars, calico cloth, pepper, cynamon, cloves, mace, nutmegs, with divers other good things, to the comfort of us all'.

Lancaster immediately took steps to secure the town, placing his commanders and giving strict instructions against stealing and looting – which, in the event, were never disregarded – 'which is a thing much to be observed in such an action; for common mariners and souldiers are much given to pillaging and spoiling, making greater account of the same than of their shares' [i.e. their percentage entitlement on the overall result of the expedition]

'A very sure watch' was kept this first night

Day 3 At first light Lancaster and Captain Venner walked the town and gave instructions for fortifying it. Using the plentiful timber available a nine foot palisade was built round the town, completed within two days. Also commenced at once was a new fort built along the narrow promontory (no wider than 40 paces across at high water), in which the cannon from the original fort were placed.

Having put in hand these military measures Lancaster turned to diplomacy. He dispatched his surgeon – who had been brought up in the Netherlands – to talk to the Dutch ships. 'Although this people were somewhat stubborn at the first, as that nation is in these causes' the doctor talked them round to agree to carry timber to England for payment. The Dutch came ashore, agreed a freight rate with Lancaster, made friends and proved staunch and faithful allies.

About midnight a great number of Portuguese (with Indian support) launched an attack. The defendants were ready for them and Lancaster had provided all the muskets with haile-shot. [small shot which scatters like hail when discharged], which drove them off, one discharge killing both a horse and its rider. Lancaster lost one man: the enemy more, but they removed their dead and wounded in the dark, so their casualties could not be counted.

Day 4 Three ships and two pinnaces appeared before the harbour. One pinnace spotted the English flags and sailed in, whereupon Lancaster sent an invitation to the squadron to come in, which they did. They turned out to be French privateers, looking for 'purchase' i.e. plunder. One of the captains turned out, too, to be an old friend – the Captain John Noyer (or Lenoir) from Dieppe who had helped Lancaster at Mona the previous year (1594) when the Edward Bonaventure had sailed away without him.

Lancaster greeted him warmly, agreed to his request for a lading of Brazil wood for his ship and his pinnace and gave him a prize caravel of 50 tons, again with a promise of lading with Brazil wood. To the two other captains (one from Dieppe and the other from La Rochelle) Lancaster also promised ladings of Brazil wood. He also gave the Frenchmen the oriental commodities left over after he had loaded his own ships.[57]

Having secured the defences, Lancaster commenced the work of loading the ships; in the case of the English ships it was re-loading, since they had come in full and now proceeded to re-load with the most valuable items available. The force was divided into two, one party loading (with their weapons in good order set and placed by them) while the other stood guard 'with their furniture in their hands'. The prize which had held wine and the Welcome's pinnace were used as lighters to carry the cargo to the anchored ships.

The Dutch handled the loading of their three ships separately.

It was on this day, too, that the deputation arrived from Olinda (about four miles away) 'three or four of the principall gentlemen of the countrey, and said that from the bishop, themselves and the rest, they would have some conference with our admiral'. There followed the set-piece drama already described,[58] with Lancaster making himself unavailable by going on board the Dutch ships until the deputation gave up and left, and then justifying his conduct to the men, with his classic description of his time in Portugal as a young man and his comments on the behaviour to be expected from Spaniards and Portuguese.

Lancaster's instructions that, for the future, anyone coming over would be warned that thereafter 'he would be hanged out of hand' had its effect. Only a few slaves came over subsequently, from which he was able to learn what was afoot.

Day 5 As the loading went forward the Portuguese, 'seeing us so busie' started during the night to cast up a trench in the sands 'about a sacar shot from our ships' i.e. about 2/3 of a mile [extreme range for a saker was about one mile]. Since this was clearly aimed at installing guns to attack the ships and impede their loading, Lancaster and his captains led an attack, at which the Portuguese and Indians fled, leaving 'four good pieces of brasse ordinance, with powder and shot and divers other necessities', and also five small country carts 'which to us were worth more than al the rest we tooke' for moving the heavy items of cargo. The platforms being constructed were destroyed. Following this engagement there were no more Portuguese initiatives for a few days.

Day 6 The next day brought more good luck. 'And this farther good chance or blessing of God we had to help us, that as soon as we had taken our cartes' a Portuguese vessel the next morning came into the harbour, with 60 negroes, 10 Portuguese women and 40 Portuguese. The women and negroes were turned away but Lancaster kept the Portuguese to draw the carts when they were laden 'which to us was a very great ease. For the country is very hote and ill for nation to take any great travell in'.

Throughout the time at Recife it was necessary, every five or six days, to go over to the mainland opposite the town to fetch water, for there was none at Recife itself. The Portuguese soon spotted this weakness and attempted to prevent the watering parties: several men were lost and injured.

Days 7-19 Loading of the ships continued. Sometime in this period an attempt was made to cut the anchor cable of the Admiral, the Consent, by night. This attempt was detected by the watch boats, and the swimmers managed only to cut the rope attaching the anchor buoy, not the anchor cable itself.

Day 20 The Portuguese were also preparing fire-ships.[' a policie learned to their cost in England' – a reference to the English fire ship attack at Calais in 1588] The first attack was made around Day 20. Five caravels filled with combustibles were brought within about one mile of the ships at anchor and then launched. (They could not be brought any closer since Lancaster had always maintained at least six boats on watch half a mile from the ships) However, with wind and tide both in their favour the fire-ships rapidly approached the fleet, and there was considerable apprehension. Foresight and detailed training once again paid off, and there was no panic or disorder. 'Our companie in the boats so played the men when they saw the fires come neere our ships.....and so we were delivered, by God's help, from this fearfull danger'. The caravels were secured by grapnels and either grounded or brought to anchor, and no damage ensued.

Days 21-25 Loading of the ships continued

Day 26 Six nights later, at around 11pm, the second fire attack was launched.

Three great rafts were sent down the river. They had many poles protruding from them to foil the use of grapnels and stores of fireworks which emitted sparks and threatened to set off the powder held in the boats and carried by the men. At first the boatmen 'durst not for fear of fyring themselves with their owne powder' close with the rafts but they dampened cloths and laid then over their equipment, and then were able to board them safely, attach grapnels and haul them ashore.

While this attack was also foiled there was intelligence from a negro slave that a third fire attack was in preparation – still more problematic 'such as we should never be able to prevent'. However the expedition sailed away before this could be launched.

Day 31 With the lading of the ships completed Lancaster gave notice that the fleet would depart that night or, at latest, the following morning. He did, however, notice fresh activity on the sand near the anchored ships, with the start of some kind of fortification. He went at once to the town (Recife) and consulted with his captains. His view was that they should depart that night 'saying that it was but folly to seeke warres, since we had no need to do it'. Other of the commanders said that it was prudent to investigate, since the wind might not be favourable for leaving the harbour. In the end, Lancaster decided that they should attack the new works in force but stay within the cover of the ships' guns: 'the ships may play upon them with 40 peeces of ordinance at the least, so that a bird cannot passe there but she must be slaine'. Lancaster said that he had been unwell for the last two days and was 'not strong enough to march upon these heavie sands'.

Accordingly, some 275 English and French men set out under the leadership of Edmund Barker (Captain of the Salomon), Captain Barker of Plymouth (2 i/c to Captain Venner), Captain Addey and the three French captains. It appears that Captain Cotton, as Lancaster's Lieutenant and 'principall leader for their land service' was in overall charge. Lancaster warned them on departure not to go further than he had indicated, and he returned on board to check that the ordinance was ready to cover the landing party if required.

The party marched along the narrow promontory with Recife behind them until they reached the works. After a ragged, ineffective salvo the Portuguese abandoned their position: the planks being laid made it clear that a gun emplacement had indeed been intended. Having destroyed the incomplete works the leaders, contrary to Lancaster's express orders, marched on to fight with some Portuguese nearly a mile away (i.e. towards Olinda) – and out of range of the ships' guns. The Portuguese retired smartly – the Anglo-French party followed, their order breaking down, and they ran into an ambush. About 35 were killed, including Edmund Barker, Captains Barker, Cotton and Noyer and the French captain from La Rochelle. The remainder retreated to the cover of the ships' guns.

Lancaster came ashore to meet the returning force 'much bewayling the death of so many good men as were lost, wondering what we meant to passe the express order that was given us', but as soon as he saw that 'our men were much daunted', he changed tack, with his customary skill, and encouraged them, saying 'that the fortunes of warres was sometimes to win and sometimes to loose'; and announced that they would leave Recife that evening.

Providentially the wind shifted to the south and by 11pm. the fleet had cleared the harbour, undamaged by some Portuguese gunfire. There were 15 ships – the three Dutchmen; four Frenchmen plus the pinnace which Lancaster gave them; three ships of Captain Venner's Plymouth fleet, and the four of Lancaster's original squadron, all fully laden.

The next morning Lancaster ordered the fleet to sail for Parajua and Potaju some 120-130 miles northwards along the Brazilian coast for fresh water and 'refreshment'. This was a small French settlement where Brazil wood cut by the Indians in the interior was exported. (Shortly after this time the settlement was overrun by the Portuguese and the French were expelled). With typical thoroughness Lancaster had sent ahead two Frenchmen (who also spoke the native language) in a small pinnace six days before, to organize the 'refreshment'.

Arriving off Peranjew at night time the fleet found 'a stiffe gale of wind' and most of the ships, not knowing the coast, put off to sea and set course for Europe, leaving Lancaster with four ships to enter the comfortable harbour and enjoy the refreshment. They then set out to chase the rest of the fleet, but did not catch them. By the time that Lancaster was in the Downs, the French ships had safely reached Dieppe, Captain Venner's fleet was back at Plymouth and the other English ships had passed up to London.

One final episode of the expedition must be recorded – a blend of farce and tragedy. English mariners in Elizabethan times had a weakness for feu de joie – at the least provocation, on meeting other ships, and on entering or leaving a harbour or anchorage, they would discharge their ordnance. Setting sail from the Downs for London, the Admiral, the Consent, loosed off a salute to the Queen's ships at anchor. Unfortunately, some powder in the gun room (on a lower deck right aft) caught fire and exploded, killing the gunner and two other men and injuring 20, of whom 4 or 5 died, and wrecking Lancaster's cabin. After initial alarm the fire was put out with help from the other ships and Royal Navy vessels, and the cargo was unharmed.[59]

With the fire extinguished and fresh men taken on board Lancaster proceeded safely to Blackwall: this was in July 1595.

Overview

The contrast with the 1591 Voyage is total. The original plan, repeatedly modified, is carried out in a cool but determined manner, without any setback, marred only by the sally on the last day, which started successfully but was unnecessarily turned into disaster.

Apart from the military and commercial triumph we see the emergence of a brilliant all-round commander. Previously we have observed only the constituent parts: they are still in evidence:- (i) the high-principled man, who can relate easily to all kinds of people and is particularly solicitous about his subordinates – even to the extent of explaining what his is trying to do, and why, and how; (ii) the skills of the naval and military professions, for example, erecting the nine foot palisade, managing the fire ship defences and issuing hail shot for the muskets (iii) the commercial skills – particularly negotiating favourable deals while remaining on friendly terms with the other parties; successively Captain Cotton, Captain Venner, the Dutch and the French. Add to these the leadership flair, which formed the English contingent into a disciplined, contented and determined force (at least after the hiccup while the Consent was separated from the other ships early in the voyage out), and then had the same effect on the international group which developed. Finally, the expedition repeatedly enjoyed the good luck which is said to favour good commanders [tanto fortior tanto felicior – the bolder, the luckier], or, alternatively, received the support of a higher power 'But (God be thanked) who was always with us and our best defence in this voyage, by whose assistance we performed this so great an attempt with such small forces....'

The Recife Raid established Lancaster as a leading commander of his day, with the unusual combination of naval/military and merchanting skills. He arrived back in England as something of a hero, attracting the fulsome praise of the pamphlet by Henry Roberts to which we have already referred. The achievements of the Raid hovered between the commercial and the political: the investing syndicate must have been delighted, and 'the authorities' must have been pleased too. It is possible that the Government 'pension' of £50 per year which Lancaster was receiving in 1601,[60] and which continued until 1610 when it was surrendered, may have been an indication of official approval of the Recife Raid.[61]

News of the Raid of course spread quickly to Europe, before Lancaster was back in England.[62] On 25th.June the Venetian ambassadors in Madrid were reporting home to the Doge and Senate (in somewhat exaggerated terms) 'News has lately been received that twelve galleons belonging to the Queen of England landed four hundred harquebusseers at Pernambuco in Brazil. They harried the country and sacked a ship belonging to the West Indian fleet, and made themselves masters of a small fort near Pernambuco. The booty amounts to 7,000 cases of sugar, 6,000 hundredweight of pepper, and other goods to the value of two millions in gold. . .'[63]

On 21st. July Drake and Hawkins reported the arrival at Plymouth of two ships from Brazil loaded with 800 chests of sugar, 12 or 14 tons of pepper and other booty: this no doubt referred to the arrival of Captain Venner's squadron.[64]

On 29th.July Henry Roberts' pamphlet eulogizing the Recife triumph of Lancaster and his colleagues in prose and verse was registered at the Stationers' Hall and went on sale in London.[65] Apart from describing the Raid in high-flown prose and verse 'An act of more resolve hath not/ Beene complisht at the sea', the pamphlet lists the 'spoyles and rich commodities...which was sinemon, sugar, pepper, cloves, mace, calloco-cloth and brassel-wood, with other commodities'. On the basis of internal evidence the accounts of the Recife Raid by Hakluyt and Roberts are reckoned to have come from the same source,[66] though Roberts does provide some additional details.[67] However, Roberts' pamphlet does contain two discrepancies. The first is the remark about Lancaster 'being a citizen of this famous cittie of London, though by birth of gentillity..' The contrast made between City men and gentlefolk is pleasing[68] but the attribution to Lancaster of 'gentility by birth' is, as we noted earlier[69] simply incorrect. Roberts seemed to have been carried away by his enthusiasm. The second discrepancy is more serious – Roberts gives a quite different account of the disastrous sally from Recife immediately prior to the departure of Lancaster's force. In his pamphlet he has Lancaster leading the sally but in the Hakluyt account he stays behind on the basis that he is feeling off colour and not up to marching on the heavy sand, and, after stressing that the force should not exceed his explicit instructions, he goes back on board to oversee the deployment of the guns in the ships to cover the shore party. Clearly, between these two accounts, only one can be correct. While the pamphlet is almost contemporary reporting, the preferred view is that Hakluyt is correct. We have already suggested that Richard Hakluyt knew Lancaster[70] and would have checked what he published about him. The re-writing of what occurred in the pamphlet is usually ascribed to Roberts' desire to exonerate the memory of Captain Cotton. When Cotton was recruited at Dartmouth he was elected 'their principall leader for their land service' and is referred to as Lancaster's 'Lieutenant' i.e. second in command: in the sally, in which Cotton was the senior officer, Lancaster's explicit instructions were disregarded.

We have no way of valuing accurately the Recife booty in total (though one source suggests £50,000 in 1605 money – which seems reasonable: compare the cargo of the carrack San Felipe taken in 1587 valued at £114,000) or discovering what accrued to Lancaster personally but it obviously established his financial independence at around the age of 40. He felt able in 1595 to invest £800 in a rentcharge [an indefinite annuity secured on land] which brought in £66 p.a., and – to confirm that he had, indeed, 'arrived' his portrait as a conquering hero was painted in the following year, 1596.[71]

Before leaving the Recife Raid we must record the views of Robert Southey, printed in his History of Brazil in 1810.[72] Southey was an extremely prolific man of letters,[73] producing poetry and ballads, plays, pamphlets, translations and a number of books, including a Life of Nelson and Lives of British Admirals. He took a considerable interest in Spain and Portugal. In his History of Brazil he accurately recounts the story of the Raid – as given above – and praises Lancaster: 'The Admiral displayed as much prudence in the management of his conquest as his valour in winning it. Not the slightest disorder was committed, nor any private pillage; perhaps no freebooters ever before or since behaved with such strict order and regularity.'

However, he appears to have had moral scruples. First, referring to Lancaster's speech to his men about his time in Portugal as a young man, he states 'there was therefore what may be called moral treason in bearing arms against a people with whom he had been so long domesticated' [We have deduced that Lancaster spent about six years in Portugal – between the ages of 20 and 26 – some 14 or 15 years earlier]. Then, obviously having reservations about privateering in general, he says 'These privateers were exceedingly religious in their profession,....the name of God was always in their mouth, and they had great hope of his blessing them in the performance of their voyage,...a voyage of which the whole and sole purpose was plunder'. Next, Southey took exception to Lancaster employing the Portuguese whom he captured to move the bulky booty in the local carts which they had taken: 'by this insolent usage of the prisoners relieving his own men, who were incapable of hard labour in that hot climate.' Finally, in another outburst against privateering, he pays James a back-handed, if inaccurate, compliment: 'Freebooters when they have enriched themselves have rarely been contented, that passion for plunder which is first their crime being righteously appointed to be their punishment. There is however reason to believe that Lancaster was satisfied with his fortune, for no further mention is made of him:[74] and the good sense with which he conducted the whole expedition renders it probable that he knew how to profit wisely by what he had won.'

It is difficult to make any useful comment on these tetchy criticisms. The morality of one age is rarely applicable to another in any meaningful way. While not a naval or mercantile historian, Southey did write on some naval subjects and should have known how 'national' wars were waged 'by contract' in an earlier period, and that privateering was regulated by the Admiralty Court and the Lord High Admiral, implementing the policies laid down by the Privy Council. The 'moral treason' outburst sounds similar to criticisms made in some quarters of the Royal Navy's attack on the Vichy fleet in WWII: despite the unpleasantness, the military and political considerations were overwhelming.[75]

8

Fame and Fortune

Lancaster returned from the Recife Raid in 1595, if not rich, at least financially independent. We do not know exactly what he made out of the voyage but he did feel able to buy a perpetual annuity in 1595 (technically a 'rentcharge', since payment was secured on land, namely the Manor of Fyll near Ashford in Kent) of £66 13. 4d. For this he paid £800. On a straight conversion the annuity might be worth around £10,000 p. a to-day but that does not give a realistic comparison. In the 1590s a craftsman might be paid between £4 and £10 p. a. (but plus his keep), a parson might get £20 p. a. , and a Royal Navy captain £50 p. a. (but again plus keep). It is likely, too, that Lancaster had ongoing income from his merchanting interests, and also, it would seem, a Government pension of £50 p. a.[1] The purchased rentcharge continued throughout Lancaster's life and then supported the charitable legacies under his will. It was finally bought out in 1929, by the then owner of Fyll Manor, by a capital paymernt of £1,500. By then the original investment of £800 had paid out £22, 268.

Within weeks of Lancaster's return the extravagantly worded pamphlet of Henry Roberts ('Lancaster his Allarums') was on sale in the streets of London, praising his military prowess, his eminence in the City of London and (incorrectly) his 'gentle birth'.

Lancaster's Portrait

The next year 1596 saw the portrait of Lancaster painted which is reproduced on the front cover. Surviving Tudor portraits are not plentiful, and this is a fine one, emphasizing the strength and energy which we associate with Lancaster. He exudes confidence, plainly dressed as a successful Elizabethan man of action.[2] His left hand is on the pommel of his sword and his right rests on a globe which shows the South Atlantic, with NE Brazil prominent and an English ship, wearing the cross of St. George off the coast: here, it would seem, is the victor of Recife. The portrait carries eight lines of latin elegiac verse;[3] gives its date – 1596, Lancaster's age – 42 and the date of his death – 6th June 1618. The portrait is to-day held by the National Maritime Museum, by whom it is attributed to the 'English School (16th Century)'. The Museum acquired it in 1971 when it was sold by Sothebys: their attribution was to the 'Flemish School'.[4] Prior to 1971 the painting had been, since the mid-19th century, in the hands of the Christie-Miller family.[5] There is an identical portrait (thought to be a copy) in the Hall of the Skinners' Company. This was presented to the Company by Arthur T. Marson, the Master in 1907-8. It appears that it was copied from the portrait held by the Christie-Millers.[6]

The portrait raises a number of issues – Is the 1596 date correct or is it a 17th century copy ? Alternatively, is it one of several 'versions' ? Since the date of Lancaster's death could only have been added after that event, was it at that point that the date of the portrait, Lancaster's age at that time, and the latin verses were also added ? What is the rationale for the verses, which seem to describe Lancaster's whole life (not just the Recife success in 1594-5) and are in extravagant terms quite alien to his character ? Who commissioned the work ? Where was the portrait kept during the long period to the mid-19th century ? For present purposes, we will side-step the stylistic questions and concentrate on the issues which bear on Lancaster's life and career.[7]

While there are a number of alternative permutations we will assume that the portrait was in fact painted in 1596, together with Lancaster's age at that time. Since the date of his death must have been added later the simplest explanation is that the latin verses were added at the *same* later date. A careful examination of the verses confirms that were composed later than the portrait and indeed after Lancaster's death in 1618. The following points are relevant:- (i) The Recife Raid is referred to ('littora occiduae bresiliae') but the victory celebrated in extravagant terms in the verses covers the whole world, particularly its wide eastern reaches ('spatiis porrectus Eois orbis'). In view of the comparative failure of the 1591 voyage, this must be based on the successful First Fleet expedition in 1601-3 (ii) The reference to Lancaster's widespread charity ('inopum pater') fits with the extensive list of charitable bequests in his will.[8] While he was always considerate of others, particularly subordinates, we have no evidence of widespread charity during his life (iii) the description of Lancaster's achievements and qualities are in the past tense ('eram') (iv) the reference to posterity in the last line also places his life in the past (v) the precise meaning of the last two lines is by no means clear, but one historian has expressed the view[9]] that they carry Laudian or anti-Puritan overtones (good works are required to achieve salvation, 'election' is insufficient on its own). This seems quite alien to the down-to-earth practical Christianity which we see in Lancaster's life, and suggests that the versifier is trying to impose his own retrospective 'spin' on Lancaster's beliefs (v) If the Laudian implications are valid this suggests a date for the verses well into the 17th century.

The one interesting biographical point in the verses is that they confirm that Lancaster was never married ('caelebs'). This was already tolerably clear from his early life as an expatriate merchant and seafarer, from his will and from the invitations extended to him to attend the Skinners' Election Day celebrations, when the other distinguished guests were invited with their wives: see below p. 135.

Did Lancaster himself commission the portrait ? Once we have established that the eulogistic verses were added later, this is quite possible.[10] If some other party was responsible, the most likely candidate might be the collegiate body with which Lancaster was most closely connected at that time: i. e. the Skinners' Company.[11] The Skinners do have fine, carefully preserved portraits of other worthy 16th century members, for example, those of Sir Thomas Smythe and Sir Andrew Judd and there is some evidence, provided by Samuel Pepys, that they did in fact have a portrait of Lancaster in their hall in the 17th century. In his Naval Minutes, gathered mainly in the period 1680-83, there is a note[12] '[Call upon] Mr Abraham Hill for the inscription upon the picture of Sir James Lancaster, an English seaman, hanging in Skinners' Hall'.[13] The interest of Pepys and his friend Abraham Hill (not a scientist but a prominent member of the Royal Society for some 60 years) seems to be concentrated on the inscription, but the reference to a picture of Lancaster *with an inscription* suggests that the picture referred to may indeed be the same as the 1596 portrait under discussion. Whether or not this is the case, it raises the question as to why a portrait of Lancaster (a respected Skinner in his day, though never an officer of the Company) was removed from the Hall. Two explanations may be offered. First, that the portrait was only on loan to the Company. Secondly, that the Company had some reason for removing it – perhaps this was the setback imposed by the Court of Chancery in 1713 when it removed the Skinners' Company as trustee of Lancaster's will and substituted the Corporation of Basingstoke, on the grounds that the Skinners had failed to pay in full the annuities secured on the real property which Lancaster had vested in the Company.[14] As mentioned above, the Skinners acquired a copy of the 1596 portrait in 1907-8. It is possible, on this hypothesis, that the presentation of the copy by the Master in 1907-8 was based on the knowledge that the

Company had once had the original portrait.[15]

Other candidates for commissioning the portrait might be one or more of the syndicate which backed the Recife Raid – they had as much reason to celebrate Lancster's success as anyone: Paul Banning, Simon Boreman, Thomas Cordell, Sir John Harte and Sir John Watts were all rich and powerful. If this speculation is correct, it might also explain where the portrait was preserved safely until it was acquired by the Christie-Miller family.[16]

Before leaving the portrait, we may comment that it does not carry Lancaster's heraldic arms, something which is often found. The short answer is that, being of humble origins, Lancaster had no right to arms by inheritance, and there is no record of his ever being granted any.[17] Lack of formal authority, however, did not necessarily deter men who had risen in the world from 'assuming' arms, either because they could trace descent from some armigerous person or because they simply happened to have the same name. A further possibility is that another party, perhaps after the subject's death, 'attributed' arms to him. There seems to be no evidence that Lancster used heraldic arms during his life. If there was, it would be reasonable, on the basis of what we know about his character, to assume that he would have had some grounds for so doing, albeit without formal authority We have already established that his forebears who migrated to Hampshire, while of humble rank, came originally from a tightly knit pool of Lancasters based on the town of Lancaster,[18] so it is quite feasible that they were indeed related to armigerous Lancasters in Lancashire or Westmoreland. The article on Lancaster in the Early History of the Skinners' Company illustrates 'his' arms. 'Argent, two bars gules, on a coulon of the second a mullet pierced or'.[19]

Lancaster was buried in 1618 in the church of All Hallows, London Wall. We have no knowledge of the mode of burial or whether there was any memorial.[20] It is quite possible that his executors, with the support of his powerful City colleagues, erected a memorial which included 'his' arms – whether assumed or attributed. There is a tradition at Basingstoke that Lancaster's arms were displayed (probably painted) on the wall of St. Michael's Church. This tradition is underpinned by a report of a Visitation of Basingstoke Church on 14th August 1686:[21]

> 'On the East end of the South isle against the wall between the isle and the Quire
>
> [1. Arms of Sir James Deane]
>
> 2. Arms: Arg. , 2 bars gu. And on a canton of the same a pierced mullet of 6 points or. The Armes of Sr James Lancaster Knight who deceased

Anno Domini 1617 [Sic: he died in 1618] and gave to this Towne by his last Will an Annuity of 118 pounds 6 shillings and 8 pence for ever to sundry pious and charitable uses'.

No such arms are in that position to-day. Moving on to the 19th century and the account provided by Baigent and Millard, it is first mentioned that in 1840 and 1841 'the Church underwent extensive reparation'. Monuments let into the floor were destroyed or covered , and replaced by memorial notices on the walls. Next, it is reported[22] that there is an old drawing which shows that 'there were formerly heraldic paintings in the style of the 16th or 17th century in the spandrels of the Nave Arches'. Six are listed, including 'V. Sir James Lancaster. Argent, two bars gules, on a coulon of the second a mullet or'.[23] The 'old drawing' appears to confirm that memorials and paintings already on the walls were also lost or moved as part of the 1840-1 'reparation'. Baigent & Millard then report[24] the current i. e 19th century, position. 'The coats given upon the two shields last mentioned were painted upon them in 1841, as well as the arms given upon the the four corner shields[25] . . . On the shield of the North East corner are the arms of Lancaster, commemorative of Sir James Lancaster, a great benefactor of the town'. The Rector of Basingstoke (in 2003) thought that Lancaster's arms might at one time have been painted on the North Wall of the North Aisle: there are some remnants of paint on that wall but they are quite indecipherable.[26]

To-day it is possible to see (with binoculars) what appears to be Lancaster's arms on the 'corner shield' mounted on the NW corner of the nave (not NE as stated by Baigent & Millard); the heraldic shield is clasped in the arms of an angel. When were there put there ? Baigent & Millard (above) describe 'an old drawing' which show that 'there were *formerly* heraldic paintings *in the style of the 16th and 17th century*' (italics added). With the history unclear, we may speculate that the Corporation of Basingstoke took the initiative in getting 'Lancaster's arms' displayed in St. Michael's church in the 17th century, soon after his death in 1618, perhaps at the same time as the summary of his legacies to the town were first displayed. Lancaster's surviving brother, Peter, might have had a hand in this, or perhaps one of the influential Basingstoke families with whom the Lancasters had intermarried, for example the Yates or Massams. Alternatively, Basingstoke may have simply followed a memorial erected at All Hallows, London Wall. We may therefore conclude that Lancaster did not himself assume the arms during his life, but that they were attributed to him posthumously.

At some time – we do not know exactly when – Lancaster acquired the lease of a large London house. Intriguingly Sir William Foster states without any qualification (and without quoting any source) that Lancaster lived at 'the Papeye', a large house with a garden and a subsidiary house, built on the site of a redundant church, St. Augustine Papeye in St. Mary Axe.[27] Perhaps Sir William had identified some unpublished clue in the records of the EIC,[28] but since the Papeye fits the description in Lancaster's will, and he was certainly living near St Mary Axe, it seems reasonable to accept that the Papeye was indeed his home. On a balance of probabilities it seems more likely that Lancaster acquired the lease of the Papeye only later, after his return with the EIC First Fleet in 1603. His purchase of his Lincolnshire estate (Maidenwell) and his farm near Basingstoke (at Pamber) took place in 1608 – this seems to tie in with the completion of the protracted negotiations between James and the EIC over his profit-share entitlement from the first EIC voyage, so the same considerations may have applied to his acquisition of a large London house.

In 1596 another English expedition set out for the East, targeting China, organised by Sir Robert Dudley. It consisted of three ships, the Bear, the Bear's Whelp and the Benjamin, under the command of Captain Benjamin Wood.[29] Sadly the whole fleet was lost without trace, it is thought somewhere off Malaya. In the same year 1596 the successful attack on Cadiz in 1596 took place – Lancaster was not involved.[30]

The 3rd Earl of Cumberland

In 1598 James again appears in the City of London 'A Team' of merchant adventurers. The Earl of Cumberland, contrary to his usual practice, in that year joined forces with a large City of London squadron of armed merchant ships for his 12th privateering expedition.[31] George Clifford, the third Earl of Cumberland,(1558-1605) was the most prominent privateer in the 1586-98 period, sending out twelve expeditions.[32] He was also a fascinating character. The Cliffords were of ancient lineage, descending from the Dukes of Normandy. Losing his father when he was 11 years old, George was entrusted to his kinsman Lord Bedford, and in due course married his youngest daughter, Lady Margaret Russell. He was educated at Trinity College, Cambridge and afterwards at Oxford and took an interest in mathematics and geography which led on to navigation and seafaring. With great charm, a winning tongue, dashing appearance and personal bravery, a born leader of men, George was widely popular (though there was some jealousy) and a favourite of Queen Elizabeth. On the other hand he was addicted to sport of all kinds, and gambling, had a quick and violent temper and was a lifelong philanderer (despite being devoted to his wife). Cumberland's privateering expeditions were not commercially successful so their military effect (which was in fact his primary objective) appears to have been under-rated at home: certainly he was feared by the Spaniards. His vessels and equipment were of the highest quality – reckoned equal to Royal Navy standards – so he ran through his own and his wife's fortunes. In general, Cumberland organized his own expeditions and rarely took partners. However, in his 12th expedition he formed a major partnership with the City of London, taking on some twelve of their armed merchantmen. There is a surviving agreement (never apparently executed, though it seems to have been acted upon). The City representatives (called 'Commissioners') were:-

Paul Banning (*Alderman*)
Leonard Holliday (*Alderman*)
John Watts (*Alderman*)
John Moore (*Alderman*)
Thomas Cordell
William Garraway
William Shute
James Lancaster
Thomas Allabaster
Robert Waldon.

So Lancaster was in good company. The Admiral (flagship) was the Malice Scourge of some 600 tons, built to the highest standards and owned by Cumberland, though Paul Banning and Sir John Hart also had some interest in her. When acquired by the EIC in 1600 the Malice Scourge had three demi-cannons, 16 culverins, 12 demi-culverins and eight sakers, giving an armament superior in weight to that of Royal Navy ships of similar size.[33] The expedition was a military triumph: it captured Porto Rico – but the city was not held. The outstanding quality of the Malice Scourge made her attractive to the promoters of the East India Company to act as their Admiral in their first voyage.[34] After some hard bargaining with Cumberland she was acquired in 1600 (for £2,700) and re-named the Red Dragon. Cumberland was an original member of the EIC (the only nobleman, described in the Charter as 'Our most deare and loving Cosin' – the City promoters preferred to work with 'men of business') and he was careful to absent himself from meetings of the Court while the purchase was being negotiated. The Red Dragon served again in the EIC second voyage in 1604.

We turn now to Lancaster's major voyage – by which he is most usually remembered – the EIC First Fleet 1601-3.

9
The First Voyage of the East India Company
1601-3

We have already noted that the efforts to organize direct English voyages to the East Indies in the 1580s, following the circumnavigations of Drake and Cavendish, all came to nothing. The 1591 Voyage, while a total failure in commercial terms, again demonstrated that such expeditions were feasible and that it was possible to ignore and/or 'work round' the Portuguese claims to monopoly in the Indian Ocean. The 1591 Voyage also encouraged the Dutch whose energy, navigational and merchanting skills, combined with the solid administration and financing of the VOC, almost immediately propelled them into the lead. As a result, the English, instead of seeing opportunities to exploit at their leisure, by penetrating the Portuguese position in the East on the back of their Armada reputation, found themselves at the risk of being sidelined by the Dutch newcomers.

The 1596 voyage, sent out by Sir Robert Dudley, and led by Captain Benjamin Wood, seems to have been targetted primarily at China, since the Queen provided a letter addressed to the Emperor to introduce the merchants Richard Allot and Thomas Bromfield.[1] The fleet cruised in company down the West African coast with Sir Walter Raleigh (on his way to his unsuccessful expedition to El Dorado) and their own voyage proved even less propitious – since nothing further was heard of them.

With knowledge of the enormous geographical spread and importance which the EIC was to attain it is difficult to appreciate its small and simple beginnings – effectively an extension of the Levant Company. The 'head office' for the new company was for some years accommodated in the house of the first Governor, Sir Thomas Smythe (who was also Governor of the Levant Company), in Philpot Lane, off

Fenchurch Street.[2] There were five or six staff. The Secretary of the Levant Company doubled as the Secretary of the EIC and, at the start, the same volume served as 'letter-book' and minute book for both companies. It is thought that the bulk of the money subscribed was derived from the profits of the Turkey/Levant and Levant Companies and that in turn most of the Levant Company capital came from the plunder seized by Drake from the Spaniards during his circumnavigation.[3]

We do not know exactly when moves were started to establish an English chartered monopoly for trading to the East Indies – the first reported subscription list was made up in 1599, so it was probably in that or the previous year: but this step was entirely predictable, indeed long overdue. We have seen the sustained effort by leading London merchants, over some 45 years, to move English traders upstream closer to the source of oriental commodities, particularly oriental spices. This is the thread which runs through the Muscovy, Venice, Turkey/Levant and Spain/Portugal Companies to the EIC – and it continued into the companies established to find the NE and NW Passages to the Pacific. The ambitions of the merchants were, in the early days, impeded by the Treaty of Tortesillas,[4] and later, during the periods of cold war and open war with Spain, by the vacillations of English foreign policy. During the long cold war Elizabeth wanted to avoid actions which might provoke the Spanish and then, in the 1590s, the aim was to avoid prejudicing efforts to make peace. In September 1599 a substantial subscription list was established[5] and the promoters sought approval through the Privy Council. This was denied on 16th October and the merchants, to avoid wasting money, postponed everything until the following year: the withdrawal for a year seems, also, to have had a tactical angle – to pressurize the authorities into making up their minds. At this stage – lobbying rather than operational planning – Lancaster appears not to have been involved. Early in 1600 the merchants submitted to the Queen a memorandum supporting the idea of an East Indies company and emphasizing how it would be feasible to 'work round' the European traders already established in the area. This was studied – and the project was approved. On 23rd. September 1600 the 'Adventurers' held their first 'court' i. e. formal meeting, and 17 directors/managers (called 'committees') were appointed, including Lancaster.[6] Now knowing that a Royal Charter would be forthcoming, the adventurers immediately 'changed gear', moving from lobbying into a period of intense operational planning. From the first minute book of the EIC it is clear that this group, initially as the court of the adventurers and by the end of 1600 as the court of the Company, met almost every day from 23rd. October to early the next year (Lancaster last attended on 17th February 1601 before boarding his flagship) to organize the entire enterprise – buying ships, equipment, victuals; employing the senior and middle-ranking officers and merchants (including James himself as Admiral or General and John Davis as Fleet Pilot); negotiating the 'profit share' of the key people; arranging for coin from the Royal Mint; and receiving advice and charts from individuals like Richard Hakluyt. The directors took the decisions and, broken down into smaller groups, went on to implement them: there were many excursions to the Thames and to the West Country. The 'trade goods' and cash embarked amounted to £27,000. Suitable presents for oriental sovereigns were provided. The Queen signed letters for delivery to them, with blank spaces left for their names to be inserted, and granted Lancaster a commission of martial law.

Two particular events during this period deserve mention. First, quite early on (3rd. October 1600), the Lord Treasurer urged the Company to appoint Sir Edward Michelborne as commander of the first fleet. The response was illuminating. It was resolved 'not to employ any gentleman in any place of charge or command in the voyage'; and the message back to the Lord Treasurer was firm but quite diplomatic, relying on 'market forces': he was asked 'to give them leave to sort their business with men of their own quality . . . . lest the suspicion of the employment of gentlemen . . . do drive a great number of the adventurers to withdraw their contributions'. Michelborne was to return to plague the EIC later as the first 'interloper' i. e. a challenger of their monopoly. Secondly, a discussion on 22nd. January 1601 concerning what share the crews would receive if any prizes were taken revealed the thinking of the directors. 'The intention was to pursue the voyage in a merchantlike course. Yet notwithstanding if any opportunity be offered without prejudice or hazard of the said voyage then Captain Lancaster will have discretion . . . ' and will make arrangements with the crew. This had a sequel: when setting out from Achen in September 1602, in company with Spielbergen's fleet, on the joint Anglo-Dutch venture which netted the San Antonio, Lancaster allotted 1/8 of any spoil to the Dutch and 1/6 to his own men (i. e. over and above their wages). At the time, the Susan had been detached to buy pepper at Priaman, so on return to England her crew petitioned to be included in the share-out. We do not know the eventual outcome, but the EIC in answer to the petition stated 'that all its sailors were engaged for a trading voyage only and that their wages were fixed accordingly'[7] Some embarrassment about recording a discussion of privateering possibilities is discernible. If there was indeed embarrassment, this probably related to the Privy Council's wish to avoid provocation to the Spanish and their subjects the Portuguese. Privateering was accepted as an alternative to trading on any voyage, and several of the directors of the EIC were long time backers of privateering activity. Indeed, a failure by a commander to seize a privateering opportunity would be regarded as a serious dereliction of duty by commercial backers. On this voyage trade was obviously the prime objective.[8]

Dutch engraving, thought to be of the Red Dragon, Lancaster's flagship

The Charter was issued on 31st. December 1600. On this occasion (unlike the earlier voyages which we have described) the financial backers and their investments are a matter of public record. The Company was – like the Turkey/Levant Company in its early days[9] – organized on a joint stock basis i. e. everything was done through the Company and in its name. The first-named backer was the Queen's favourite the Earl of Cumberland;[10] Sir Edward Michelborne is listed,[11] and then the City knights, the aldermen and some 200 other individuals, mostly City men. Lancaster and his cousin Sir James Deane were amongst them. The total subscribed was around £60,000.[12] The Charter named Sir Thomas Smythe as Governor and 24 committees (directors), amongst them Lancaster. The ships and the command structure were as follows:-

> 1. Admiral, the Red Dragon (ex Malice Scourge) (600 tons). Captain Lancaster (also principal factor), general or admiral of the fleet. Captain Davis, Pilot Major i. e. fleet pilot. William Broadbent, Master. Crew of 202.
>
> 2. Vice Admiral, the Hector (300 tons). Captain (John) Middleton (also principal factor in the Hector). Henry Napper, Master. Philip Grove (de Greve – he was Dutch), second fleet pilot. Crew of 108.
>
> 3. Rear Admiral, the Ascension (260 tons). William Brand, Captain and principal factor. Roger Hankin, Master. Crew of 82.
>
> 4. The Susan (240 tons). John Havard, Captain and principal factor. Samuel Spencer, Master. Crew of 88.
>
> 5. Victualler, the Guest or Gift (120 tons)

Apart from the victualler the ships were all of the race-built galleon type, with proven records. Purchas describes them as 'four tall shippes'[13] The EIC itself described the ships (excluding the Guest) as 'four of the best merchant shippes of the kingdome'.[14]

We can now set out, in abridged form, the events of the voyage.[15]

1601 [1600 old style until 31st. March]

13/2 Fleet departed from Woolwich

1/4 Lancaster wrote to Mr. Skynner (H. M. Treasury) from the Downs about paying his Government pension during his absence[16]

12/4 Easter Day. Arrived at Dartmouth and provisioned

18/4 Left Dartmouth, anchored in Torbay until 20/4. Wind turned fair; weighed, set course for Canary Islands

5/5 Sighted Alegranza, 'the northern most iland of the Canarias' [a tiny island to the north of Lanzarote], set course between Forteventura and the Grand Canaria and fell into calms south of Grand Canaria.

7/5 Left Grand Canaria with NE wind

11/5 21 ½' N.

20/5 8' N.

20/5 to

21/6 Mainly becalmed with contrary S winds off the coast of Guinea. At 2' N chased and took a Portuguese ship out of Lisbon. She had been in company with two carracks and three escorting galleons, all five of which had been lost. The prize held 146 butts of wine, 176 jars of oil, 12 barrels of oil and 55 hogsheads and vats of meale 'which was a great help to us in the whole voyage after'

30/6 Crossed the line, lost the north star, set course SSW and doubled Cape St. Augustine [The extreme NE tip of Brazil, close to Pernambuco and Recife] on 16th July.

20/7 19' 40' S. Unloaded the Guest [the victualling ship], took her masts, sails and yards, stripped her upperworks for firewood and left her adrift.

24/7 Passed Tropic of Capricorn, course ESE. Many men were sick 'by reason of our long being under the Line (which proceeded of our late coming out of England . . .)' Lancaster wrote to his commanders suggesting a call at Saldania or St. Helena for refreshing.

1/8 30' S. 'Met the SW wind to the great comfort of all our people'. However, when 250 leagues out from the Cape the winds turned contrary for 15/16 days, and more men were succumbing to scurvy – so that even the merchants took a turn on the helm and in the tops with the sailors – but eventually the wind returned to SW.

9/9 Anchored in Table Bay. Lancaster in the Dragon anchored first and sent his crew round by boat to help the other ships anchor, secure their sails, lower their boats &c. He was able to do this since he had, to some extent, protected his men against scurvy by dosing them with citrus juice. 'He brought to sea with him certaine bottles of the juice of limons, which he gave to each one as long as it would last, three spoonfuls every morning fasting, not suffering them to eate anything after it until noon. This juice worketh much the better if the party keep a short dyet, and wholly refraine salt meat, which salt meat and long being at the sea is the only cause of the breeding of this disease.'[17]

Lancaster went ashore to seek victuals. He handed out trifles – knives and pieces of iron – explaining 'in the cattels language (which was never changed at the confusion of Babell)' what he wanted 'Moo' for oxen and 'Baa' for sheep, 'which language the people understood very well without any interpreter'. Lancaster in his usual manner 'sent the people away very well contented with their presents and kind usage'.

Next, Lancaster ordered that part of each ship's company should take sails ashore and make tents with them to house the sick, and build fortifications around the encampment in case of trouble.

Lancaster then turned back to the trading arrangements, laying down that, when the native inhabitants brought down sheep and cattle, only 5 or 6 men, appointed for the purpose, should deal with them and the rest (not less than 30 muskets and pikes) should keep some 200 yards away, in rank, with their muskets ready in their rests. The narrator comments 'I take this to be the cause why we lived in so great friendliness and amitie with them, contrary to that which lately had befallen the Hollanders, which had five or six of their men slaine by their treacherie'.

Following this system, the third day at Saldania, 'the people brought downe beefes and muttons'. Both sides seemed well contented. The English gave two 8 inch pieces of iron for an ox, and one piece for a sheep, and in this way over 10-12 days 1000 sheep and 42 oxen were purchased. After that, the natives would not bring any more: the English speculated that this was because they thought that some permanent settlement was planned.

'These oxen are full as big as ours, and were very fat, and the sheepe many of them much bigger, but of a very hairie wool, yet of exceedingly good flesh, fat and sweet, and, to our thinking, much better than our sheepe in England'.

'The people of this place are all of a tawnie colour, of a remarkable stature, swift of foot, and much given to picke and steale; their speech is wholly uttered through the throats, and they click with their tongue in such sort, that in seven weekes which we remained here in this place, the sharpest wit among us could not learn one word of their language; and yet the people would soon understand any sign we made to them. '

Lancaster sent six sheep and two rams to be released on Robben Island 'for the reliefe of strangers that might come thither'.

The refreshing at the Cape was a success. Of the original fleet total of 480, 105 men were lost on the way to the Cape, leaving around 375. After seven weeks of refreshing all but 4 or 5 had recovered, 'wee made account we were stronger at our departure out of this bay than wee were at our coming out of England, our men were so well inured to the southerne climates'.

Before leaving we had a sermon and communion, and Lancaster's Jewish servant/interpreter was christened, Lancaster standing as godfather.[18]

24/10 Dismantled camp and loaded the ships

29/10 Sailed, passing Robben Island 'exceeding full of seales and pengwines'

1/11 Rounded Cape of Good Hope

26/11 Off Cape Sebastian in Madagascar [The most southerly point]. Set course eastwards for Cirne (Mauritius) but contrary winds prevented us. As scurvy was recurring Lancaster and the commanders decided to make for the Bay of Antongil to refresh the men. [Two thirds of the way up the east coast of Madagascar: oranges and lemons were available there, which it was recognized would 'cleere ourselves of this disease': the Apsley pamphlet is even more specific 'which is the best remedy against the scurvy']

17/12 Sighted S tip of St. Mary Island [Off Antongil] Anchored between St. Mary and Madagascar and obtained oranges and lemons. In a great storm three of our ships lost their anchors but after 16 hours the storm subsided and they returned to recover their anchors.

23/12 Left St. Mary

25/12 Anchored in Antongil Bay [Named after the Portuguese explorer, Anton Gil]. On an island in the bay there was a notice of five Dutch ships which had passed only two months before. It looked as though they had lost 150-200 men from sickness while in the Bay.

26/12 Landed to attempt to obtain victuals. Initially, the quantities offered were tiny, the prices were too high, and the local sellers very tricky. 'For all these people of the south and east parts are very subtill and craftie in their bartering, buying and selling, that unless you hold a neere hand with them, you shall hardly bring them in trade in any plaine sort'. So Lancaster took charge and organized the trading so that those appointed to buy went ashore on the bank of the river, while the other boats stood off 15 or 20 yards with their arms ready. Measures were made, and prices set (in glass beads) for oranges, lemons, plantains and other commodities, and it was made clear that dealing would only be on those terms. After some hesitation, successful buying began ('and our trading was francke and round, without any contradiction or words') of 15 ¼ tons of rice, 40 or 50 bushels of peas and beans, great store of oranges, lemons and plantains, eight beeves and many hens.

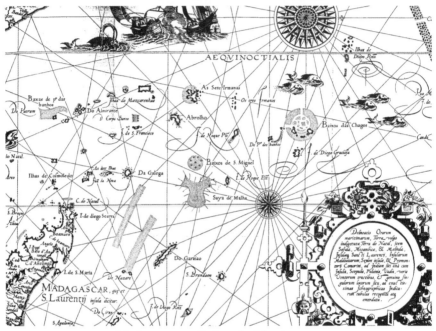

Madagascar to Ceylon, the island groups

1602

1/1 Commenced building the pinnace (the frames for which had been brought from England), trees being felled to provide the planking. She was of 18 tons 'very necessary and fit to goe before our ships at our coming into India'.

7/1 Five of the boys took a ship's boat and deserted but were recovered after two or three days.

17/1 The surgeon of the Ascension, Christopher Newchurch, tried to poison himself. He was relieved of his post and should have been put ashore but Captain Hayward of the Susan interceded for him and took him to serve as a sailor

27/2 The fleet lost at Antongil, mainly through the flux, [Dysentery: it was thought that this was caused by drinking unwholesome water taken in the rainy season when the rivers flooded] the master's mate, the preacher and the surgeon with 10 other common men, out of the Dragon, and out of the Hector the master with some other two. In addition, 'by a very great mischance' the master and the boatswain's mate of the Ascension were killed, when they were going ashore to bury the master's mate of the Dragon. 'As it is the order of the sea to shoote off certaine peeces of ordinance at the burial of any officer' the gunner shot off three pieces which were loaded with shot which struck the Ascension's boat, 'so that they that went to see the burial of another were both buried there themselves'.

6/3 After two months and eight days in 'this tempestuous and unfortunate bay' set course from Antongil to India.

16/3 Reached an island called Rogue-Pize at 10 ½ S [Foster identifies it as Agalega, but it is shown at the same latitude further east on the chart on p. 110] Lancaster sent away a boat but no safe anchorage was found. The island was attractive, with many fowl and coconut trees and a pleasant smell off the land, so that if an anchorage could be found it would be a good place for refreshment. The sailors killed many fowl with their oars 'which were the fattest and the best that we tasted all the voyage'[Probably boobies: see Tuck p. 250]

30/3 6' S. came upon a ledge of rocks. [Probably the Chagos Islands, of which the best known to-day is Diego Garcia: John Davis made this identification in his Router] Some 40 miles further on other rocks were encountered, though with 40-50 fathoms of water in between. After 2 ½ days the fleet, led by the pinnace, escaped from this danger in 6' 43'

9/4 Sighted the island of Nicobar, anchored and then had to move and re-anchor following a change of wind. Local people came out in canoes, offered some victuals at high prices, and gum made up to look like amber 'and therewith deceived divers of our men; for these people of the east are wholly given to deceit. '

20/4 Set course for Sumatra but contrary winds forced the fleet to go to the island of Sombrero about 35 miles northwards [There is a Sombrero Channel, but no island: Markham suggests identification with Nancowry Island: see Markham p. 72n.] The Dragon lost an anchor in foul ground.

29/5 Left Sombrero

2/6 Sighted Sumatra

5/6 Anchored at Achen. 16/18 ships in the roads from Gujerat, Bengal, Calicut (Malabar), Pegu (Burma), Patani (Malaysia) Two Dutch merchants came aboard, stating that the King (Ala-uddin Shah) [He had murdered the previous King in 1585 and usurped the throne] was eager to welcome strangers 'and that the Queen of England was very famous in these parts, by reason of the warres and great victories which she had gotten against the King of Spain'.

Lancaster sent Captain John Middleton (of the Vice-Admiral), accompanied by four or five gentlemen to the King to announce that he had a message and a letter from the Queen. to deliver to him. Middleton was well received by the King, who invited Lancaster to call on him the following day.

7/6 Lancaster went ashore with 30 men in attendance to the house of the Dutch merchants. A nobleman sent by the King called and asked Lancaster to hand over the Queen's letter: Lancaster declined, explaining that it was the custom for ambassadors in his part of the world to deliver letters to the King in person. Lancaster did however show him the superscription which he studied and noted and went to report to the King.

The King soon sent six elephants, with trumpets drums and streamers, to collect Lancaster and his party. The largest elephant took the Queen's letter in a great gold basin.

When the party eventually entered the presence Lancaster 'made his obeysance after the manner of the country' [It was known as 'giving Doulat'. The hands are placed together and raised above the head. At the same time the visitor bows and says Doulat'(prosperity): see Foster 130n.] The King returned the salute and Lancaster began his presentation. The King soon interrupted and invited Lancaster to sit down and refresh himself. Lancaster did so, presenting the letter and also the official gifts –a silver fountain, a great standing cup, a rich-looking glass, a head-piece with a plume of feathers, a case of daggers, a rich sword belt and a fan of feathers. The King handed all these to his courtiers except for the fan with which he had one of his woman fan him.

The feast then commenced. Rice wine was served 'as strong as any of our aquavits' and Lancaster obtained the King's consent for him to mix it with water, or to drink water alone.

After the banquet the King ordered his women to provide music and to dance 'and this they account a great favour, for these are not usually seene of any but such as the King will greatly honour. ' The King then presented gifts to Lancaster and invited him to choose a house in the city to live in. Lancaster declined the latter, explaining that, for the time being, he preferred to stay on board.

June-August At his next audience the King and Lancaster discussed the Queen's letter. The King appeared to approve what was requested and referred Lancaster to two noblemen for the detailed negotiation. This occurred a few days later and the nobleman in charge (a 'bishop') asked Lancaster to submit his arguments in writing – which he did. The negotiations were conducted in Arabic, with Lancaster supported by the Jewish interpreter whom he had brought from England.[19]

When he next saw the King (on the occasion of a cock fight) Lancaster, through his interpreter, asked how the discussions were going. The King told him that he wished to enter into agreement with the Queen and that his response would be prepared shortly, and five or six days later the King delivered them to Lancaster with his own hand.

As soon as the negotiations had been concluded Lancaster's merchants set out to buy pepper. Little was forthcoming, this being attributed to the latest crop being disappointing. The merchants, however, heard that pepper might be had at Priaman on the south coast of Sumatra. [Priaman is about half-way between Achen and the Sunda Strait, almost exactly on the Equator] Accordingly, Lancaster sent the Susan, with Henry Middleton as captain and chief merchant. [He commanded the EIC 1604 Voyage. To be distinguished from John Middleton, captain of the Hector, who died at Bantam]

Lancaster was concerned at this development, particularly as his chief pilot Captain John Davis had told the merchants before they left England that pepper could be had at Achen for 4 Spanish rials a hundredweight when, as it turned out, they had to pay almost 20.[20] Lancaster was also worried about how he was going to fill his ships.

An Indian came to Lancaster's house selling hens. He was employed by a Portuguese captain who was staying in the house of the Portuguese ambassador. Lancaster guessed that he was a spy so his hens were bought and he was well received. Eventually Lancaster talked to him and he revealed that a plan was being hatched to send a force from Malacca to attack the English fleet. Lancaster told him to report back and promised him his liberty. In the meantime Lancaster requested the King to prevent the ambassador's servants leaving for Malacca – which he did. Eventually, it came out – as Lancaster had suspected – that the hen-seller was a double agent.

On 24th June a Dutch pinnace of 50 tons named Lam arrived at Achen. She had become separated from the fleet led by Joris van Spielbergen, of Middleburg, which – it was thought – had been lost. Lancaster bought the pinnace. Spielbergen, however, turned up with the rest of his fleet, the Schaep and the Ram, on 6th September.

September – Lancaster was ready to leave Achen. Knowing that the Portuguese Ambassador was due to go to Malacca he requested the King to delay his departure, explaining why. 'Only stay him but tenne dayes, till I be gone forth with my ships'. 'Well' said the King and laughed, 'thou must bring me a fair Portugall maiden when thou returnest, and then I am pleased'. The King complied and delayed the Ambassador.

Lancaster introduced his two merchants, Starkie and Styles, who were to stay behind and continue to buy pepper.

Lancaster was approached by the Dutch commander Spielbergen who – like the English – had little cash with which to buy commodities. He suggested that they join forces. Lancaster agreed, cutting him in for an 1/8 share 'of what should be taken'.

11/9 The combined English and Dutch fleet sailed towards the Straits of Malacca (the Ascension, by now two-thirds laden, came too as Lancaster did not want to leave her unprotected at Achen). Lancaster was 'dangerously sicke'

4/10 'Laying off and on' in the Malacca Straits: Hector sighted a large Portuguese ship the San Antonio. She was engaged and captured. Lancaster took charge, evacuating all the crew of the prize and putting only four men aboard, so that they handled all unloading and transfer to the ships of the fleet according to Lancaster's orders; thus avoiding the pilfering &c. 'which otherwise would hardly have been avoided in such businesse as this'.

The prize was of 900 tons, out of San Thome [Now a suburb of Chennai (Madras)] bound for Malacca, carrying 950 packets of calicos and pintados, other packets of merchandise and much rice and other goods. The Indian cottons were unloaded over five or six days, and then, a storm arising, the crew was put back on board and the ship left at anchor with the remainder of her cargo.

Lancaster did not board the prize 'and his reason was, to take away suspicion both from the mariners that were there and the merchants that were at London, least they might charge or suspect him for any dishonest dealing by helping himself thereby. '

Lancaster was heartily relieved by this 'and very thankful to God for it, and . . . he was much bound to God that had eased him of a very heavy care, and that he could not be thankful enough to him for this blessing given him. For . . . he hath not only supplied my necessities to lade these ships I have: but hath given me as much as will lade as many more ships as I have if I had them to lade. So now my care is not for money, but rather where I shall leave these goods that I have, more than enough, in safety, till the return of the ships out of England. '[21]

21/9 The fleet left the Straits of Malacca to return to Achen. A waterspout was seen nearby 'which we feared much . . . if they should light in any ship she were in danger to be presently suck down into the sea'.

24/10 Anchored at Achen. The merchants were well and safe and reported their kind entertainment from the King. Lancaster selected gifts from the prize and presented them to the King who appeared pleased at the success against the Portuguese 'and jestingly said, that he had forgotten the most important business that he requested at his hands, which was the faire Portugall maiden he desired him to bring with him at his returne'. Lancaster diplomatically replied 'that there was none so worthy that merited to be so presented. '

The Ascension was loaded with the pepper, cinnamon and cloves which the merchants had managed to buy 'which was scarcely the ship's full lading, but at that time there was no more to be had, nor that year to be hoped for. ' The unsold part of the merchandise brought from England was re-embarked and the fleet prepared to leave. Lancaster's resolution was to make for Bantam in Java where he hoped to buy more pepper at better prices with his newly acquired 'commodities'.

Lancaster went for his farewell audience with the King, who handed over his letter (in Arabic) for the Queen; gifts for the Queen and a further gift for Lancaster himself. The King then asked if the English preserved the Psalms of David, and being told that they sung them daily,[It was the custom to sing a psalm at the change of the watch] said 'I and the rest of these nobles about me will sing a Psalme to God for your prosperitie, and so they did very solemnly'. Lancaster and his party responded by singing another psalm, and then took their leave. The King wished them a safe journey home and promised 'if hereafter your ships returne to this port you shall find as good usage as you have done'.

9/11 The Dragon, Hector and Ascension left Achen, and, on 11th November Lancaster dispatched the Ascension for England.[22] The two remaining ships sailed along the coast of Sumatra towards Bantam to meet up with the Susan. They passed through dangerous rocky islands 'but thankes be to God, who delivered us from many other dangers, as he did also deliver us from these. '. Continuing for [the account reads 'from'] Priaman the Line was passed for the third time.

26/11 Met up with the Susan at Priaman. Henry Middleton had bought 600 behars of pepper and 66 behars of cloves. [A behar is equal to 387 ½ lbs or 176 kilograms] Pepper cost less at Bantam but was not grown there being brought from Manangcabo some 30 miles inland. The only local product was gold, washed out of the rivers. Although within 15' of the Line it is 'a place of good refreshing and is very wholesome and healthfull' Lancaster instructed the Susan to load 100 behars of pepper to complete her cargo and to sail for England.

4/12 The Dragon and Hector set course for Bantam.

15/12 Entered Sunda Straits and anchored under Pulopansa, an island nine miles from Bantam.

16/12 Entered the roads of Bantam 'and shot off a very great peale of ordnance out of the Dragon, being our admiral, and out of the Hector: such a one as had never beene rung there before that day'.

17/12 Lancaster sent John Middleton (his Vice Admiral) ashore to call on the King announcing that they carried a message and a letter from the Queen of England and requesting safe conduct to deliver them. Middleton returned with a nobleman to welcome Lancaster ashore.

Accordingly he went with the nobleman, taking some 15 supporters, to call upon the King (who turned out to be a boy of 10 or 11 years) sitting with some 16 or 18 noblemen in a round house. Lancaster made his obeysance and 'the King welcomed him very kindly'. He delivered the Queen's message, with some presents, 'which the King received with a smiling countenance' and referred him to one of the noblemen, his protector, 'for further conference'. Conversations of 1 ½ hours with the protector produced an invitation to come ashore and trade without molestation, which was confirmed by all the noblemen, followed by an invitation from the King to select a house to stay in.

Within two days the merchants brought their commodities ashore and began to sell them. One of the noblemen came to Lancaster and explained that it was the local custom for the King to buy first, before his subjects, Having learned that the King would pay reasonable prices, Lancaster directed that this course be followed.

1603

Within five weeks sufficient goods were sold to load both ships, with 276 bags of pepper over. Of these each bag contained 62 pounds and cost 5 ½ rials each. In addition, the charge for anchoring two ships was 1500 rials and the customs duty 1 rial on every bag.

'We traded here very peaceably, although the Javians be reckoned among the greatest pickers and theeves of the world. ' After one or two 'abuses' the King had authorized Lancaster to kill anyone found in the house during the night 'so after foure or five were thus slaine, we lived inn reasonable peace and quiet. But, continually, all night, we kept a carefull watch. '

Master John Middleton, captain of the Hector, fell sick on board his ship. (Lancaster had laid down early in the voyage that when he was ashore his second i/c should remain on board).[23] Lancaster went to visit him but he died the same night. [It appears that he was not replaced as captain, but that the Master, Alexander Cole (phonetically rendered by Purchas as Sanderbole) took command]

10/2 The ships were fully loaded and ready for departure. Lancaster left eight men and three factors, under Master William Starkey, at Bantam to sell the remaining commodities and to accumulate cargo for the next English ships. He also commissioned a 40 ton pinnace, with 12 men and

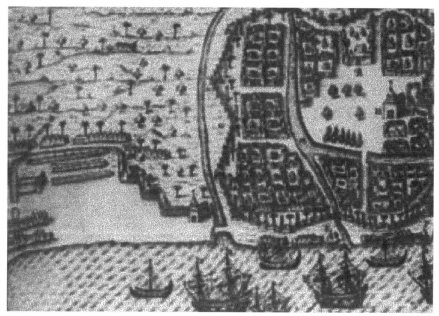

Plan of Bantam

two merchants, loaded with 'commodities', to sail to the Moluccas [the Spice Islands proper], trade there and establish a 'factorie' to await the arrival of the next English ships.

Finally, Lancaster went to take leave of the King, who handed over a letter and gifts for the Queen, and some gifts for Lancaster. 'And thus the generall tooke his leave of the king, with many kind countenances and good words'.

20/2 The fleet weighed anchor, 'shot off our ordinance' and set course for England.

22/2-23/2 Passed the Straits of Sunda

26/2 Cleared the land and set course SW.

28/2 8' 40' S of the Line

13/3 Passed the Tropic of Capricorn steering SW with a SE gale.

14/4 In 34' S judging Madagascar to be to the N.

28/4 A furious storm and raging sea, for a day and a night. Forced to furl all sails. Leaks were sprung which lasted for the rest of the voyage.

3/5 Another severe storm which, the following morning, caused the Dragon's rudder to fall clean off. 'Now, our ship drave up and downe in the sea like a wracke, which way soever the wind carried her, so that sometimes we were within three or four leagues of the Cape Buena Esperanza, then cometh a contrary wind, and driveth us almost to 40 degrees to the southward into the hayle and the snow, and sleetie cold weather.' Throughout the Hector stood by the Dragon and the Hector's Master (Alexander Cole) frequently came on board to offer help. Eventually, an effort was made to dismantle the mizzenmast and use it as a steering oar: this failed. Lancaster then instructed the carpenter to make a new rudder, which he did but it was not possible to hang it properly as most of the 'rudder irons'[Gudgeons] had been lost with the original rudder. The rudder was hung and the ship set her course but, being insecurely fastened, it came off after four or five hours.

At the failure of this attempt, the most promising so far, the crew became restive and wished to abandon the Dragon and take passage in the Hector. Lancaster showed his steel, 'Nay, 'he said, 'wee will yet abide God's leisure, to see what mercie he will shew us; for I despaire not to save ourselves, the ship, and the goods, by one meanes or other, as God shall appoint us'. Further, he secretly commanded the Hector to part company at night and sail for England, taking a letter from him to the Governor of the Company.[24] In the morning, however, the Hector was still there, 'for the master was an honest and a good man and loved the generall well, and was lothe to leave him in so great distress'. The Hector did however, keep her distance a few miles away Lancaster peevishly commented 'These men regard no commission' [i. e. obey no orders].

With better weather and a smooth sea, a final effort was made to attach the newly built rudder. The Hector sent over her best swimmers and divers and it was secured by the two surviving 'irons'. Fortunately, the makeshift rudder held, but by now the fleet was to the north west of the Cape [They could tell by the latitude] so that it was not possible to reach any part of mainland Africa. It was therefore decided to make for St. Helena. On the way a last disaster struck: the main yard fell from the mast and knocked a man overboard.

5/6 Passed the Tropic of Capricorn

16/6 Sighted St. Helena and, after three months at sea, came to anchor close under the land, near the Portuguese chapel. Some writings ashore showed that Portuguese carracks had left only eight days earlier.

'In this iland there is very good refreshing of water and wild goats'. Lancaster devised a careful plan to maximize the catch of wild goats. Four men, plus the best shots, were sent to camp in the middle of the island. Each marksman was assigned four men to carry the goats which he had shot to an appointed rendezvous. A further 20 men were sent each day to bring the carcasses back to the ships. 'So there was no hoyting [Boisterous behaviour] or rumour [In this context, clamour] in the iland to fear the goats withal'

The ships were attended to and the Dragon's rudder checked, and all the sick men

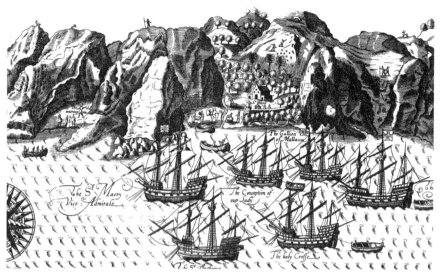

A 1590s view of St Helena: note the wild goats

5/7 recovered their health, so the ships set sail on a NW course.

13/7 Passed Ascension Island

19/7 Passed the Line

29/7 Sighted Fogo Island. [One of the southern islands in the Cape Verde group] Becalmed

7/8 16' N

12/8 Passed the Tropic of Cancer

29/8 Passed the Island of Sainte Marie [Santa Maria in the SE of the Azores Group]

7/9 By sounding fixed ships 120 miles from Land's End.

11/9 Anchored in the Downs 'for which, thanked be Almightie God, who hath delivered us from infinite perils and dangers in this long and tedious navigation'.

Overview

The First EIC Voyage may, from an operational point of view, be regarded as successful. All the ships came home safely and performed well (the loss of the Red Dragon's rudder was due to extreme weather – and their survival and recovery showed outstanding leadership and seamanship); the pilotage and navigation was exemplary – the escape from the maze of the Chagos Islands was managed coolly and without any damage; discipline and morale were maintained; visits ashore for refreshing were well managed and effective. If the fleet did not reach The Spice Islands themselves, it filled its holds at reasonable prices without needing to do so.

Commercially, too, the expedition could hardly be faulted – and Lancaster was not to know that their pepper in London would be worth far less than expected.[25] At the three ports where trading took place on this voyage – Achen, Priaman and Bantam – friendly relations were established at once and freedom to trade on acceptable terms was obtained. While providing for the present voyage, Lancaster at the same time laid the foundations for ongoing trade, establishing 'factories', appointing expatriate factors and leaving precise instructions for safeguarding existing stock, acquiring more, buying and selling at discretion in the meantime and generally managing the EIC presence. The ability to plan with confidence several years ahead (when communications between England and the East Indies took at least a year) while at the same time managing the current voyage with great skill marks Lancaster's outstanding calibre and underlines his vital contribution to the future of the EIC. The departure from Bantam captures the moment when a one-off trading voyage is transmuted into the opening chapter in a very long story. We quote below from Lancaster's instructions to the commander of the pinnace ordered to Banda; to the hierarchy of merchants to remain in Bantam, and to the merchants instructed to establish the new factory at Banda, to give a flavour of Lancaster's style – but to appreciate their overall impact it is best to read them in full.[26]

From the 'Remembrance for Master Keche, Master of the Pinnace'

'Firste, as soone as I am gone, you shall procure from the marchauntes resident heare of such and soe many goodes as they shall appointe you, and by all meanes, after you have taken them in, procure such provisions that they may be kept drie, for a little wett bringeth in theis goodes much damadge. I doubt not you will be carefull in this pointe . . .

When God shall send you to Banda and you have delivered your marchandizes, you maie laie upp your ship, and you and your men lie att the marchauntes howse and assist them in their business all you cann. But I thinke yt good to look to your ship, that she be not lost, but husband her, soe that, yf occasion should be proferred by any enymies aland, you maie have some helpe by her by the sea . . .

And hereby I doe acknowledge to have consorted with you from the 1 of February 1603, for as long as you shall be in the marchauntes service, for 8li. the monneth.

Thus God send His blessinge upon you in all your affaires.

In Bantam, this 12 of February 1603. '

From the 'Remembrance for Master Starkie, Thomas Morgan, and Master Scott'

[Starkie and Morgan died, so Scott took charge as Lancaster had directed]

'As sone as our shipps be dispatched from hence, with as much convenient speede as may be made I would have you to dispatch the pinnace for the Moloccos to the iland of Banda; and lade in her of all sortes of commodities as you can learne to be vented there . . . .

Alsoe lade in her 500 rials of 8 att the least; for yt may chaunce they maie have neede to use some money . . .

For the sales of your commodities, you must use your owne discretions; always holdinge this in mynde, the tyme of comeing of our shipps; and procure 20,000 bagges of pepper (as neere as you cann) to be in readynes against their comeing . . . Myne opinion is to putt yourselves out of commodities as soone as you cann and putt yourselves into peppers, for in soe doinge you may chaunce to benefit the Company in the defraying your chardges, for they shall be at above 850li. the year chardge in thies partes.

When you have bought any store of pepper, yf the Holland ships come and the prise ryse, you may take the benefit and sell to the Companies most profit; onelie, have a reguard not to be unfurnished at the expectation of our shippinge . . . .

And for the boyes, lett them not want apparel and necessaries that apperteyne unto them, for soe they shall doe you better service. Lett the cookes boye be bound for 7 yeares; and to have the freedome of London in his tyme, accompte the 2 yeares that he hath served in our shippe.

Thus I end, desiring you to meete together in the morninges and eveninges in prayer. God, whom yee serve, shall the better blesse you in all youir afaires. Thus I wish His blessings to be always upon you, to preserve and keepe you, and to putt His feare in your hartes. Amen.

Foget not to husband your commodities, that there be nothiinge spoyled nor come to decay under your handes. '

From the 'Remembrance for Thomas Tudd, Gabriell Towerson, William Chasse, and Thomas Dobson

[Towerson took charge when the other three died]

'As soon as the pynnace is laded by the marchauntes resident here in Banda . . . you shall imbarke yourselves in her . . . and saile directlie with your said goodes to Banda, unless you touch in some place necessarie for your refreshing. And make no longe staye, and have especiall care of your safetie and how you put any man aland in any place, for the people in those partes, their whole bodyes and mindes be all treason; and therefore open your eyes in this behalfe.

And when God shall send you to Banda, take a howse or howses for your business, as you think most fitt for the Companies best profit, and make sale of your commodities, always advaunceing the price the best you may.

In your provision you shall make in nutmegges and maces, have you a greate care to receive such as be good, for the smallest and rotten nutmegges be worth nothinge at home; soe that their fraight and principall will be lost. Of maces the fairest and best will be soonest sould, and to best rekoninges.

I make accompte the Compaie will fraight some 2 shipps for that place of the burthen of 600 tonns, more or less; and therefore have a care to get their ladinge in tyme and aforehand, that it may be redie by such tyme as the shipps be with you (which I hope will be Michaellmas come twelvemonneth or before). Yt doth greatlie ymporte you to be carefull and procure ladinge, for this is your whole business there, and therefore ar you sent.

Alsoe I would have you agree together loveinglie, like sober men; for your owne discords, yf you suppress them not, will be to the marchauntes greate losse and hindrance and to your owne undoing. Therefore governe yourselves soe that there be no brabbles amonge you for any cause . . . .

And for the paying of your companie their wages, doe yt sparinglie, and remit soe much as you cann till their retourne. But when necessitie requireth, rather doe yt in comoditie than money, yf you in your discretions see such occasion.

I would have you to paie no wages to Thomas the barber, and fit him with clothes meete, not to exceed in any thinge, for he is another mans prentice, and seeketh onelie to wast his masters . . . '

Even allowing for the boost to English prestige from the Armada victory the expedition did establish that courtesy and fair dealing (it might be called 'gentlemanly behaviour' even if practised by men who at home would not be classed as gentlemen) could generate and develop commercial goodwill and long term relationships. Sometimes the natives of the East Indies failed to distinguish between the European traders – particularly between the Dutch and the English[27] – but generally the behaviour of the English, who did not seek to buy spices by force or duress or establish fortified bases, made them more popular. customers. At the same time, it must be admitted that the ruthless policy of the Dutch over time enabled them to establish and enforce a monopoly of trading in Indonesia, followed by colonial exploitation which lasted until WWII, bringing immense wealth to the Netherlands.

It is really only in the financial area that the Voyage fell short, and that cannot be laid at Lancaster's door. Once again a late start meant a slow passage out (which in turn meant heavy losses from scurvy – although Lancaster's preventive measures with lemon juice showed what could be done)[28] so that the extended time spent in the voyage when added to the time taken to realise the cargo on return, depressed the real rate of return on the investment. By the time that the accounts had been completed (this was not until 1609), it had taken nine years to realise a profit of 95% – a little over 8% p. a.[29] For the first trading voyage of a newly established enterprise the financial arithmetic was, of course, only part of the story. The First Fleet was intended to be exactly that – the first of many – and the success, and thus the profits, of future voyages were in part due to the foundations laid by Lancaster and his fleet.

Lancaster personally distinguished himself on the voyage, showing leadership, concern for his officers and men, personal courage, diplomacy and charm, and securing advantageous trading rights. He also took charge himself where it was necessary – organising trading for victuals and supplies, preventing stealing and pilfering, organizing the replacement rudder in the Dragon, even managing the goat hunt at St. Helena. It is interesting to note that he was quickly on friendly terms with the much older King of Achen, his much younger son, the child King of Priaman and the Dutch Admiral Spielbergen. He appeared to take equal pleasure in befriending the hen-seller, conducting long kindly conversations, getting information out of him and at the same time exposing him as a double agent.

Part Three
Swallowing the Anchor

[A maritime term to indicate giving up, or retiring from a life at sea: see OC p. 850]

10

The Second Fleet of the East India Company

Lancaster reached England from the EIC First Fleet Voyage in September 1603. While we have no direct evidence the next few months must have been extremely hectic, both for him and for all the other EIC directors. The latter had received some prior notice – from the arrival of the Ascension in June – as to how matters had fared, but they had barely six months to deal with the reception of the First Fleet and the preparation and dispatch of the Second Fleet, which sailed in March 1604. The first priority was to get the First Fleet's cargo into safe storage, not an easy task when a sack of pepper could confer lifelong financial independence on a sailor or stevedore.[1]

Apart from a new monarch (Elizabeth died on 24 March 1603 and James I succeeded), 1603 saw a bad outbreak of plague, and a resulting collapse in trade. Suddenly there was more pepper (a million pounds in weight) than the English domestic market could absorb, North Europe was well supplied by the Dutch, and – to make matters worse – James I had just personally acquired a cargo of pepper,[2] which he insisted on realising ahead of the EIC. As a result the directors distributed pepper as a dividend in kind, delegating realisation to the shareholders, some of whom took six or seven years to dispose of it – the price being driven down in the meantime.

These trading problems impinged on the cash flow and the EIC had to borrow money to pay off the First Fleet crews, while trying to raise fresh capital for the Second Fleet. There was considerable resistance to subscribing, in the light of the modest financial showing of the First Fleet, but the directors had no alternative. First, it was commercially essential to maintain the momentum which the directors had planned and Lancaster had set in motion; secondly, the EIC was committed by its charter to dispatch a fleet each year, and, thirdly, there was the threat to their monopoly posed by the interloper Sir Edward Michelborne hovering in the background. The directors demanded that the original subscribers must now find a new £200 for each £250 which they had put up for the First Fleet, so they did well to raise £60,000 in new capital.[3]

The Second Fleet consisted of the same four ships as the First. Lancaster would have been the obvious choice for Admiral but the directors appointed Henry Middleton, who had commanded the Susan. Sir William Foster said of Lancaster (who was around 50) 'his health was poor and he had had enough of adventure and hardship'.[4] No corroboration of his poor health has come to light (and he had 15 active years of life remaining) though Sir William may have picked up some clue), but it would seem very natural that Lancaster, after 30 years almost continual absence abroad or at sea, was ready to come ashore. Giles Milton takes a slightly different line, 'Lancaster had no intention of commanding this new expedition: wealthy, knighted and understandably reluctant to tempt fate by sailing to the East Indies for a third time, he graciously accepted the desk-bound post of director. He was placed in charge of planning the new expedition and his influence is everywhere apparent . . .'[5]

The Instructions of the EIC to Captain Middleton[6] (we can see Lancaster's hand here) directed him to concentrate on cloves, nutmeg, mace and cinnamon, and to sail to the Spice Islands themselves. Middleton was also ordered (this was obviously inserted by a hand other than Lancaster's) to 'propound to yourself the good example of your late predecessor, Sir James Lancaster'. The Second Fleet proved a success – although the Susan was lost – and it returned early in 1606.

In 2nd. October 1603 Lancaster received the honour of knighthood from James I at Winchester. It would be interesting to know whether, and in what terms, the King discussed the East Indies trade with him, since less than a year later[7] he authorised Sir Edward Michelborne, the 'interloper', to sail to the East Indies in breach of the monopoly which Queen Elizabeth had granted to the EIC[8] – with disastrous consequences both for the Company and for England's reputation. It is sad to record that Michelborne had persuaded John Davis to serve as his pilot – possibly, as we have already suggested,[9] because Davis felt he had been unfairly treated after his sterling service with the First Fleet; and sadder still that he was killed in an attack by Japanese pirates off the Malay Peninsular. When Lancaster was knighted it is intriguing to note that he was described as being 'of Hertfordshire':[10] we have no explanation for this – perhaps he had taken up (temporary) residence in that county.

11

Non-Executive Elder Statesman

During most of the next 15 years Lancaster appears to have served as a director of the EIC, but we cannot be certain – since the Minutes of the Court have been lost for the periods 1603-1606, 1611-1613 and 1615-1617: but even when not so serving he was called upon to help on occasions.[1] The comparatively few mentions of his involvement with EIC business show that he was employed in a 'non-executive' director/elder statesman role – taking charge where his experience or special knowledge justified, offering advice, and on one occasion where 'weight' and 'gravitas' were required, acting in conjunction with the Governor and the Deputy Governor.

It is convenient to describe at this stage the drawn-out negotiation in which Lancaster was engaged with the EIC as to his exact entitlement to 'profit share' in the First Fleet venture under the employment contract settled in 1600 which appointed him as Admiral. The original terms are not clear, but these arrangements generally were along the lines 'if the venture shows a 100% profit then £x will be payable, if 150% then £y, and so on'. In 1608 a 'Committee was 'appointed on one side by Sir James Lancaster and Sir Henry Middleton, and on the other by the Company, to examine the order of 14th January 1607, touching the true interpretation of the allowance of the profit of adventure'.[2] It will be in mind that the accounts for the First Fleet were not settled until 1609, so the profit figure – to which the profit share formula had to be applied – was not yet known. In view of this it is not clear what was being discussed – was it the meaning or interpretation of the profit share formula, or were they trying to arrive at a 'horse traded' figure of profit share, to avoid the need to wait until the accounts for the First Fleet had been completed. The financial results of the First Fleet were calculated in 1609, when a 95% profit was established. It looks as though James' final entitlement figure was 'horse traded', rather than precisely calculated, and he seems to have received altogether (there were some payments 'on account') something in excess of £2,000 – perhaps equivalent to £300,000 to-day.

We do not know how closely Lancaster had kept up with the Skinners' Company while he was abroad or at sea. Obviously, he would not have been able to take part in the administration of the Company and there is no suggestion that he was invited to become an officer or join the Court: but it is clear from the references to him in the Court Minutes of the Company that he was treated with respect, for example, in 1605 and 1606 he was invited (with other important guests and their wives) to attend the Election Day Dinner.[3] Again, there is no evidence as to whether Lancaster continued as a merchant. We have seen that he was a consummate 'people's person' and took great delight in 'doing deals' – in which he seems almost always to have been successful.[4] Further, as we will see, he invested in several NW Passage exploration projects and in one mineral exploration expedition after he had 'come ashore'; so it is reasonable to assume that he maintained some interest in normal import-export business – probably as an investor or non-executive partner, rather than as a day-to-day trader.[5]

In 1604 Lancaster appears as a member of the Minerals and Battery Works Compan, being listed with the other investors – courtiers, City men, gentry – in the new charter which James I granted in that year. The Company had originally been chartered by Queen Elizabeth in 1568,[6] together with its sister compeny the Mines Royal Company. These two corporations carried into effect the strategy attributed to William Cecil (Lord Burghley) for importing into England the foreign know-how (particularly German) for mining and working metal ores. The Mines Royal Company received the monopoly for working mines in the counties of Yorkshire, Cumberland, Westmorland, Cornwall, Devon, Gloucester and Worcester, and in Wales. The Minerals and Battery Works Company was granted the monopoly of (i) mining in the other English counties and in the Irish Pale (ii) of mining 'calamine', that is zinc ore which, combined with copper, produces brass and (iii) of 'battery' which covered the hammering of iron to make 'plate' for armour and other purposes, making brass and the casting of guns. There is no real explanation why two companies were needed but in the event they worked together and the lines of demarcation were not too strict: for example, both companies 'drew' wire. Why did Lancaster join the Minerals and Battery Works Company ? And, When ? The Letters Patent of 1604 recite that the original grantees and all or most of their assignees are dead and then goes on to state that 'the said Powers and Priviliges &c. are since come unto' the listed members, including Lancaster, who are duly incorporated 'by the name of The Governours, Assistants, and Society of the City of London of and for the Mineral and

Batteryworks'. So, in priciple, Lancaster could have joined the Company at any time prior to 1604: in practice, the choice is between (i) the 1595-1600 period which was his first long spell in England, and (ii) 1603-4 when he relinquished full-time employment and was perhaps seeking non-executive or less-than-full-time roles. Neither of the sister 'mineral companies' proved particularly profitable,[7] and, as a result, the monoply activities were often 'farmed out' to non-members from around 1570-80. From this we may deduce that Lancaster's reason for joining was probably not for the investment return. A possible explanation is Lancaster's expertise in ordnance and armour: he had been serving in armed merchantmen since 1581-2, he had seen military action in Portugal in 1580-81 and had commanded a successful amphibious operation at Recife in 1594-5. His expertise was recognised by the Court of the EIC which in 1617 appointed him to chair a committee to consult with all the English gunnery experts and to recommend on future policy for arming the Company's ships.[8] It may be therefore that Lancaster was invited to join the Battery and Works Company to make available his ideas on cannon design. In 1604 Lancaster was not one of the officers of the Company, but that is consistent with a limited technical input. It seems unlikely that further evidence on Lancaster's involvement will emerge: there is a full manuscript record of the Court minutes of the two 'mineral companies' from 1568 to 1713 but unfortunately there is a gap between c. 1590 and c. 1615.[9]

On a balance of probabilities it looks as though it was in or about 1604 that Lancaster acquired his London house, The Papeye.[10] We know that it was a leasehold interest, and that it was probably for a term of years (since he left the lease to Mrs Owfield),[11] but we do not know how much money would have been needed to acquire it; we may assume that his wealth accumulated to date was sufficient. In February 1607 at a Court Meeting of the EIC, it was decided that a smaller group would meet later at Lancaster's house. If by that time the Papeye was indeed his house it would have been less than 10 minutes walk from the EIC headquarters in Sir Thomas Smythe's house in Philpot Lane, off Fenchurch Street, to the north end of St. Mary Axe.

The Papeye was a large house with an interesting history.[12] The site was originally occupied by the church of St. Augustine Papeye[13] and a graveyard: they are clearly shown in Agas' 'bird's-eye' map c. 1592.[14] The church was built under the Wall where St. Mary Axe then formed a T-junction with Camomile Street and Bevis Marks. The church had served its own parish but by 1428 there were only 10 parishioners and the parish was therefore combined with All Hallows, London Wall. In 1442 a Fraternity of the Papeye was formed to support poor and decayed priests and the redundant church and its land became part of its endowment, the church serving as the chapel of the Fraternity.[15] The Fraternity was suppressed in around 1548. The church was then demolished and various buildings were erected: eventually they became a private house,[16] and, by Lancaster's time, there seems to have been a main house, gardens and a subsidiary house.[17] According to Stow previous occupiers had included Sir Francis Walsingham, Secretary of State to Queen Elizabeth, but this must have been some years earlier, and does not help with dating Lancaster's acquisition.[18]

In his will Lancaster left legacies to three male and two female servants, and Mrs. Owfield is mentioned as having at least one servant.[19] He left some quite valuable sounding chattels e. g. 'plate', a collection of 'china' (presumably oriental porcelain), furniture and a library, and by his will directed that his household and the employment of his servants should be continued for three months after his death, in order to give them time to seek new positions; so it seems that life in the Papeye was on quite a comfortable scale. Even if he could afford to do so it seems unlikely after a Spartan existence at sea that Lancaster would, around the age of 50, have suddenly adopted a lavish or luxurious lifestyle. This is, to some extent, confirmed by the fact that when he purchased a substantial estate in Lincolnshire and a farm in Hampshire (in 1608) neither had a mansion house – it appears that he was looking only for sound investments.

Over the last 15 years of his life Lancaster seems, on the limited evidence available, to have devoted himself to the affairs of the EIC, to the Skinners' Company, to continued involvement in trade, perhaps to the business of the Minerals and Battery Works Company, to his family and several charitable projects in North Hampshire, to acquiring agricultural property (in Lincolnshire and Hampshire) and to a new field of interest – the search for a NW Passage as an extension to the activities of the EIC. He also, in his last few years, urged the EIC to develop an alternative route to the East Indies via the Magellan Strait. The latter appears not have been followed up, perhaps because – under pressure from the Dutch – the EIC was beginning to switch its attentions from the Indonesian islands towards India. At some stage someone must have suggested to Lancaster that he should put himself forward for election as an alderman but, as we will see, when he stood for election in 1612, another candidate was chosen.

We will follow these developments on a chronological basis, with diversions as necessary to cover Lancaster's relations with the Puritans, his acquisition of agricultural land and his involvement with the NW Passage.

In 1604 the Court of the Skinners' Company instructed their Clerk (the 'chief executive' of the Company) to speak to Lancaster about a loan being sought from the City by James I.[20] We do not know the circumstances, or the outcome, but it looks as though the Court hoped that, with his newly acquired wealth, Lancaster might feel able to contribute more than his 'normal' contribution as a member of the Company. It appears that the Skinners' Company was in some financial difficulties, so this may have been the explanation.

In 1605 Lancaster was invited, with other dignitaries, to attend the Election Day dinner in June.[21] In the same year occurred the upset for Peter Lancaster, which we have already described.[22] In September Peter was elected (at around the age of 46) as Second Warden of the Skinners' Yeomanry, but in December he lost this position when he demonstrated that his net worth was less than £100 and that he was unable to pay his share of the loan to the King, namely £4. It is perhaps surprising that his brother James Lancaster did not bail him out, but we know no more.

In 1606 Lancaster was again invited by the Skinners to their Election Day dinner.[23] On the last day of the year he attended a Court of the EIC.[24] No doubt he had been attending these meetings regularly since 1603[25] but with the Minute Book lost we have no record.

For 1607 we have a regular Minute Book for the EIC, so Lancaster's participation as a director is recorded, and from these accounts, we can get a feel for the kind of activity in which he was engaged during the 'blank' periods for which the minutes have been lost. Early in January he was asked by the Court to provide advice to Captain William Keeling on the conduct of the Third Voyage to the East Indies, in particular the best route from the Cape across the Indian Ocean. This resulted in the 'Hints'[26] They give very precise instructions to ensure that (i) voyages set out from England 'early enough' (ii) that the voyage across the Indian Ocean is planned to catch the monsoon winds. From a reference in the minutes of this meeting, and in the minutes of two further meetings in January, it is clear that there is a ongoing discussion on the profit share to which Lancaster was entitled in respect of the First Fleet voyage.[27] At a meeting of the Court in February it was agreed that the captains, masters and the two mates of each ship (of the planned Third Voyage) should meet separately with Lancaster at his house.[28] This lends support to the suggestion that by 1607 he had moved into the Papeye in St. Mary Axe as his London home, less than ten minutes walk from Sir Thomas Smythe's house in Philpott Lane. The Court also directed that copies of the 'Hints' should be given to the chief merchant or captain of each ship 'for their better instruction'.[29] At the same February meeting the Court considered the diet of the men in the Red Dragon, suggesting that some notice was being taken of Lancaster's efforts to prevent scurvy in the First Fleet. She was to load one cwt. (hundredweight) of the root of saxifrage and a quarter cwt. of aniseed for beverage 'very wholesome for the preservation of men's health', and some 'lemon water'. If the intention was to prevent scurvy, it was unsuccessful; Captain Middleton put in at the Cape in July 1604, contrary to his instructions, to refresh his men, many of whom had contracted the disease.[30] At a Court in August the Governor, Sir Thomas Smythe and Lancaster expressed the view that the 'Union' (a ship being considered for the Fourth Voyage) would be fit but that her repairs would probably prove expensive.[31] At the meeting of the Court in September Lancaster requested that he be paid £2000 on account of his outstanding profit share at Michaelmas i. e. at the end of September, for 'some extraordinary use thereof'. We cannot be sure but it looks as though he may have identified the country estate for which he had been looking – he completed the purchase of the Maidenwell Estate in Lincolnshire in the following year 1608. The Court went some way to meeting this request, agreeing to pay £1500 on account in October 'in regard of his former good service and his counsel given and to be given to the Company'(and a further payment of £300 two months later). At a Court meeting in December 1607 Lancaster expressed the view that a shallop (rather than a pinnace) would be more suitable for a purpose under discussion (evidently for the Fourth Voyage), and, after an interview, he approved one Richard Rowles as a suitable commander.[32] At a later meeting in the same month on 23rd. December a further £300 was approved for payment to Lancaster in respect of his profit share.[33]

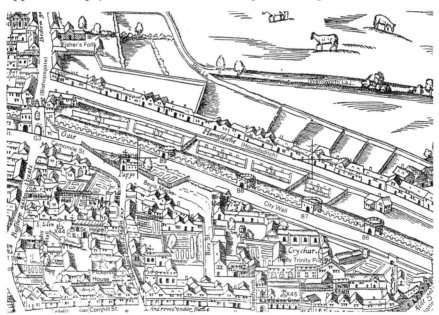

The Papeye, Lancaster's London house, at the north end of St Mary Axe

12

Maidenwell and Pamber

It is convenient at this point to digress to describe Lancaster's agricultural investments, both made in 1608. Since neither Maidenwell nor the farm at Pamber[1] included a mansion house, it looks as though he had been looking simply for agricultural investments. The location of the Pamber property might, however, suggest that he was seeking to provide a farming tenancy for one of his kinsmen in Hampshire.

Maidenwell is a hamlet 5 miles south of Louth in East Lincolnshire. The nucleus of the estate included land at Maidenwell, Farford (now Farforth), Abie and Claythorpe and consisted originally of some 337 acres. There was a dwelling house and garden. The estate was referred at the time of James' death as the Manor of Maidenwell. The estate lies about 450 feet above sea level on the Lincolnshire Wolds, and appears to have been good quality arable land – it was certainly sold as such in 1977.[2] After James' death the trustees of his will (the Court of Chancery in 1713 substituted the Corporation of Basingstoke for the Skinners' Company as trustee) acquired further adjoining land on several occasions, so that when it was finally sold (in 1977) the estate had increased to some 1415 acres.[3] Lancaster acquired Maidenwell in 1608 from Sir George Anton and

The Maidenwell Estate, Lincolnshire

Edmund Shuttleworth. We have no information on how Lancaster managed Maidenwell or indeed whether he ever went there. After his death it was in the hands of the Skinners' Company, as trustee of his will, for about 100 years.[4]

The Court of Chancery removed the Skinners' Company as trustee because they were unable to pay in full the annuities charged on Maidenwell, and Lancaster's other real property, out of the income which they received from them.[5] Whether this was due to poor management or the fluctuations in the fortunes of farming we are unable to say. In modern times Basingstoke Corporation (as the substituted trustee of Lancaster's will) has done very well with the estate (after allowing for the additional capital which they invested to enlarge it): inflation over the years increased the income while the amount of the charged annuities remained the same – the difference accrued to Basingstoke.[6] Maidenwell has always been somewhat remote, but it has two claims to attention.[7] First, the estate included the largest arable field in the entire United Kingdom, known as Burwell Walk and measuring over 189 acres.[8] Secondly, the estate received a secret visit from Charles Stuart, the Young Pretender: the exact date is not known. The tenant of the estate, one Mosely, was a Catholic and supporter of the Young Pretender, who arrived by sea at Saltfleetby and made his way to Maidenwell. During his stay Charles visited Lincoln and attended an entertainment, at which he was recognized: with Mr. Mosely's help he had to hurry back to his ship on the coast.

In the same year, 1608, Lancaster also acquired 'three messuages or tenements' in the parish of Pamber, known as Long Towe, Wilboroughs

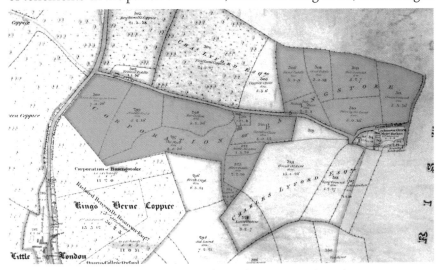

Frog Lane Farm, at Little London, near Basingstoke

and Goldecke. This is in Hampshire, about eight miles north of Basingstoke, near the village of Little London. It was a small farm of less than 100 acres. It too came into the hands of the trustees of Lancaster's will on his death. In modern times it has been known as Frog Lane Farm. It was sold by Basingstoke Corporation in 1898.

Sir James Deane: a memorial in St Olave's, Hart Street, in the City of London

1608 saw the death of Lancaster's cousin, Sir James Deane, Master of the Drapers' Company and Alderman on 15th May at Hackney.[9] Lancaster was appointed the senior of four executors, and Paul Banning, a long-time City supporter and colleague of his, was among the overseers of the will. At the time of his death, Sir James Deane owned the manor of Deane and Ashe (and the advowson – the right to appoint the priest), other property in and around Basingstoke, a manor in Cambridgeshire and a house with land in Hackney (possibly Sutton House, which still survives in the hands of the National Trust) Although he had been married three time Sir James' main family beneficiaries were his nephews and nephews-in-law. There were a number of important charitable bequests, charged on the Manor of Deane and Ashe: – (i) an annuity to support the almshouse which he was building at the time of his death in London Street, Basingstoke, and their occupants (They are still occupied as such: see the picture overleaf) (ii) £10 p. a for a Lectureship In Basingstoke (iii) an annuity of £10 p. a. to augment the stipend of the master of the school attached to the Fraternity of the Holy Ghost in Basingstoke (iv) other bequests to benefit the poor in Basingstoke, and also in specified locations in London (v) £1 p. a. to maintain the causeway between the Angel Inn and the Church in Basingstoke. Lancaster was entrusted, during his life, with the nomination of the Lecturer and the schoolmaster (under items (ii) and (iii) above). As senior executor Lancaster must have spent much time in and around Basingstoke.

Before leaving 1608 we may note that Lancaster attended EIC court meetings at least in February, April and December. It is interesting to note that at the April meeting the receipt was minuted of a letter received for Lancaster from Henry Sydall, one of the factors at Bantam. It had taken a year to reach England.[10]

Sir James Deane's almshouses in Basingstoke

In 1609 Lancaster appears at an EIC Court meeting in May and the minutes of a meeting in July indicate that the long discussion over profit share arising from the First Fleet was finally resolved. A dispute was also resolved over the salary of a junior factor whom Lancaster had appointed at Bantam

We noticed that Lancaster, under the will of his cousin Sir James Deane, was entrusted with picking the Basingstoke Lecturers. Since the lectureship attracted the interest of the Puritans, it is a convenient point to consider Lancaster's relations with them.

13
Lancaster and the Godly Mafia[1]

In the course of his life Lancaster was close to a number of prominent Puritan divines and may have been related to one or more of them by marriage,[2] in particular the father and son Thomas and Samuel Crooke (sometimes Crookes) and Stephen Egerton. We will consider here how these Puritans came into his life and what, if any, effect these contacts had on his character and behaviour; and describe the manoeuvres to get a Puritan appointed to the Basingstoke Lectureship. First, as to the precise nature or definition of Puritanism, it will be best to leave this perennial debate to the attention of specialist scholars. We may adopt the practical position that while it is impossible to define Puritanism with any precision it is not difficult to recognize a member of the tribe: the famous description of Dean Hutton of York made in 1573 will suffice, 'At the beginning it was but a cap, a surplice, and a tippet; now it is grown to bishops, archbishops, and cathedral churches, to the overthrow of the established order, and to the Queen's authority in causes ecclesiastical'.[3]

Thomas Crooke was born in the 1540s and educated at Trinity College, Cambridge. By 1578 he had obtained his first degree, then a degree in divinity, and become a Doctor of Divinity. In the meantime (i) he publicly supported Thomas Cartwright, Professor of Divinity, in his criticisms of the Church of England (Cartwright was dismissed and went abroad) (ii) he was, in 1573-4, appointed rector of Great Waldingfield in Suffolk. In 1578 Crooke appears as a member of Pembroke Hall, Cambridge – a move probably due to his Puritan leanings. At Great Waldingfield he married, produced two sons and remained until 1582, having in 1580-1 been appointed Chaplain ['Reader in Divinitie'] to Grays's Inn, a benefice which he held until his death in 1598. Gray's Inn clearly regarded Crooke as a great catch. It is not easy to see why – perhaps they wished to please Lord Burghley, himself a member of the Inn, who introduced him,[4] or perhaps it was the quality of his preaching [Or perhaps the quantity. The editor of the Pension Book of Gray's Inn 1569-1669 comments (on p. xxxvi) 'I do not know whether we are to draw any conclusion as to his sermons from the fact that soon after his appointment an 'hower glass' was bought for the Chapel'] The Inn paid Crooke a stipend of £66. 13. 4 [100 marks](partly financed by an annual levy on all the members) and provided him with accommodation (two members of the Inn were ejected to make room) and his 'commons'. (The previous chaplain, also a Puritan – who had been expelled from Cambridge for his extreme Presbyterian views – was paid only £4 per year). In 1586 Thomas Crooke was invited by the Skinners' Company 'with Mr. Graunte and other learned men' to examine a Mr. William Hatche who had been put forward to be headmaster of Tonbridge School, then (as now) managed by the Company[5] Thomas Crooke had two sons Samuel b. 1575 and Helkiah b. 1576. Helkiah was a famous doctor who became physician to James I. Samuel was also a distinguished scholar. After Merchant Taylors' School he went as a scholar to his father's (second) college Pembroke Hall, Cambridge. He was chosen to be a fellow but the Master vetoed the appointment, no doubt on account of his Puritan tendencies. Soon afterwards he was elected the first Dixie scholar at the recently founded Emmanuel College.[6] Samuel was appointed reader in rhetoric and philosophy, took holy orders in 1601 (as required by the Emmanuel statutes) and immediately started to preach in the villages around Cambridge – unprecedented behaviour for a college fellow. In 1602 Samuel was appointed rector of Wrington in Somerset where he remained until his death in 1649. He married Judith Walsh, daughter of a clergyman in his father's part of Suffolk but there were no children. He was an extremely active and popular preacher (clergymen at that time did not normally preach at all) and he became a zealous advocate of church reform along presbyterian lines and, during the Civil War, an active recruiter for the Parliament. When the Royalists recaptured Somerset in 1643, Samuel was bullied into a grovelling recantation, being by then 70 years of age.[7] In age Lancaster was closer to the father, Thomas Crooke, and it seems likely from the legacies in Lancaster's will that he had got to know some of Thomas' relations and parishioners in Great Waldingfield, suggesting that the friendship originated with the father.[8] It is at this time too that he may have met the Rev. M. Walsh, another Suffolk minister and his daughter Judith.[9] While we have no direct evidence, it seems probable that Lancaster made Thomas' acquaintance early in his life, either in Suffolk i. e. before 1582 (He was around 28 in that year), or when Thomas was Chaplain at Gray's Inn i. e after 1580, or possibly when Thomas spent time at the Skinners' Hall in 1586. A meeting at Gray's Inn in the mid to late 1580s seems most likely: at that time non-members of the Inn were permitted to attend services in the Chapel. From the manoeuvres over the Basingstoke lectureship later[10] it seems unlikely that the friendship originated with Lancaster's own family in Hampshire. Lancaster left £50 and his library to Samuel Crooke's wife Judith, and £5 to Samuel for a mourning ring.

We have no indication at all as to how and when Lancaster met Stephen Egerton, another Puritan divine, but they clearly became friends, since he left him a legacy of £4. Lancaster appears to have enlisted Egerton to help him identify candidates for the Basingstoke lectureship.[11] Egerton was about the same age, being born c. 1555. He was a graduate of Peterhouse, Cambridge and suffered suspension and imprisonment for refusing to conform. He was appointed to the living of St Anne's, Blackfriars in 1598 and remained there until shortly before his death in 1622.

Did these associations affect Lancaster's religious beliefs or his conduct and mode of life in general? It appears that they did not. Lancaster comes across, throughout his life, as a man of high principles; his religious observances appeared to be those of a practical merchant and naval/military commander; he seemed to delight in the company of everyone he met, irrespective of their rank, race and religious persuasion and was always most solicitous to those under his authority; in short, he appears to led a practical Christian life, avoiding the complications of dogma and ritual.[12]

As we have noted Sir James Deane, in 1608, by his will established a Lectureship at Basingstoke and Lancaster as senior executor was authorized during his life to approve the appointment of the lecturers.[13] Such lectureships were around that time very common all over England. Their purpose was, like the earlier meetings of clergymen known as 'prophesyings' – which were banned by Queen Elizabeth who considered that they presented a political risk – (i) to harmonise and standardise the teachings of the reformed Church of England, and (ii) to educate both the laity and the less well educated ministers in these authorized doctrines. While those who established them, like Lancaster and his cousin, probably considered them as a public spirited way for wealthy individuals to benefit their communities – just like the educational endowments which they also funded – the Puritans apparently saw them as an opportunity to pursue their own agenda – to spread their ideas throughout the Church – and they therefore plotted to get their men appointed. This policy – harnessing the support, particularly the financial support, of conventionally religious individuals, to promote Puritan ideas – was not confined to lectureships. It is instructive to study the manoeuvres of the founder of Emmanuel College (Sir Walter Mildmay) to enlist a network of rich individuals, particularly in London, to fund his new seminary for 'godly preachers'.[14] In his own will, in 1618, Lancaster left legacies to augment the stipend of the Lecturer, to support students of divinity at Oxford and Cambridge and poor godly preachers; but he also left legacies to benefit education in Basingstoke and Kingsclere, the poor in his parish in London, the main London hospitals and the prisoners in the London prisons and 'compters'. It is difficult to see here more than the public spirited generosity of a wealthy bachelor who had already provided for his kinsmen and friends.

As has been pointed out[15] the combination of the 'hidden agenda', described above, with the acrobatic semantics employed by the Puritans, designed to convince themselves, each other and the authorities that they were 'conforming', was over time broadly successful in diffusing the less extreme Puritan ideas throughout the Church of England – an interesting case-study on whether the ends can justify the means.

We can now glance briefly at some Puritan plotting over the Basingstoke Lectureship. Samuel Crooke wrote in 1609 to yet another prominent Puritan divine, Samuel Ward,[16] offering him the Basingstoke lectureship 'on behalf of' Lancaster.[17] The letter begins and ends with the mantra 'Imanuel', its tone is conspiratorial and the references to the townsfolk of Basingstoke less than flattering 'having been till this time blinded by ignorance and superstition'; 'the spirit of Popery which there haunteth'.[18] Ward is asked to direct his answer to 'my Brother Egerton's house in Blackfriars; you may send your letter open to him if you will'. In the event, Ward apparently did not rise to the bait, and there is no trace of other Puritan candidates. While the names of the first holders of the lectureship (prior to 1634) have not survived[19] it was later normally held by the rector of Basingstoke.

14

Arctic Exploration and the Northern Passages

In 1610 Lancaster became involved in exploration for the NW Passage. We have suggested that his interest was inspired by his daily contact over the three years of the First Fleet voyage (1601-3) with John Davis, his Fleet Pilot.[1] Although he never sailed in Arctic waters Lancaster became interested, later in his life, in this area and, in particular, in a North West Passage as a short cut from England to the East. With his customary energy and pertinacity he was also, near the end of his life in 1614, still urging the EIC to exploit the Magellan Strait route to the Spice Islands as an alternative to the Cape.[2]

We may set the scene with a brief overview of the search for the Northern Passages. While there were other motives for Arctic exploration, for example fishing, whaling, furs, trading, mineral recovery, colonization, the main thrust in the 16th century was to find a passage to China and the East. The search involved amazing doggedness, bravery, consummate skill in seamanship and navigation, appalling loss of life – and proved a total failure, apart from the by-product advantages mentioned above. As we will see, there was also a thread of irony running through the whole story. The search for Northern Passages was based on the belief of the ancients that the land mass of the earth is surrounded by sea, so that, as a matter of symmetry, the Southern Ocean south of America, Africa and Asia must be 'balanced' by a similar mass of ocean encircling the north of America and Asia. Although the reasoning may be questioned the conclusion turned out to be true – eventually: but the Passages have generally been impassable, except by icebreaker or submarine. The search was carried out mainly by Northern Europeans, particularly the English. The objectives were, first, to find a shorter route, and secondly, to avoid the political and religious obstacles presented by the compact between the Papacy, Portugal and Spain – formalized in the Treaty of Tordesillas

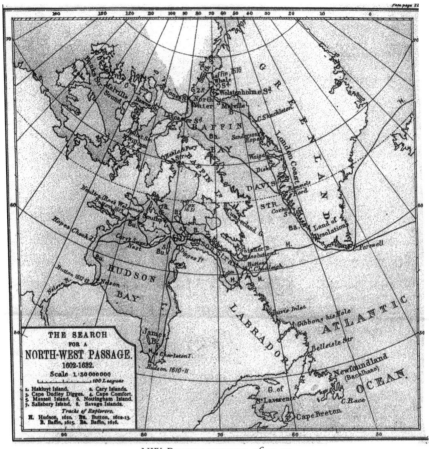

NW Passage voyages, 1602-22

in 1524, which purported to exclude other nations from the lands and seas beyond Europe and the Mediterranean.[3] As the 16th century progressed and the Reformation spread the religious sanctions weakened but the political 'cold war' vacillations between England and Spain still steered English mariners and their merchant backers towards a way of 'working round' the monopoly claimed by Portugal and Spain. Persuading Queen Elizabeth to permit frontal assaults on the monopoly was a difficult, unpredictable business. In 2002 Gavin Menzies[4] put forward the claim that in the matter of the Northern Passages, as in other parts of the world, the Chinese forestalled the Europeans.[5] He maintains that in 1422-3 one of the last Chinese treasure-ship fleets, after sailing up the east coast of America, visiting Rhode Island and Massachusetts, entered the Davis

Strait and sailed up the west coast of Greenland and then possibly sailed on towards the North Pole (at that date under 200 miles away). Then, turning east, the fleet passed north of Iceland and sailed back to China passing north of Scandinavia, Russia and Asia, producing detailed and accurate charts of the northern coasts of the land mass.[6] As a navigator himself, Menzies' argument is based on working back from the charts to the hydrographers who drew the charts, to the fleets who carried them and to the Chinese Empire – which was the only country able to afford such a monumental undertaking across the world at that date. Menzies argues that all this was possible because of a comparatively warm period in the Arctic in the first half of the 15th century.[7] These bold claims have been hotly contested by professional historians.

The final irony in the search for a Northern Passage is the apparent failure to distinguish between (i) the scientific/geographical question – does a passage exist ? and (ii) if yes, is it commercially useful since we will never know when it is going to be passable ? This failure to think the issue through may have been due to the fact that the decision-takers and providers of funds were not seafarers (Lancaster was an exception, though he had no experience of Arctic conditions), and had no concept whatever of the unpredictable nature of Arctic ice, whether considered on a day-to-day, seasonal or longer-term basis. The hard-nosed commercial viability point was indeed made (but not heeded) by an experienced and successful whaling captain who had visited northern waters every year over a long period; by Sir William Monson and by Sir Richard Grenville (the hero of the Revenge). With his customary independence of mind, Sir William made two points (i) Would it in fact produce a shorter route than round the Cape ? (ii) The availability of a passage would be unpredictable.[8] Grenville was more specific 'Nowe consideringe the sea and ayre under the Artike circleare so congeled that they are navigable only 3 monethes in the yeare, whereof it is requisite to reserve at leaste one monethe to retorne, if the said passadge sholde not be met withall'.[9]

In the debates in the EIC as to whether the Company should fund Northern Passage exploration the usual line was 'It costs comparatively little by our standards in relation to the benefit which would ensue, so let's do it'. Fleets consisted of one or two ships, of very small size (by EIC standards) e. g. 40-60 tons, with crews to match and small arms (no cannon) and needing to be victualled for less than six months – unless they planned to over-winter. Much of the drive behind English efforts to find a northern passage to the East came from the international merchants, principally from London, who had been trying to follow the Oriental Spice Trade up-stream towards its sources since the middle of the 16th century. While these individuals may in some cases be concealed behind the corporate façades of e. g. the Merchant Adventurers, the Muscovy, Spanish/Portuguese, Turkey, Venetian and East India Companies, they are the same group – whom we have already met – headed by Sir Thomas Smythe, Sir Edward Osborne and Richard Staper. Lancaster of course joined this group, initially as an employee, but, eventually, as a principal. In the second half of the 16th century efforts concentrated first on a North East passage and, while none was found, regular trade with Russia was established. Interest then switched to the North West side

Martin Frobisher made three expeditions in 1576, 1577 and 1578 and discovered the Sound or Strait which bears his name, but not much else, though he started an abortive gold rush.[10] Significant discoveries were made by John Davis, the famous navigator who commanded three expeditions in 1585, 1586 and 1587: his success stemmed from his combination of seamanship, navigational and leadership skills. He sailed to around 72 degrees N.

It seems likely that it was Davis who aroused Lancaster's interest in Arctic matters, and the North West Passage in particular, during the First EIC Voyage 1601-3 during which he served Lancaster as Fleet Pilot and must have been in daily contact with him.[11] Their backgrounds and temperaments were similar and Lancaster may well have absorbed Davis' life-long enthusiasm for the North West Passage. It is tragic that Davis was to die on his next voyage to the East in 1605, at the hands of Japanese pirates, having joined the 'interloper' Sir Edward Michelborne – apparently aggrieved by his treatment by the EIC. Had he survived he would surely have been associated with Lancaster in backing/leading further Arctic exploration. Davis' career was quite like Lancaster's;[12] he was a Devon man, of yeoman stock, born c. 1550 at Sandridge on the River Dart, and from childhood was friendly with Humphrey and Adrian Gilbert and Walter Raleigh. He had good schooling and went to sea young, becoming a commander by the age of 30. Through the Gilberts and Walter Raleigh, Davis was introduced to Sir Francis Walsingham, who favoured Arctic exploration, and to William Sanderson (sometimes Saunderson), a rich merchant, who became Davis' main financial backer.[13] West Country merchants also invested in Davis' first and second voyages. When Davis returned from his third voyage, in 1587, he had identified two promising leads for the N-W. Passage search (i) the 'Furious Overfall' – the rough water at the mouth of what was later to be named Hudson's Strait (leading to Hudson's Bay), and (ii) 'Sanderson his Hope' a cliff on the Greenland Coast in 72 degrees N.[14] This was the furthest point north which Davis reached and, with its clear, deep water it suggested free access to the north – and perhaps thence westward to the NW Passage. However, by

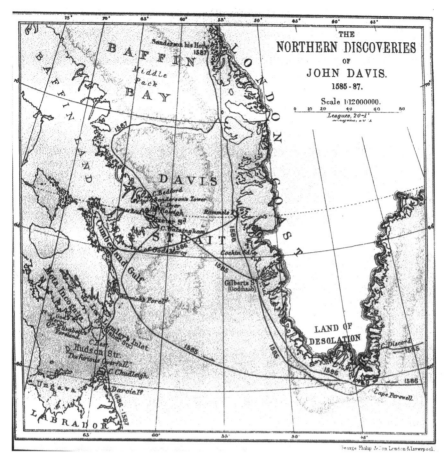

The NW voyages of John Davis

that time (1587) no one was interested in further Arctic exploration: all thoughts were concentrated on the Spanish Armada. Davis was given command of the Black Dog in the Armada campaign, a small ship of some 20 tons, but with the important role of attending the Lord High Admiral in Ark Royal, and probably acting as a pilot.[15] In 1589, like many others, Davis went into privateering. With the backing of Ralegh and probably Sanderson, he took two ships, the Drake and the Barke of Lime (probably Lyme, now Lyme Regis) to join an expedition put out by the Earl of Cumberland.[16] Davis had met Cumberland some years before and on his first Arctic voyage had named Cumberland Gulf after him.[17] Davis' ships met up with Cumberland's squadron in the Azores. The cruise was a success: 13 prizes were taken and Davis received his share, securing his financial independence. He undertook further privateering in 1590 (when Lancaster was similarly engaged).[18] Now equipped with capital, Davis took a ship to join Cavendish's Second Voyage (1591-3),[19] having in mind to pass the Straits of Magellan with the fleet and then to break away to sail north to attempt the North West Passage from its western end. Cavendish's autocratic behaviour and jealousy, and the difficulties of the voyage, combined to turn the whole venture to disaster. Cavendish abandoned his fleet and the survivors returned to England only through Davis' heroic leadership. His investment in the voyage was all lost. Financially ruined, Davis returned to Devon in 1593 and devoted himself to his practical navigation manual, publishing 'The Seaman's Secrets' in 1594. He also perfected the 'Back Staff' which he had been developing at sea: this was designed to simplify the taking of the sun's elevation in the sky.[20] 'Davis' Back Staff' remained the standard instrument for this purpose until the reflecting quadrant was introduced in 1731, leading in turn to the modern sextant. In 1595 Davis also published an address to the Privy Council, 'The Worlde's Hydrographical Description'; explaining the advantages of continuing to seek the North West Passage, but it fell on deaf ears. After two years ashore Davis was back commanding a merchant ship in 1594, and he was employed in the Cadiz Raid of 1596 and the 'Island Voyage' (to the Azores) in 1597. We do not know the details of his service (probably as a pilot) but in this way Davis acquired the Earl of Essex as a patron. At this time, English and Dutch interest in direct

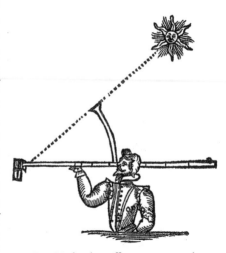

Davis's back staff, precursor to the sextant

voyages to the East was mounting, stimulated by Lancaster's first voyage in 1591-3 and Linschoten's coup in bringing back to the Netherlands a complete merchant adventurer's guide to the East.[21] Essex despatched Davis to offer his services to Cornelius de Houtman, reckoning that this would be to England's longer-term advantage. Houtman's fleet sailed in 1598 and returned in 1600. So far as Davis was concerned, the voyage in many ways resembled Cavendish's Second Voyage. Houtman was autocratic, brutal and jealous of the handful of Englishmen in his fleet: but when the ships were attacked by the forces of the King of Achen (who had shown considerable kindness to Davis personally) it was the

Englishmen who led the counter-attack which saved the day. Davis was back in England in the middle of 1600, in time to join Lancaster as Fleet Pilot on the First EIC Voyage.

We may now return to May 1603 when the Admiral of the EIC First Voyage, the Red Dragon, lost her rudder and was drifting helplessly between the Cape of Good Hope and Antarctica.[22] Lancaster refused to abandon his ship and wrote his famous farewell letter to the Governor of the EIC. , 'I will strive with all diligence to save my ship, and her goods, . . . by the course I take in venturing mine owne life, and those that are with me. I cannot tell where you should looke for mee . . . because I live at the devotion of the wind and seas'.[23] The last paragraph of the letter is intriguing, since it has no connection whatever with the plight of the Red Dragon or indeed with the First Fleet expedition, 'The passage to the East India lieth in 62 ½ degrees by the north west on the America side'. It seems reasonable to assume that, over the previous two years Davis, with his unquenchable enthusiasm for the North West Passage, had converted Lancaster to his views, and the latter decided to give them maximum impact by including this tip in what might well have turned out to be a message from beyond a watery grave. There is, however, a question to which we have no answer. Davis was a meticulous navigator. As we noted above, he had identified two promising areas for further exploration towards the North West Passage. 'Saunderson his Hope' lies around 72 degrees N. The mouth of Hudson's Strait is at 62 degrees N. 62 ½ degrees N is the latitude of Frobisher Bay – which is indeed a bay i. e. a cul-de-sac, having no further relevance to a North West Passage. Half a degree or 30 minutes is 30 nautical miles.[24] In any event this occasion is the first direct connection recorded between Lancaster and the Northern Passages, and no doubt it explains his support for further exploration when he came ashore. He may have already been indirectly involved, since the EIC (formally incorporated only a few weeks before Lancaster left England) and some of its leading lights had been supporters of this exploration for some time.

After Davis' voyages for the North West Passages there was a long hiatus. The expeditions of George Weymouth (1602) and of John Knight (1606), both backed by the EIC. , achieved nothing.

More solid achievements were realised by Henry Hudson's Voyage in 1610, although he died at the hands of mutineers after wintering in the Arctic.[25] It is with this voyage led by Hudson that James became an active investor in Arctic exploration, as one of a heavyweight City syndicate. The group consisted of Sir Thomas Smith (Smythe), Lancaster, Sir Dudley Digges, Sir William Cockayne, Sir Francis Jones, Sir John Wolstenholme, Richard Wyche,[26] Ralph Freeman and William Stone, 'all names well known in Arctic geography'.[27] Hudson had gained valuable experience in three earlier voyages, two towards Spitzbergen and Novya Zemlya and one to the east coast of America, when he named the Hudson River and visited Chesapeake Bay, Sandy Hook and Manhattan Island. He entered and named the Hudson's Strait and Hudson's Bay and named Cape Digges for one of his patrons, Sir Dudley Digges. The survivors of the expedition, some mutineers and some 'bystanders', were brought back to England in 1611 by the skill of Robert Bylot, who was to distinguish himself later.[28]

In 1612 this same City of London syndicate (including Lancaster) was formally incorporated by Royal Charter into 'The Company of Merchants of London, Discoverers of the North-West Passage'.[29] Lancaster became a committee (director). In May 1612 the Company sent out two ships commanded by Captain (later Sir) Thomas Button, under the patronage of Henry, Prince of Wales, in whose names the formal instructions were issued.[30] Robert Bylot was among the crew.[31] Button sailed into Hudson's Strait, entered Hudson's Bay, crossed to its western side, which he explored, and wintered in the south of the Bay in the Nelson River, at what is now Port Nelson and headquarters of the Hudson Bay Company. The ships returned safely in the autumn of 1613, and Button argued that a North West Passage did exist. Separately from Button's expedition. 1612 also saw a voyage by two small vessels out of Hull commanded by John Hall sent out by Sir Thomas Smith (Smythe), Lancaster, Sir William Cockayne and Master Ball. Hall had been employed in 1605, 1606 and 1607 by the King of Denmark to prospect for minerals on the west coast of Greenland, and it seems that this voyage had similar objectives, with no reference to the North West Passage. The pilot was William Baffin.[32] On entering Rommels Fjord (about 66 degrees N) on 21st. July 1612 Hall 'was slain by a savage',[33] apparently in revenge for killings and abductions carried out by a Danish party (which included Hall) on a previous visit. The expedition returned to Hull.

In 1614 a single ship, the Discovery, was sent out commanded by a Captain Gibbons, who had served as a 'volunteer' with Sir Thomas Button (to whom he was related) in 1612-3. Button appears to have thought highly of Gibbons, and the Discovery was one of the two ships in Button's expedition; further there is circumstantial evidence that the EIC was persuaded by Sir Thomas Smith to contribute £200 to the venture.[34] Gibbons, however, was unlucky. He was caught in the ice and trapped for 20 weeks in a bay thought to be Nain Bay in Labrador. Contemporary mariners called the bay 'Gibbons his Hole'.[35]

In 1615 and 1616 the N-W Passage Company sent out the Discovery, captained by Robert Bylot and with William Baffin as mate and navigator, to carry out two expeditions. As already noted both men had extensive Arctic experience and Baffin was in the mould of John Davis, an outstanding seaman and navigator. The 1615 expedition entered Hudson's Strait, sailed along its northern side and explored the area to the north of Southampton Island. The 1616 Expedition followed Davis' other 'lead' – northwards up the Davis Strait into Baffin Bay. By 30th May they had reached Saunderson his Hope – the furthest north achieved by Davis in 1587 at 72 degrees N. Early in July, around 74 ½ degrees N. , they named Sir Dudley Digges Cape, Wolstenholme Sound and Island and Whale Island. They named Sir Thomas Smith Sound and Hakluyt Sound just short of 77 degrees N – the furthest point north which they reached – and on their way back south on the American side named Alderman Jones' Sound and Sir James Lancaster's Sound. They were back in Dover by the end of August, having made substantial new discoveries and established the possibility of whaling. However, Baffin felt that there was no N-W Passage to be found either via Hudson's Bay or at the north of Baffin Bay.[36]

The work of exploration went on after Baffin's two voyage with Bylot (Baffin himself took service with the EIC in the East, hoping – like Davis – to find an opportunity to seek the N-W Passage from its western end) but this marked the end of Lancaster's association with it. With hindsight it is not difficult to see that the critical element was navigational skill.[37] There was no shortage of able and courageous seamen, but progress depended on the ability to fix and record the position of the ship and of features observed so that charts could be improved and other explorers could follow. Many expeditions brought back colourful descriptions of places and events – but no indication whatever of where they were. In navigational skill, John Davis and William Baffin stood head and shoulders above the others.

Lancaster was thus involved in five Arctic expeditions both as an investor and as a director: – (i) Hudson's last voyage in 1610 (ii) Button's 1612 voyage (iii) Hall's 1612 voyage seeking minerals in Greenland (iv) Bylot and Baffin's 1615 voyage and (v) Bylot and Baffin's 1616 voyage. The professionalism of these expeditions may well reflect the contribution made by Lancaster as the only naval commander among the investing syndicate. While no profit was realized, the amounts invested were comparatively small,[38] the quest for the NW Passage was successfully pushed forward and useful intelligence was gained for the development of whaling. Lancaster's name (like the names of his fellow adventurers) is permanently recorded in the Arctic at Lancaster Sound at 74 degrees N.

15

Last Years

As a footnote to 1610, Lancaster relinquished his Royal pension of £50 p. a. on 4th May whereupon a pension of the same amount was granted to one Martin Basil.[1]

We have no sighting of Lancaster in 1611. In 1612 he was put up for election as an alderman in Cordwainer Ward. The other candidates were Edward Barnes a Mercer, Richard Mills a Butcher and Robert Bright a Salter. Barnes was elected but immediately discharged on payment of a fine of £500.[2] We have no explanation for the outcome. At that time the aldermen were generally drawn from the Great Companies, but as Lancaster was a Skinner this would not have counted against him, and – as we have seen – he was treated with great respect by that Company, despite having held no office. Beavan mentions Lancaster 'one of the founders of the East India Company and commander of its first fleet' in a list of rejected candidates, with the comment 'It is interesting to note one or two cases in which men of eminence, actual or prospective, were included in the four whose names were returned to the Court of Aldermen for selection of one to fill a vacancy in that body, but were not chosen either on those or any subsequent occasions'.[3] Since the aldermen were elected to participate in the work of civic government i. e. it was not an honorific appointment, the explanation may be that at 58 years of age (having been away from the City almost continuously for 30 years and now in a non-executive role) Lancaster was reckoned to be 'past it'. Had he stood for election soon after his triumphant return from the First Fleet voyage in 1603 the result may well have been different. Age as a bar would also explain why he did not stand again – as many candidates did.[4] In the same year (1612) Lancaster was appointed an overseer and witness of the will of Sir Leonard Holliday, Master of the Merchant Taylors and

Lord Mayor in 1605. Lancaster and Holliday had served together as 'Commissioners' representing the City's interest in the 12th Privateering Expedition put out by the Earl of Cumberland in 1598[5] and they were both original directors of the EIC. We have already mentioned that in the same year, 1612, the NW Passage Company was incorporated and the expeditions of Sir Thomas Button and John Hall were dispatched.

Nothing was reported of Lancaster in 1613. In 1614 the Court of the EIC requested him to produce the original document issued by the King of Achen setting out the privileges which he granted to the English merchants in 1602.[6] In Court meetings in March, April and July Lancaster urged that the EIC should plan a westabout voyage to the Indies via the Magellan Strait. The Court sought his opinion both on the plan itself and on who should be employed.[7] His reasoning is not recorded – perhaps he thought that navigation outside the monsoon area would be preferable or that access to the Spice Islands would be easier from the East (following the experience of Drake and Cavendish).

In 1615 and 1616 Lancaster was involved, as we have already noted, in the Bylot/Baffin expeditions seeking the NW Passage.

1617 was the last year in which Lancaster participated in the affairs of the EIC: the significance of his interventions seems to have been maintained. On 30th September he and a Committee were asked 'to confer with the master gunners of the land and report on the lengths and weights of the ordnance for shipping' – unfortunately there is no trace of the outcome. In November, at the invitation of the Court Lancaster joined the Governor and the Deputy Governor in an interview with Captain Best (who led the Tenth Voyage in 1612) and who had proved quite troublesome over several years. The purpose of the interview was 'to inform him how distasteful his courses are to the Company'.[8] It looks as though Lancaster was enlisted to add gravitas and seniority to the Company's reprimand.

At a Court meeting in December 1617 – Lancaster's final appearance – the last surviving chapter in a sad little tale was played out.[9] In March 1617 Captain Alexander Childe of the 'James' reported to the Court that he had suffered a mutiny on board in Jask Road (just outside the Straits of Hormuz on the Persian side), the ringleaders being Richard Weekes, a quartermaster, and John Byrde. The case ran its course, Weekes was convicted and his sentence was considered. Tantalisingly, we have no explanation of the circumstances. On 14th November 1617 it is reported that Weekes is suing for mercy 'acknowledging his folly and craving favour' ('Folly' sounds more like disobedience than any form of physical violence), but on 2nd. December the Court decided that Weekes was not to be pardoned. However at a later meeting in the same month, the Court decided after all to pardon Weekes 'for the sake of Sir James Lancaster and referred for future employment'. A possible explanation of this happy outcome is that Richard Weekes was a member of the Basingstoke Weekes family into which James' sister had married; with the likelihood that James had helped him into employment with the Company. In any event this final reference to Lancaster in the Court minutes indicates the respect and affection which his colleagues continued to feel towards him.

In 1618 the Court of the EIC in April revived Lancaster's enthusiasm for a voyage via the Magellan Strait, but we do not know what happened subsequently.

16

Death, Will and Estate

Lancaster died at the Papeye in St. Mary Axe in June 1618. His will, dated 14th April 1618,[1] stated that while 'being weake in bodie, yet, thanks be given to Almighty God, of good and perfect memory', so it appears that his health had deteriorated, and that he was proceeding to put his affairs in order. On 2nd. April 1618, too, Lancaster transferred his real property[2] to three of his colleagues, Sir William Cockayne, Richard Wyche and Robert Bateman, for them to hold upon the trusts to be declared by his will.[3]

The assets were the real property mentioned above, the lease of the Papeye, chattels and a library in the house, and, presumably, some cash, shares in the EIC and the Minerals and Battery Works Company and so on. Valuing the land at £3,500 per acre and translating cash to current values by a multiplier of 140, the present-day value of the estate might be around £2 million.

As executors Lancaster appointed 'my very loving and trusty good friends Mr. Joseph Jackson and Mr. Leonard Parker of London, Merchants'; they received legacies of £120 each plus £5 each for a mourning ring – we know nothing further about them. It is possible that they were partners with Lancaster in the ongoing import-export business which we have suggested he continued after coming ashore. As overseers Lancaster selected Richard Wyche ('of London, merchant'),[4]

Lancaster's Arms:
argent, two bars
gules, on a coulon of
the second a mullet
pierced or

John Tailor ('servant to Mrs. Owfield'), Aramis Hope ('my ancient servant') and Aramis Moore ('notary public'). Witnesses to the will were Abraham Cartwright, John Owfield,[5] Nicholas Matthew (possibly a servant of Lancaster), Samuel Reynolds (Lancaster's servant – he received a legacy of £30 and his master's clothing) and 'My brother Master Lancaster' (presumably Peter – who also got a legacy of £200 and a lease of land).

Lancaster was generous to his family and 'cousins'. Beyond them (the borderline is hazy in places) are friends, acquaintances and servants. For a list of these legacies (which in value totalled some £2,000 (say around £300,000 to-day) and a consideration of the relationships between Lancaster and the legatees, see Appendix XII.

Mrs. Thomasine Owfield (sometimes 'Owfeild')

From the context of Lancaster's will she appears to be part of his household at the Papeye. Two (possibly more) intriguing questions arise, Who was Mrs Owfeild, and, What was her relationship with Lancaster ? As to her identity, a reasonable hypothesis is that she was the widow of one of Lancaster's colleagues, possibly with some relationship by marriage. On this basis, one Roger Owfeild and his wife Thomasine appear to fit the bill. This Roger was an original member of the EIC (and therefore known to Lancaster at least since 1600) and a member of the Fishmongers' Company, who stood, unsuccessfully, for alderman in 1602.[6] After his death in 1608 his widow Thomasine figures in the records both of the Fishmongers' and the East India Companies. The minutes of the Court of the Fishmongers' Company indicate that Roger's widow in June and September of 1609 continued to pay the rent due under a lease.[7] On 20th November 1609 the Court authorised the sealing of two leases in favour of the widow Mistress Thomazen Owfield. A similar reference occurs in the EIC records which mention that a Mrs Thomasine Owfield in 1614 received a transfer of EIC shares:[8] the transferor is not named but we may guess that they were being transferred to her by her late husband's executors.

This hypothesis has now been confirmed as almost certainly correct by examination of the wills of Roger and Thomasine Owlfeild. In Roger's will [dated 1608] he appoints some of his good friends as overseers to ensure that his will is given effect to and his children are properly brought up: the first named of these overseers is Sir James Lancaster Knight, indicating that the families were close. Similarly, Lancaster appointed a John Owfeild as a witness to his will: this might well be the John Owfeild to whom Thomasine refers in her will as 'a kinsman, of Billiter Street, a fishmonger' – no doubt a relation of her deceased husband Roger.

What then was the relationship between the rich widow and Lancaster ? We learn from Roger's will that, while he and Thomasine had two sons and seven (possibly eight) daughters, he left a substantial estate, with one third of the residue passing to the widow. When Lancaster died 10 years later, it seems clear that Mrs Owfeild did not need the lease of the Papeye *for any financial reasons,* so it seems reasonable to conclude that he left her the lease and 'the tapestry hanging of my chamber' (and other valuable sounding chattels), and also £450 to be distributed at her discretion amongst poor householders, *because she was already living in the house* – as indeed the context of Lancaster's will suggests. In her own will, 20 years later, Thomasine requested that she be buried in St Katherine Creechchurch 'as neere to the body of my late deceased husband . . . as conveniently may be' and she left money to the poor of that parish, but she also left money for the poor of the parish of All Hallows in the Wall, in which the Papeye was situated. When Roger died in 1608 the nine or ten children were growing up and one of the daughters was about to marry. Assuming that he and his friend Lancaster were approximtely the same age, Roger would have been in his mid-fifties at his death. Lancaster lived on a further 10 years and Thomasine a further 30, so it seems reasonable to assume that she was considerably younger than her husband – and certainly young enough to attract a new admirer. It is quite possible, therefore, that the husband's friend formed a romantic relationship with the widow.

We may turn now to Lancaster's charitable bequests, which illustrate his devotion to the Skinners' Company, Basingstoke and Kingsclere, the needy, mainly in London, ('inopum pater': see the verses on Lancaster's portrait in Appendix VI) and, it may be argued, to the Puritan cause. The annuities (as opposed to the cash legacies) were charged on his real property. The Skinners' Company received an annuity of £58 6s. 8d. to be devoted, as to £35 for acting as trustee of the will,[9] £3 6s. 8d. for an annual dinner and £20 for widows of freemen of the Company. To Basingstoke Lancaster left annuities of £40 to supplement the stipend of the Lecturer established by Sir James Deane in 1608; of £45 to the poor of the town at discretion, people of honest report and such as frequent the lecture; of £20 towards the maintenance of the free school (organized by the Fraternity of the

St Mary's, Kingscelere

St Michael's Basingstoke

Holy Ghost), of which £16 was to go to the usher and £4 to the master or usher at discretion; and of £13 6s. 8d. for a petty schoolmaster. Total £118 6s. 8d. Kingsclere received annuities of £20 to maintain the school master in the free school and of £10 to the churchwardens for the distribution of bread every Suinday.

Lancaster left an annuity of £60 to support three students of divinity at Oxford and Cambridge and of £20 to support four honest and godly poor preachers. There were charitable cash legacies as follows:- £20 to each of the following parishes – Whitechapel, St. George's in Southwark, St. Mary Overy's in Southwark, St Giles without Cripplegate and All Hallows in London Wall; to Christ's Hospital £30, St. Thomas' Hospital £13 6s. 8d. , St. Bartholemew's £13 6s. 8d. , and to the Masters of Bridewell £13 6s. 8d; for poor prisoners £4 to each of the prisons at King's Bench, Marshalsea, White Lyon, Newgate and Ludgate and £13 6s. 8d. to each of the 'compters' (debtors' prisons) at Wood Street and the Poultney.

We have already mentioned the £450 which Lancaster left to Mrs. Owfield to distribute at discretion to poor householders. Finally, he left £20 to the poor of Basingstoke and the same amount to the poor of Kingsclere.

Out of the residue of the estate Lancaster directed his executors to purchase land or houses in the City of London to the annual value of £30-40, and to make them over to the Skinners' Company. The additional income was to supplement the annuities

The Benefactions Board in St Michael's, Basingstoke

to Basingstoke and for the divinity students and the godly preachers by specified amounts,[10] and any surplus was to go to Mrs Owfield to be distributed at her discretion. Lancaster's surviving executor did in due course buy houses near the Swan Inn in the parish of St. Lawrence Poultney and devised them to the Skinners' Company to be consolidated with the rest of his real property.

The will contains some feature demonstrating Lancaster's modesty and consideration for others. He directed ' my bodie be interred in the night season for the avoidance of trouble', and that his house be kept running at the cost of his estate for three months to give time for my servants to find other masters and in the meantime to have meat drink and wages behaving as they have in times past.

Lancaster was buried in All Hallows, London Wall, his parish church, but the church was demolished and rebuilt in 1765-7 so we have no record of his tomb or of any memorial. As already noted, Lancaster's arms are displayed on a corbel in the NW corner of the nave in St. Michael's, Basingstoke and his legacies to that town are recorded on the west wall of the church. A similar record is maintained in Kingsclere church of his legacies to the free school and the poor of that parish.

Part Four
Taking Stock

17

Lancaster ~ the Man

In tracking Lancaster's life and career we pass through periods of feast and famine. During the 7-8 years of his three main voyages we have detailed accounts of what he was doing, virtually on a day to day basis, and particularly in respect of the Recife Raid. To this we may now add detailed knowledge of his family (where virtually none was available before) resulting from the examination of previously unpublished family wills, especially that of his mother. Revisiting published material has also yielded more information – for example about his role in the Earl of Cumberland's 12th expedition and his involvement as investor and director in five NW Passage voyages. However, there still remain periods which are either totally blank or which yield less than we would like. However, since Lancaster's main characteristics are marked and constant, it is probably safe to ignore the periods of famine and extrapolate directly from the information which we do have.

Our best sources are the direct evidence of the 1596 portrait and the documents produced personally by Lancaster – the Hints, his letter to Sir Thomas Smythe from the rudderless Red Dragon and his instructions to the staff whom he left behind in the East in 1603. The evidential weight of the accounts by Hakluyt, Purchas, May and Apsley is difficult to assess. Where words are put directly into Lancaster's mouth by the author or 'narrator', for example the speech at Recife about the attempt of the local Portuguese to talk him out of his booty, we may reasonably assume that these were indeed his words and feelings. In other cases, we cannot be so sure but, in looking at a close-knit military or naval unit – where community attitudes and values develop from the inter-relation between officers and men – some licence may be claimed to assign to Lancaster what may be called 'ship's company' attitudes or sense of humour. If he was not the originator he was probably in sympathy or 'on the same wavelength'.

We will deal first with Lancaster's personal characteristics, and move later to his relations with others – colleagues, subordinates, foreigners and so on. We may start with the portrait, and Lancaster's physical appearance. From his stance with his right hand on the globe he appears to be of a good height for the 16th century, say 5' 10" to 6' 0" and well built without being either thin or overweight. His facial features are strong with a high, broad forehead, widely spaced piercing eyes, and a pronounced aquiline nose. The strength of his features is reinforced by the sharply trimmed beard and moustache (like his hair, of a definite reddish hue)). His face suggests determination and energy, though some wariness may be discerned. If we did not know otherwise, he might even seem fierce and intimidating. No doubt with the Recife triumph only a few months old the artist wished to convey a military victor at the height of his powers (He was just 42 years old). While smart and neat Lancaster's dress is plain and sober, quite unlike that of an aristocrat or courtier.[1] His pose, too, proclaims his victory, with his left hand on his sword pommel and his right on the globe.[2] The overall impression is of vigour and purpose, but totally devoid of pride, swagger or pretension.[3] The portrait is of a man who gets things done, does not aspire to 'rank' but knows his own worth.

Despite nearly 20 years at sea Lancaster's health seems to have been good. He was seriously ill, to our knowledge, only twice, first, when the Edward Bonaventure lay off the south of Ceylon waiting for Portuguese prizes in December 1592 ('Our capitain at that time lying very sicke, more likely to die than to live'), and, secondly, in the joint operation with Spielbergen in the Malacca Strait in September 1602 ('Our general dangerously sicke'). Significantly, both occasions were in tropical areas. At Recife in 1594 he declined to join the disastrous sally 'for I have not bene well these two dayes and I am not strong to march upon those heavie sands'. This sounds nothing serious. In 1604, according to Sir William Foster, ill-health prevented Lancaster from taking command of the Second Fleet.[4] Since he personally led his men into battle twice at Recife, and would have probably led the final sally, had he not been 'off colour', he must then at least have been in good physical condition (he was around 41 in 1595).

We have already considered Lancaster's religious beliefs[5] and concluded that, as a man of action spending much of his time abroad or at sea, he was a down-to-earth Christian untroubled by the niceties of ritual or dogma. He regulated his personal conduct according to Christian principles, organized regular worship and was always mindful of a God who would look after him and his men if they deserved it.[6] As we will see, below, with regard to his attitude to foreigners, Lancaster was reasonably tolerant of other faiths, though we do not see him confronted with zealous anti-Protestant Spanish Catholicism. In the 1591 Voyage 'We . . . tooke a pangaia (a small vessel) which had a priest of theirs in it, which in their language they call a Sherife;[7] whome we used very courteously' [November 1591]. He negotiated happily with 'the chiefe bishope' of Achen, who represented the King.[8] At their final departure from Achen Lancaster and his men sang psalms with the King and his retinue, saying that they sang them every day (perhaps at the changing of the watch, which was customary).[9] In the First EIC Voyage at the Cape he stood godfather for his Jewish interpreter who was christened after a sermon and communion.[10]

Regarding Lancaster's leisure pursuits we know little: indeed his character and career suggest an unremitting commitment to business. As a country boy James had no doubt been brought up to ride and shoot and perhaps to fish. He is found shooting an 'antilope . . . of the bignes of a colt' 'for the pot' for the ship's company at the Cape in August 1591, and he organised the goat hunt at St. Helena in a very professional manner, but there is no account of him riding (except on an elephant at Achen). In December 1592 off Madagascar he took with the hook 'exceeding great store of bonitos and albacores . . . as many in two or three howers as would serve fortie persons a whole day'. His failure to acquire a home outside London – when he had become wealthy enough to afford it – suggests that his interest in country pursuits was not that strong. Lancaster obviously enjoyed music (he joined in the singing of a psalm for the King of Achen), and music and acting (including the recently published plays of Shakespeare) were popular on board English ships, being encouraged to keep the men busy and out of mischief.[11] For Lancaster these interests may have originated in his time as an apprentice in London. His will refers to 'china' and some attractive sounding furniture and artefacts, so he may have taken advantage of his time in the East to pick up some treasures. He bequeathed his 'books or library' to Mrs. Samuel Crooke but we do not know what kind of books he collected.

We may probably conclude that, like many self-made men, Lancaster concentrated his time and efforts on pursuing his professional and commercial interests.

We may pass to examine his sense of humour. In his Hints he explains the dangers of the Bassas da India (rocks in the passage between Africa and Madagascar) thus: 'Yf you be not very carefull to looke out night and day, you shall feele them before you see them' – a touch of dry, professional humour not to be found in the Admiralty Pilots. It seems to have been customary to comment on prizes which yielded food and drink in a jokey way: on the 1591 Voyage the contents of a Portuguese caravel 'wine, oyle, olives and capers were better to us than gold'; on the Recife Raid in 1594 a cargo of 80 tons of Canary wine 'came not unto us before it was welcome' and, with regard to another cargo of wine 'The Spaniards, having their free passage and an acquittance for the delivery of their wines were all set ashore upon Tenerif; making a quicke returne of their long voyage intended into the West Indies'. Arriving at Recife and capturing the fort and the town, 'The day of our arrival was their Good Friday, when by custome they usually whippe themselves; but God sent us now for a generall scourge to them all, whereby that labour among them might well be spared'. Discussing the sally on the final day at Recife under the cover of the ships' guns, Lancaster said 'If any power should come against you, the ships may play upon them with 40 pieces of ordinance at the least, so that a bird cannot passe there but she must be slaine'. An example of gallows humour: at Antongil (in Madagascar) on the First EIC Voyage a peal of ordnance fired to mark the death of an officer killed two of his fellow officers on their way to the funeral 'So they that went to see the burial of another were both buried themselves'. We have already noted James' diplomatic quip that he had not been able to find a Portuguese maiden beautiful enough to be handed over to the King of Achen.[12]

Lancaster was skilled and experienced in four professions – diplomacy, commerce, soldiering and naval command. (We will deal with leaderships and command skills later) By the time that he had finished working with the Royal Navy in 1589 (aged around 35) he was trained and competent in the last three departments. While such 'doing' skills are not essential to taking charge and directing others, it is generally found that the more effective commanders are those who can, if necessary, 'do it themselves' or show their men how to. When Lancaster left Bantam in February 1603 he left instructions for the factors remaining and the master of the pinnace:[13] they were models of their kind, covering the commercial essentials – what to buy and where, the importance of quality, care over storage, judicious selling and so on – but also 'pastoral' guidance about keeping a happy community and looking after the young apprentices. In the course of the voyages, he set up the practical arrangements for trading, understanding that for trade to flow smoothly in useful volumes, orderly conditions must be established.[14] Ashore he understood, and took care of, security from thieving and fire risks. He never for a moment forgot the overall purpose of his voyages – turning a profit for his backers. After days of worrying about where he could find sufficient pepper at reasonable price, the relief when (in concert with Spielbergen) in September 1602 he captured the Santo Antonio – with its vast cargo of Indian cottons – was palpable.

When his commercial experience and skill were combined with his special brand of charm, Lancaster was a master deal-maker, as we will describe below.

He had less opportunity to show his soldierly experience, since most of his activities were afloat – or at least amphibious. We may instance his personal leadership and courage on storming the fort at Recife, and in attacking and demolishing the gun platform on the sands, the speedy and effective fortification of Recife Town; the issue in advance of 'haile shot' for the muskets which shattered the only attack which was made on Recife Town itself; and his anxiety to get back on board, prior to the final sally, to direct covering fire from the ships' guns.

In naval operations we have many examples of his professionalism: the repair of the Saloman's mast at Dartmouth (on the way to Recife in October 1594)'by the earnest care and industry of the general'; the organization of the initial landing at Recife, with the determination to leave the boats empty and unusable; arranging the night watch in the river at Recife; organizing the loading of the booty and the re-packing of the English ships; the constant attention to keeping watch against enemy activity and any pilfering or misbehaviour by the men; quietly sending ahead to set up a 'refreshment' stop 100 miles up the coast from Recife; on the First EIC Voyage, organizing a regime with lemon juice for the men in the Red Dragon; organizing a tented (but fortified) camp at the Cape to allow the sick men to recover; being ready on arrival at Achen with (previously prepared) written submissions to support the request for permission to trade; on capturing the Santo Antonio, carefully controlling who was allowed on board, and refraining from boarding her himself, to avoid suspicions of misconduct.

We can turn now to consider Lancaster in his professional and social inter-action with others. We will deal first with his attitude towards foreigners, since it is important that the comments by some modern writers, based on his famous speech to his men at Recife,[15] are kept in context, and not permitted to migrate into the currently trendy zone of 'racism'. It has already been suggested that the 'lifelong grudge against Portugal' interpretation of Sir William Foster and the 'moral treason' accusation of Robert Southey cannot be sustained. Lancaster and his crews were relaxed and friendly with the Europeans they fell in with – French, Portuguese and Dutch (though the last-named tended to be wary, and had to be 'won over').[16] There were virtually no contacts with the Spanish – which could have presented problems – particularly if the Englishmen had any friends or colleagues who had fallen into the hands of the Inquisition. Beyond Europe Lancaster and his men[17] were intensely curious but tolerant, and took things as they found them, for example,

'Indians' and black African slaves working and fighting with (and sometimes betraying) the Portuguese in Brazil. Native people are praised and admired, when appropriate, e. g. fine stature and fleetness of foot at the Cape; kind warnings in East Africa against the Portuguese; generous and lavish hospitality at Achen. But, conversely, where criticism is considered due, there is no holding back. The three main areas which come in for criticism are stealing, commercial dishonesty, and attacking and killing Englishmen – all matters of some importance to merchants and seamen far from home who are already having to face deadly natural perils every day. The observations, objective if sometimes full-blooded, are therefore not judgemental, but guides to those who may follow – to keep away, be very vigilant, take precautions &c. – rather like sailing directions to avoid 'treacherous' rocks or sandbanks.[18]

Some examples illustrate these points:-

(i) **The inhabitants of the Comoros Islands**. 'But looke to yourselves; for, after their tournes are served of such thinges as they need, they will employ all their wittes to betrauy you in what they cann.'[19] The same inhabitants 'which are Moores, of tawnie colour and good stature, but they be very treacherous, and diligently to be taken care of.'[20] The same incident reported by May 'finding the people blacke and very comly, but very treacherous and cruell, for the day before we departed they killed thirty of our men on shore'.

(ii) **Zanzibar**. 'These Moores informed us of the false and spiteful dealing of the Portugals towards us, which made them believe that we were cruel people and man-eaters'.[21]

(iii) **The Hollanders at Recife** 'Although this people were somewhat stubburne at the first (as that nation is in these causes) yet being satisfied with good words and good dealing, they . . . were so satisfied that they went thorow with a fraight [made a deal for carrying the booty to England]; and then we joined with them and they with us, and they served us as truly and faithfully as our own people did, both at watch and ward by sea and all other services'

(iv) **The 'Portugals' at Recife**.[22]

(v) **Nicobar on the First EIC voyage.** They 'brought gummes to sell instead of amber and therewithal deceived divers of our men; for these people of the east are wholly given to deceit. '

(vi) **Bantam on the First EIC Voyage**. 'Wee traded here very peaceably, although the Javans be reckoned amongst the greatest pickers and theeves of the world. But the general had commission from the King (after he had received an abuse or two) that whosoever he took about his house in the night, he should kill them; so, after four or five were thus slaine, we lived in reasonable peace and quiet'.

(vii) **The Planned voyage from Bantam to Banda**. 'And wheresoever you be come, trust none of the Indians, for their bodies and soules be wholly treason, and yt will be very dangerous to touch in any unknown place; therefore avoied yt. '[23] Same trip – instructions to the merchants being embarked: 'And make no long staye, and have espetiall care of your saffetie and how you putt any man aland in any place, for the people in thoise partes, their whole bodies and mindes be all treason; and therefore open your eyes in this behalfe. '

Lancaster's most striking, and endearing, characteristic was his ease with people – 'inter-personal skills' in the current jargon. Perhaps this came from his large family and secure background and upbringing. He seemed to take pleasure in relating to people of all ages, races, colours, religions and so on – his own ship's company, when encouraging them and – when necessary – explaining his plans; on the Recife Raid successively with Captain Cotton, Captain Venner, the Dutch and the French, and also the 'Portugall' who rescued the sailor who got lost at Maio; with the aged king at Achen, his middle-aged son, the boy king of Bantam, the Indonesian hen-seller, the Jewish interpreter; the native inhabitants at the Cape (with whom he communicated quite unselfconsciously with 'Moos' and 'Baas'); and his City of London colleagues as he moved up through the ranks.

This ease and charm produced tangible results as well as pleasure (i) when James needed help it was forthcoming; on the 1591 voyage the French captains de la Barbotiere, Felix and Lenoir (or Noyer) rendered assistance at Mona and Saint Domingo (and were generously thanked and rewarded for their kindness at Recife in 1595) (ii) James was a remarkable deal-maker, witness the privileges negotiated at Achen and Bantam, the joint ventures agreed with Captain Cotton, Captain Venner, the Dutch and the French at Recife, and Spielbergen at Achen, and he invariable managed to combine favourable deals with real, lasting friendship – an unusual combination.

As a natural diplomat Lancaster knew when to defer and when to stand firm. He had no problem with 'giving doulat' i. e. making obeisance, to the Kings of Achen and Bantam (the latter being only a child),[24] and he was not too proud to sit 'upon the ground as the manner is'. However, when the King of Achen's courtier asked him to hand over the letter from Queen Elizabeth, he declined, explaining that English ambassadors delivered their sovereign's messages only to the monarch personally. Again, he declined (for the time being) the King's offer of a house, explaining that he preferred to remain on board, and had no hesitation in asking the King if he might drink the arrack served at the first feast diluted with water, or even drink water on its own.

His character and conduct also generated respect, loyalty and affection. Leaving aside the aberration of the mutinous company on the 1591 Voyage,[25] his officers and men were clearly devoted to him and would follow him anywhere, and this feeling spread effortlessly to the enlarged multi-national force at Recife of English, Dutch and French. When the Red Dragon was drifting helplessly off the Cape, the Master of the Hector (Alexander Cole) flatly disobeyed Lancaster's order to sail for England with his farewell message to the Governor of the EIC: Cole 'was an honest and a good man, and loved the general well, and was lothe to leave him in so great distress'. Cole continued to stand by the Red Dragon, but at a distance, no doubt wishing to be beyond the range of further instructions from the Admiral. Again, the King of Achen obviously became fond of Lancaster. In June 1602 he 'did anoint the genrall with rich ointment, and called him his sonne', and in his letter to Queen Elizabeth the King referred to him with 'God continue his welfare long'. The last direct reference to Lancaster in the EIC records (in December 1617) describes the Court pardoning Richard Weekes (possibly a kinsman by marriage) 'for the sake of Sir James Lancaster'.

We should consider, too, Lancaster's relations with women. In these enlightened times a man who does not marry is almost automatically labelled homosexual or asexual. In times past, indeed until quite recently, attitudes were more perceptive and less judgemental. In Lancaster's time, expatriate merchants and seafarers often were compelled to postpone marriage – and then never got round to it. In the meantime local, overseas liaisons of all kinds were quite normal. Lancaster's expeditions had problems with sailors who went on 'runs ashore' and we have no reason to think that the officers were better behaved, though they may have been more discreet. All the members of Lancaster's party seem to have enjoyed the performance by the King of Achen's exotic dancing girls. He himself conducted a risqué negotiation with the King under which, light-heartedly, the King agreed to delay the departure of the Portuguese ambassador (so that the English fleet could escape from their surveillance) provided that Lancaster procured him a beautiful Portuguese maiden. Lancaster returned later to Achen empty-handed and explained, diplomatically, that he had been unable to find any candidate beautiful enough for the King. We have already noted that there was no evidence that Lancaster had any romantic relationship with Mrs Thomasine Owfield, the widow who seems to have shared his London house. However, since extra-marital relationships were not unknown, we should not rule it out either. Another possible object of his affections was one of his maidservants, Agnes, who received a disproportionately generous legacy in his will.[26] It looks possible, too, that Lancaster was a long-term admirer of Judith Crooke nee Walsh (the wife of Samuel Crooke), since he left her a legacy of £ 50 and 'my library or books which heretofore I have promised her'.[27] We may guess that she was some 20 years younger than Lancaster, and that he may have met her, before she was married, through Thomas Crooke (Samuel's father), who was a fellow minister with Judith's father the Rev. M. Walsh in Suffolk.[28]

We turn finally to Lancaster's leadership qualities and management style. The point of departure must be his interest in, and consideration for, other people, noted above, which conditioned all his dealings with other people of whatever rank. But leadership requires more than making oneself pleasant. Of the other ingredients, the first, already discussed, was his experience and skill in commercial, military and naval matters. We may add:-

(i) his capacity to make detailed plans , including the evaluation of objectives against risks

(ii) his ability to adapt to circumstances and thus to amend what has been planned [Particularly noted on the Recife Raid]

(iii) his meticulous attention to detail, particularly on security and keeping watch and on curbing the natural tendency of his men (which he well understood) towards relaxing and looting

(iv) his willingness, where appropriate, to explain to his colleagues and subordinates what he is seeking to achieve. We have covered in detail Lancaster's famous speech at Recife. Equally notable were his words on the way to Brazil when Captain Barker in the Salomon had become temporarily detached, and the men wished to abandon the plan to attack Recife; and his courageous and determined address on the rudderless Red Dragon, 'Nay, wee will yet abide God's leasure, to see what mercie he will shew us: for I despaire not to save our selves, the ship, and the goods, by one meanes or other, as God shall appoint us'.

(v) encouragement and kindly words, whatever the task in hand. A good example was the building of the galley-frigate at Maio in the Cape Verde Islands on the way to Recife in 1594 'Where the carpenters applied their work, still cheered unto it by the general's good gifts bestowed among them and kind usage of the rest of the commanders, not without great care of the captaine for the safety of them all, by keeping good watch'

(vi) patience and understanding where things have gone wrong. This was particularly marked after the disastrous sally at Recife, when Lancaster swiftly turned from reproach to encouragement: 'At our returne into the towne the admiral came to us much bewailing the death of so many good men as were lost, wondering what we ment to passe the expresse order that was given us. With this losse our men were much daunted, but our admiral began again to encourage them, declaring that the fortune of the warres was sometimes to win and sometimes to loose'

(vii) extending mercy, even in the case of serious offences. In January 1602 at Antongil Christopher Newchurch, surgeon of the Ascension took poison. He was very ill but did not die and was dismissed from his post, and should have been put ashore. However, Captain Hayward of the Susan sought permission to take him into his ship as an ordinary sailor and Lancaster allowed this. Again, in June 1602 at Achen, one Thorougood, a sailor in the Red Dragon was condemned to be hanged for mutiny and contempt 'but by great intreaty he was forgiven'.

It is clear that Lancaster had all these qualities and skills in abundance, and that he also had the essential, final ingredient of leadership – authority or power of command. A quick glance at his portrait is sufficient to confirm this. As a result he received loyal and devoted service, and the respect and affection of his men.

To round off this section we may note a public spirited action typical of the man. At Table Bay in September 1601 the EIC First Fleet managed, eventually, to buy livestock, obtaining over 1000 head at trifling cost, bartering pieces of iron. Before setting sail Lancaster set down on Robben Island 'six sheep and two rammes for the relief of strangers that might come thither; which shortly after was found there by certaine Flemmings, to their relief, because they could get no cattell of the country people'.

18

Lancaster in his Time

Four hundred years later any meaningful assessment of Lancaster must be related to contemporary conditions and people. While trained by Drake, and showing himself a pupil quick to learn, Lancaster was not in the same class as that lifelong naval commander, as brilliant in his strategic thinking as in his operational performance: but it is possible that he might have been, had he been put to naval service in the Royal Navy or as a privateer from the start, instead of being trained basically as a merchant. A similar comparison may be made with Ralegh with regard to fighting qualities, but there are marked dissimilarities – if Lancaster lacked Raleigh's intellectual, literary and oratorical skills he also was without his intolerable pride, his selfishness and his innate duplicity. It is easy to differentiate Lancaster from Martin Frobisher – who was a ferocious and effective fighting commander with virtually no other attractive or useful qualities.[1] Turning to Lancaster's commercial contemporaries, he does not bear direct comparison with the 'Merchant Princes' like Sir Thomas Osbourne, Richard Staper, Thomas Cordell, Sir Thomas Smythe and Sir John Watts. They started with the advantages of wealth by inheritance or marriage, and connections in the City, and built enormous fortunes by merchant adventuring without moving away from their London base. But Lancaster, if he was not lucky enough to start with such advantages, undoubtedly had the qualities – as a merchant and leader – to achieve similar success.

However, what sets Lancaster aside from his contemporaries is his virtually unique combination of naval/military, commercial and leadership talents, making him, it is suggested, a top-rank performer in the field which he developed for himself. It seems clear, from the way in which his career developed, that he was in essence a merchant and he saw naval/ military skill as a means of protecting his trading activity (for example in the Mediterranean or, on longer voyages, when stopping for victuals or 'refreshment') and as a means of extending it through privateering ('purchase') in more distant markets.

An overall assessment of Lancaster's life and career can, it is suggested, be made at two levels. At the first level, we see an interesting and attractive character in the later part of Elizabeth's reign who built a successful career from humble beginnings, which touched many aspects of English life at home and abroad and demonstrated the openness and opportunities of Tudor England.[2] He might therefore fairly be described as a talented and useful player in the Second Division.

At a second level, in a wider context and a longer time-span, Lancaster has some claim to a pivotal position. He turned into reality the dreams of Sir Edward Osborne, Richard Staper and Thomas Cordell (and those who followed them) to pursue the oriental trade, particularly in spices, towards its source. In a sense the EIC was simply doing what other Trading Companies were doing in other parts of the world, but the field of operation was vastly greater and the EIC represented the new world power which had fought off the Spanish/Portuguese Armada. With the backing of the Queen and the EIC Lancaster achieved this in the First Fleet voyage. We may therefore re-classify him as an outstanding player in a new, distinct category – as a seaborne merchant adventurer. In the First Fleet expedition we see combined in one individual the roving ambassador (with blank letters from his Sovereign to deliver to friendly Heads of State, the naval/military commander (with the authority of martial law) deploying his armed merchant fleet, and the chief merchant who is engaged simultaneously in buying and selling to make up the current voyage and in laying down long-term plans for an international trading organization. Once the sui generis nature of the role is recognized it is suggested Lancaster measures up to his leading contemporaries.

If in this way we raise Lancaster to his rightful position, we can look forward into the future to make out some of the later developments which can legitimately be traced back to him and the First Fleet – the EIC extends from mere 'out and back' voyages to providing a trade and carry service (becoming known as 'the country trade') throughout the Indian Ocean region (with Indian cottons being bought instead of being 'purchased' on the high seas); the EIC develops in Europe a re-export trade in oriental products; the EIC spearheads the new British Empire in the eastern hemisphere; the English language, the English style and pattern of trading, and to some extent English culture, spread across the Orient; and eventually India becomes the largest democracy in the world. In this way, too, Lancaster and the EIC have some claim to have fathered the commercial globalization which has emerged at the end of the 20th century.

The opportunities for the EIC (and for the Dutch and the French), displacing the Portuguese, came originally from the voluntary withdrawal by the Chinese from naval, commercial and political dominance in the Indian Ocean region in the 15th century. It is ironic that to-day China is rapidly re-emerging as a world commercial power.

Appendix 1
Lancasters in North Hampshire

All authorities trace the surname Lancaster (with its variants Lankester, Lanchester &c.) ultimately to Lancaster ('the camp on the River Lune' in Roman times), the old county town of Lancashire. By the 16th. century most Lancasters outside Lancashire are found in Cumbria (Cumberland) and the English Midlands. Some had moved further afield e. g. around London, and, as we will see, several have been located in or near to Basingstoke around 1500. A general migration over a long period from the north west of England to the south east is well established; so we may conclude that we are dealing with 'incomers' settled in North Hampshire.

The main published sources on Lancaster and his life[1] have little to offer on his origins. They state that he was born in Basingstoke in or around 1554 and his father was probably also named James – because someone of that name held land in the Winchester Field[2] in 1544 i. e. at about the right time. Some further details of James' family are deduced from his will – but this was written 64 years later, in 1618.

We can augment this very scanty account in two ways, first, by re-working various published sources, and, secondly, by deploying hitherto unpublished information.

For any historical enquiry affecting Basingstoke and its 'outer hundreds'[3] the first port of call must be the *History of Basingstoke* by Baigent and Millard,[4] an excellent Victorian work of local history: it does not disappoint. There are numerous references to Lancasters in all kinds of contexts, throughout the 16th. century, and later.

In the 1500-1530 period the references are to Hugh and Richard Lancaster. Hugh died in 1524-5 and Richard at about the same time: we may call these 'The First Generation'.[5]

In the 1530-1560 period we find John and James Lancaster, with a William Lancaster appearing after 1550. These three we may label 'The Second Generation'. This is where we should look for James' father and we may now confidently assert that he is indeed the James mentioned here: he was the eldest son of Hugh Lancaster (above). The John mentioned here was almost certainly one of the sons of Richard Lancaster.[6]

The earliest reference in B & M to a Lancaster in the Basingstoke area is 1504, so we may tentatively propose that The First Generation arrived as adults about 1500. We have no means of telling whether the brothers were already married or whether they married Hampshire girls – the latter is perhaps more likely.[7]

This first sorting of the material extracted from B & M provides an outline framework for the Lancaster family in the district. We can fill in most of the gaps from hitherto unpublished information, gleaned from family wills held in the Hampshire Record Office.[8] As a result we now have quite a crowded canvas: an overview can be obtained by looking at the 'family tree' charts in Appendix II.

Having filled the canvas it is necessary to discover or deduce as much as possible about James Lancaster's family to form the background for his birth, early life and launch into the world.

It appears that Hugh and Richard (perhaps with one or two other brothers or relations) moved south as economic migrants around 1500. We have already noted the long-term trend of movement from NW to SE England. Hugh and Richard were 'drapers', which in the 16th. century probably meant weavers of woollen cloth.[9] Basingstoke since mediaeval times had been active in breeding sheep and manufacturing woollen cloth.

The brothers seem to have prospered.[10] By 1508 Richard had a property – probably a house and workshop combined – in Church Street, then as now one of the main streets in the centre of Basingstoke.[11] This house caused some problems. Already in 1508 it obstructed the highway near the Mote Hall.[12] Later, its cellar was reckoned a danger to passers-by at night, so Richard was ordered to improve the cellar door.[13] From the reference to the Mote Hall – which stood in the middle of Church Street where it entered the market [i. e. further west than the Willis Museum (previously the Town Hall) which to-day occupies the apex between Church Street and Wote Street] – it looks as though Richard's house was at the very top of Church Street. It was probably on the west side of Church Street – because the top house on the east side ('Brightwise') seems to have been occupied by William Lancaster, Lancaster's uncle.[14]

In 1514 Richard acquired a property known as 'Skydmore's' from one Thomas Cresswell.[15] The annual rent of 9s. 1½d. suggests that it was quite extensive and corroborates that it is the same property held later by

The Mote Hall, Basingstoke 1657- 1831. In 1832 the 'new' Town Hall (to-day the Willis Museum) was built, to replace the Mote Hall, at the apex of Church Street and Wote Street i.e. slightly to the east of the Mote Hall which stood across the entrance to Church Street. The picture is of special interest since it appears to include two of the Lancaster houses in the town. On the left the house partly obscured by the Mote Hall (approximately on the site of Lloyds TSB to-day) almost certainly belonged to Hugh, our Lancaster's great uncle and afterwards to his descendants, Lancaster's cousins. On the right the three houses illustrated were demolished to make room for the new Town Hall and the owners were compensated. Of these three houses the left-hand one with the Inn sign was almost certainly the house/ale-house belonging to Lancaster's Uncle William.

John (thought to be Richard's son) even though John did not figure in his father's will.[16]

By 1521 Hugh was paying rent for a property known as 'Donte's' and 'Heyron's'.[17] It was probably at the bottom i. e. the northern end, of Wote Street, near the site of the present Bus Station.[18] By 1541-2 his son James (father to our James Lancaster) had taken over the rent on this property, and had added an additional property.[19] It seems likely that Donte's and Heyron's was the family home, which descended from Hugh to James senior and thence (probably) to John, James Lancaster's elder brother.

By his will in 1522 Richard left two messuages with two gardens, a croft and 34 acres of land: he also (among other charitable legacies) left 3s 4d. to the Chapel of the Holy Ghost.[20] Hugh left a house and some land[21] to his eldest son James, father to our James Lancaster.

Both brothers had good sized families – Hugh had four sons and two daughters, Richard two sons and two daughters.

Hugh's eldest son was James (the father of our James Lancaster) and he inherited his father's house and land, subject to his mother's life interest. It looks as though both brothers combined weaving with farming.

Richard died in 1522 and Hugh in 1525: both were buried in St. Michael's Church in Basingstoke.

Passing to The Second Generation, James Lancaster's father married Elizabeth Seagrave, whose father Thomas was described as a mercer.[22]

James Lancaster and Elizabeth had four sons and three daughters and apparently continued to prosper, combining weaving with farming. James senior was still in 1541/2 paying rent for the same property as his father (Donte's and Heyron's: see above), plus another one,[23] and, as noted above, he is recorded in 1544 as holding land in the Winchester Field.[24] In 1557 James senior contributed 4d. to the Fraternity of the Holy Ghost towards the cost of getting the Fraternity re-established by a new Royal charter.[25] By 1571 when he apprenticed James Lancaster to the Skinners' Company, James senior described himself as 'husbandman' i. e. a man who farmed his own land but was not classed as a 'yeoman'.

Of the four sons, the eldest was John, destined (it would appear) to remain in Hampshire and take over the draper's business and the land, next came our James Lancaster and then Peter[26] who were apprenticed by their father to members of the London Skinners' Company; the youngest, Richard survived his mother (who died in 1581) but then disappears from sight. The three daughters married successfully and produced families. Agnes married Richard Yate, of a leading Basingstoke family, the second daughter, Elizabeth, married a member of the local Weekes family, and the third, Alice, married one Hopwood, probably also a local man.

James Lancaster's elder brother John produced a son (who in turn had two daughters) and three daughters, two of whom married into well-known Basingstoke families (Crosse and Massam): the third married 'Nicholl, a stockingman', probably also a local man.

James Lancaster never married and it appears that this equally applies to Peter, who outlived James, and also to Richard. We hear a little more about Peter's career in the Skinners' Company,[27] but we know nothing about Richard's life. It looks therefore that in this line there were no male Lancasters after the death of John's son, but through the daughters and granddaughters a connection was established with some of the leading Basingstoke families. The Lancaster name survived in the Basingstoke area until the 18th. century, no doubt through one or more of the other lines.

Reverting to the other two representatives of The Second Generation, John (almost certainly the son of Richard Lancaster[28] was elected a tithingman in 1540;[29] in 1541 he paid 9/1 ½ rent for a property called Skydmore's,[30] and in 1544 he is reported as holding land in the Holy Ghost Field.[31]

William seems to have been the younger brother of James senior and thus an uncle to our James Lancaster: he was an innkeeper and, in addition, appears to have been a draper.[32] By 1546 he occupied a property called 'Brightwise' which stood at the top of Church Street, on its east side – approximately where the west end of the Willis Museum is to-day.[33] This was his home and also, it appears, an inn or alehouse; later known as The Royal Oak.

We can turn now to some other members of the family. Richard Yate, whose will we noted above, was a glover but also a farmer,[34] and his second son (also Richard) who married James' sister Agnes, was a tanner. The Lancasters 'outside' Basingstoke, based on Odiham and Kingsclere, (the evidence for whom is scanty) are represented by a man (or possibly two men) named William.

A connection between James Lancaster and Kingsclere is 'needed' because in his will his second charitable beneficiary (after Basingstoke) was Kingsclere, and hitherto there has been no explanation why a wealthy unmarried testator should benefit a town some miles away from his birthplace. It now seems likely that there were Lancaster relations living there.[35]

At Overton (9 miles west of Basingstoke) there was a John Lancaster, another draper, who died in 1562. We know that he was a relation because he figures in the wills of both Richard and Hugh Lancaster, in one case as a 'backstop' legatee,[36] in the other as an overseer of the will. As Richard died in 1522 and Hugh in 1525 it seems reasonable to guess that John was contemporary with The Second Generation, perhaps, therefore, he was a nephew to Richard and Hugh. This John may also explain the often repeated (but as yet unexplained) statement that James Lancaster and Sir James Deane were 'cousins'. John's wife was Edith Deane nee Harte. She had previously been married to one James Deane [obviously not the Sir James Deane we are considering] and they had a daughter Elizabeth.[37]

John Lancaster of Overton died in 1562, leaving (apart from his step-daughter Elizabeth Deane) only one son, named William. He is probably the William Lancaster recorded as holding 30 acres of land at Overton in 1575.[38]

The Deanes probably took their name originally from the village of Deane, some seven miles west of Basingstoke. The family was prominent in and around Basingstoke. Sir James was a member of the

London Drapers' Company, became Master, and was elected an Alderman but resigned within a year through ill health. He was knighted in 1604. The Deanes were ahead of the Lancasters in climbing the social ladder: a pedigree was established for the family on the Visitations of the Heralds to Hampshire.[39] The Deanes owned land in and near Basingstoke and in 1589 Sir James purchased the manor of Ashe (near Deane), together with the advowson (the right to appoint the priest) of the church of Deane and Ashe, from Ralph Fynes, Lord Say and Sele. Lancaster collaborated with Sir James over local charitable matters – endowing the Basingstoke Holy Ghost School and establishing a Lectureship in Basingstoke – and he was the first named executor of Sir James' will in 1608. They may also have collaborated on business matters in London. Certainly Deane became an original member of the East India Company in 1600 where Lancaster was one of the first directors. In view of the relationship between the families and the fact that the Lancasters were engaged in the drapers' trade it is perhaps surprising that Lancaster's father did not apprentice James and Peter to the Drapers' Company instead of the Skinners': we do not know the reason.

From this description of Lancaster's relations and their activities we gain an impression of an energetic, hard-working family, determined – like most incomers or immigrants – to make their way in their new community. Over the first half of the 16th. century the Lancasters' fortunes prospered.[40] It is sad that James and two of his brothers produced no issue and that James, once he had succeeded in life and 'come ashore', did not establish himself as a Hampshire gentleman,[41] preferring – it seems – to spend most of his time in London among his City peers. The family became well established in Basingstoke, and their daughters married well, but they did not rank amongst the leaders in the community nor attain office either in the town[42] or in the Guild or Fraternity of the Holy Ghost.[43] Basingstoke later acquired a reputation for oligarchy, with a few families predominating over a long period,[44] so perhaps this tendency was already developing in the 16th. century.

The drive to succeed displayed by the Lancasters who settled in North Hampshire is reflected in the decision of James' father to establish two of his younger sons as London apprentices – a step taken at that period by many ambitious middle class families all over England – and also in James' own career.

Appendix II
Pedigrees

Chart I: Lancaster's Immediate Family

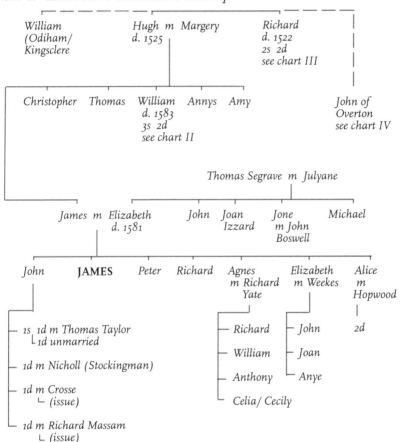

Chart II: William Lancaster's Family

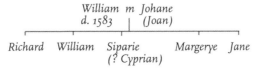

Chart III: *Richard Lancaster's Family*

Richard m Maude
d. 1522

Richard   William   ? John   Felyce   Margarey

Chart IV: *Family of John Lancaster of Overton*

John Harte

John   Edith   m firstly James Deane
           née Harte
                         Elizabeth

                         m secondly John Lancaster
                                     of Overton
                         William

Appendix III
Descriptions of the Main Spices

(from Mrs Beeton)

MACE.—This is the membrane which surrounds the shell of the nutmeg. Its general qualities are the same as those of the nutmeg, producing an agreeable aromatic odour, with a hot and acrid taste. It is of an oleaginous nature, is yellowish in its hue, and is used largely as a condiment. In "Beeton's Dictionary" we find that the four largest of the Banda Islands produce 150,000 lbs. of it annually, which, with nutmegs, are their principal articles of export.

MACE.

THE CLOVE.—The clove-tree is a native of the Molucca Islands, particularly Amboyna, and attains the height of a laurel-tree, and no verdure is ever seen under it. From the extremities of the branches quantities of flowers grow, first white; then they become green, and next red and hard, when they have arrived at their clove state. When they become dry, they assume a yellowish hue, which subsequently changes into a dark brown. As an aromatic, the clove is highly stimulating, and yields an abundance of oil. There are several varieties of the clove; the best is called the *royal clove*, which is scarce, and which is blacker and smaller than the other kinds. It is a curious fact, that the flowers, when fully developed, are quite inodorous, and that the real fruit is not in the least aromatic. The form is that of a nail, having a globular head, formed of the four petals of the corolla, and four leaves of the calyx not expanded, with a nearly cylindrical germen, scarcely an inch in length, situate below.

THE CLOVE.

CINNAMON.

CINNAMON.—The cinnamon-tree (*Laurus Cinnamomum*) is a valuable and beautiful species of the laurel family, and grows to the height of 20 or 30 feet. The trunk is short and straight, with wide-spreading branches, and it has a smooth ash-like bark. The leaves are upon short stalks, and are of an oval shape, and 3 to 5 inches long. The flowers are in panicles, with six small petals, and the fruit is about the size of an olive, soft, insipid, and of a deep blue. This incloses a nut, the kernel of which germinates soon after it falls. The wood of the tree is white and not very solid, and its root is thick and branching, exuding a great quantity of camphor. The inner bark of the tree forms the cinnamon of commerce. Ceylon was thought to be its native island; but it has been found in Malabar, Cochin-China, Sumatra, and the Eastern Islands; also in the Brazils, the Mauritius, Jamaica, and other tropical localities.

THE NUTMEG.

NUTMEG.—This is a native of the Moluccas, and was long kept from being spread in other places by the monopolizing spirit of the Dutch, who endeavoured to keep it wholly to themselves by eradicating it from every other island. We find it stated in "Beeton's Dictionary of Universal Information," under the article "Banda Islands," that the four largest are appropriated to the cultivation of nutmegs, of which about 500,000 lbs. are annually produced. The plant, through the enterprise of the British, has now found its way into Penang and Bencoolen, where it flourishes and produces well. It has also been tried to be naturalized in the West Indies, and it bears fruit all the year round. There are two kinds of nutmeg,—one wild, and long and oval-shaped, the other cultivated, and nearly round. The best is firm and hard, and has a strong aromatic odour, with a hot and acrid taste. It ought to be used with caution by those who are of paralytic or apoplectic habits.

LONG PEPPER.

LONG PEPPER.—This is the produce of a different plant from that which produces the black, it consisting of the half-ripe flower-heads of what naturalists call *Piper longum* and *chaba*. It is the growth, however, of the same countries; indeed, all the spices are the produce of tropical climates only. Originally, the most valuable of these were found in the Spice Islands, or Moluccas, of the Indian Ocean, and were highly prized by the nations of antiquity. The Romans indulged in them to a most extravagant degree. The long pepper is less aromatic than the black, but its oil is more pungent.

BLACK PEPPER.—This well-known aromatic spice is the fruit of a species of climbing vine, and is a native of the East Indies, and is extensively cultivated in Malabar and the eastern islands of Borneo, Sumatra, and Java, and others in the same latitude. It was formerly confined to these countries, but it has now been introduced to Cayenne. It is generally employed as a condiment; but it should never be forgotten, that, even in small quantities, it produces detrimental effects on inflammatory constitutions. Dr. Paris, in his work on Diet, says, " Foreign spices were not intended by Nature for the inhabitants of temperate climes; they are heating, and highly stimulant. I am, however, not anxious to give more weight to this objection than it deserves. Man is no longer the child of Nature, nor the passive inhabitant of any particular region. He ranges over every part of the globe, and elicits nourishment from the productions of every climate. Nature is very kind in favouring the growth of those productions which are most likely to answer our local wants. Those climates, for instance, which engender endemic diseases, are, in general, congenial to the growth of plants that operate as antidotes to them. But if we go to the East for tea, there is no reason why we should not go to the West for sugar. The dyspeptic invalid, however, should be cautious in their use; they may afford temporary benefit, at the expense of permanent mischief. It has been well said,

BLACK PEPPER.

that the best quality of spices is to stimulate the appetite, and their worst to destroy, by insensible degrees, the tone of the stomach. The intrinsic goodness of meats should always be suspected when they require spicy seasonings to compensate for their natural want of sapidity." The quality of pepper is known by rubbing it between the hands : that which withstands this operation is good, that which is reduced to powder by it is bad. The quantity of pepper imported into Europe is very great.

THE GROWTH OF THE PEPPER-PLANT.—Our readers will see at Nos. 369 and 399, a description, with engravings, of the qualities of black and long pepper, and an account of where these spices are found. We will here say something of the manner of the growth of the pepper-plant. Like the vine, it requires support, and it is usual to plant a thorny tree by its side, to which it may cling. In Malabar, the chief pepper district of India, the jacca-tree (*Artocarpus integrifolia*) is made thus to yield its assistance, the same soil being adapted to the growth of both plants. The stem of the pepper-plant entwines round its support to a considerable height; the flexile branches then droop downwards, bearing at their extremities, as well as at other parts, spikes of green flowers, which are followed by the pungent berries. These hang in large bunches, resembling in shape those of grapes; but the fruit grows distinct, each on a little stalk, like currants. Each berry contains a single seed, of a globular form and brownish colour, but which changes to a nearly black when dried; and this is the pepper of commerce. The leaves are not unlike those of the ivy, but are larger and of rather a lighter colour; they partake strongly of the peculiar smell and pungent taste of the berry.

Appendix IV
Selected Merchants and their Interests

Name	Dates	City Company	Alderman	Lord Mayor	Venice Company 1563	Spain/Portugal Company 1577	Barbary Company 1580	LEVANT TRADE Turkey Company 1581	Levant Company 1592	First Indies Voyage 1591-4	Recife Raid 1594	Cumberland 12th. Voyage 1598	East India Company 1600	See notes below
ALLEN, William		Skinner				Grantee								
BANNING, Paul	1588-1616	Grocer	1593		Grantee				Grantee		Backer	Commissioner	Director	
BOREMAN, Simon											Backer			1
COCKAYNE, Sir William	d.1626	Skinner	1612	1619-20		Grantee					Backer	Commissioner	Director	2
CORDELL, Thomas		Mercer	1595			Assistant		Grantee	Grantee		Backer		Director	
FORMAN, Thomas		Skinner				Grantee								
GAMAGE, Anthony	d.1579	Ironmonger(M)				Grantee								
GARRAWAY, William	d.1625	Draper	1573					Grantee	Grantee			Commissioner	Director	3
GARRETT, William								Grantee					Grantee	
HART, Sir John	d.1604	?	1580					Grantee	Grantee					
HASSELL, Percival		Skinner				Grantee								
HEWITT, Sir William		Clothworker(M)	1550	1559-60		Assistant								
HEYDON, John		Skinner				Assistant								
HOLLIDAY, Sir Leonard	d.1612	Merchant Taylor	1594	1605							Backer	Commissioner	Director	4
HOWE Roger									Grantee				Director	
MASSAM, William	d.1600	Grocer	1582			Assistant		x	Grantee					
MERSHE, Sir John		Mercer				President							Grantee	
MIDDLETON, John	?-1560	Skinner											Grantee	
MIDDLETON, Robert		Skinner											Director	
MIDDLETON, Sir Thomas	1550-1631	Grocer	1603	1613				x			Backer	Commissioner	Director	5
MORE John	c.1548-1603	Skinner(M)	1597											6
OFFELEY, Hugh	d.1594	Leatherseller(M)	1588			Grantee		Grantee(G)	Grantee(G)					7
OSBOURNE, Sir Edward	?1530-91	Clothworker	1573	1583-4		Assistant		Governor	x					
PULLYSON, Sir Thomas	d.c.1616	Draper(M)	1573	1584		Assistant					Backer			
SALTER, Master Sute														
SALTONSTALL, Sir Richard	1521-1601	Skinner(M)	1588	1597-8		Assistant			Grantee				Governor	8
SMYTHE, Sir Thomas	?1558-1625	Skinner	1599			Grantee		Governor	x				Governor	
STAPER, Edward		Skinner				Grantee								
STAPER, James		Skinner				Grantee			Grantee					
STAPER, Richard	1540-1608	Clothworker(M)	1594			Assistant	Grantee	Grantee	Grantee				Director	
STARKEY, Thomas	d.1594	Skinner(M)	1576			Assistant	Grantee	Grantee	Grantee					
TOWRESONNE, William		Skinner				Assistant								
WALKEDEN, Robert	d.1586	Skinner				Grantee	Grantee		Grantee					9
WATTS, Sir John	c.1550-1616	Clothworker(M)	1605	1606-7		Assistant	x		x		Backer	Commissioner	Governor	10

GENERAL NOTE

These men were initially Lancaster's employers, later financial backers and, later still, colleagues, partners and co-directors.

NUMBERED NOTES

1. Boreman — Interest in the Salomon. Worked in Seville until 1576. Son sailed in Recife Raid 1594-5
2. Cordell — Owner of Merchant Royal and Edward Bonaventure, prt owner of others. "One of the most important promoters o[f] privateering"
3. Garraway — Part owner (with Thomas Cordell) of the Merchant Royal.
4. Howe — Had an interest in the Salomon.
5. Sir Thomas Middleton — A man of great influence in the 1590s. Shipowner, privateer, a major sugar merchant. Married a daughter of Sir Richard Saltonstall.
6. More — Had an interest in the Salomon. One of the leading promoters of privateering in the West Indies in the early 1590s.
7. Offeley — His daughter married Sir James Deane, Lancaster's cousin.
8. Sir Richard Saltonstall — A leading City merchant, he also assisted the Government in raising money. He was Peter Lancaster's second matter.
9. Walkeden — Lancaster's second master.
10. Sir John Watts — Merchant and shipowner. "The greatest of the merchant promoters of privateering". Son sailed in Recife Raid 1594-5.

Appendix V
Some Merchant Ships and their Employment

	Levant Company Records 1581	Hakluyt Voyages 1582	Fenton's Voyage 1582-3	Hakluyt Voyages 1583	Levant Company Records 1584	The Worthy Fight 1586	Hakluyt Voyages 1586	Levant Company Records 1583-88	Cadiz Raid 1587	Armada Fleet 1588	Coruña Lisbon Expedition 1589	Levant Company Records 1590	The Valiant Fight 1590	First Indies Voyage 1591-4	Hakluyt Voyages 1591-5	Recife Raid 1594-5	Levant Company Records 1595	Levant Company Records 1600	Cumberland 12th Voyage 1598	First Voyage 1600-3
Ascension	x				x								x		x			x	Rear	Rear
Centurion											x		x		x				x	x
Consent																			x	
Crescent													x							
Edward Bonaventure	x		x		x	x		x	x	x	x	x		Rear		Admiral				
Elizabeth									x	x			x							
George Bonaventure									x	x										
Guest (or Gift)																				x
Hector							x							x						Vice
Jesus								x												
Margaret & John	x								x	x		x	x							
Merchant Royal					x	Admiral		x	Rear		x	x		Vice					Vice	
Minion													x							
Penelope														Admiral						
Red Dragon ex Malice Scourge																			Admiral	Admiral
Richard													x							
Salomon		x						x	x		x		x			Vice				
Samuel								x	x		x		x							
Susan/Suzanne	x	x										x								
Susan Parnell										x								x		
Thomas Bonaventure	x				x				x	x		x								
Tiger	x					x	x	x			x	x								
Toby	x					x		x	x		x	x								
Violet												x								
Virgin									x		x					Rear				
White Lion																				
William & John						x		x										x		

SOURCES

1. Levant Company Records, from Epstein, The Early History of the Levant Company
2. "Hakluyt's Voyages" from Hakluyt's Principal Navigations
3. The Worthy Fight and the Valiant Fight from Hakluyt's Principle Navigations
4. The 1591 Voyage, the Recife Raid and the First EIC voyage from the accounts by Hakluyt and Purchas
5. Fenton's Voyage from An Elizabethan in 1582 (based on the diary of Richard Madox)
6. The Armada Fleet and the Cadiz Raid, from Laughton and Corbett
7. The Coruña/Lisbon Expedition 1589, from Monson's Tracts
8. Cumberland's 12th Voyage, Williamson, George, Third earl of Cumberland

Appendix VI
Verses on Lancaster's Portrait

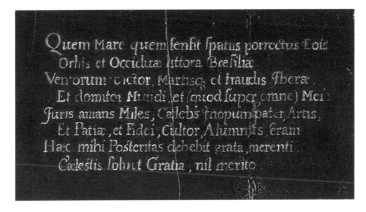

The following text has been tentatively transcribed from the portrait:-

Quem mare quem sensit spatiis porrectus Eois
Orbis et Occiduae littora Bresiliae
Ventorum victor martisque et fraudis Iberae
Et domitor mundi et (quod super omne) Mei.
Juris amans miles, caelebs inopum pater, artis
et pat<r>iae et fidei, cultor, alumnus, eram
Haec mihi posteritas debebit grata; merenti
Caelestis soluit gratia, nil merito.

A. Translation by Professor James Carley

The sea saw me; the globe extended to the eastern spaces
and the shores of western Brazil saw me.
I was victorious over the winds and in war
and over the Spanish deception.
I conquered the world and above all myself.
I was a knight who loved justice, a celibate father of the poor,
A pupil and supporter of the arts and my country and my faith.
Grateful posterity will be under obligation to me for these things.
Divine grace sets free (i. e. saves) the meritorious, not his (own) merit.

B. Tentative Translation by the present writer

I made my presence felt at sea, in the eastern reaches of the far-flung world and, in the west, on the beaches of Brazil. I have triumphed over the winds, the bad faith of Iberia and in war. I have tamed the world and, above all, myself. I was a soldier who loved what is right, a bachelor who was a father to the needy, a follower and supporter of the arts, my homeland and integrity. Grateful posterity will deservedly be in my debt for these achievements but undeservedly heavenly grace effaces them.

Appendix VII
Instructions given by Lancaster at Bantam
1602

1. A Remembrance for Master Keche, Master of the Pinnace

First, as soon a I am gone, you shall procure from the marchauntes resident heare your ladeing of such and soe many goodes as they shall appointe you, and by all meanes, after you have taken them in, procure such provisions that they may be kept drie, for a little wett bringeth in theis goodes much damadge. I doubt not you will be carefull in this pointe.

Your ladeing being received, you are to take in Master Towerson, Thomas Tudd, William Chase, and Thomas Dobson; and then sale directlie for the iland of Banda, not touching in any place by the waie without greate cause. And wheresoever you be come, trust none of the Indians, for their bodies and soules be whollie treason, and yt will be very daungerous to touch in any unknowne place; therefore avoied yt.

When God shall send you to Banda and you have delivered your marchandizes, you maie laie upp your shipp, and you and your men lie att the marchauntes howse and assist them in their busines all you cann. But I thinke yt good to looke to your shipp, that she be not lost, but husband her, soe that, yf occasion should be proffered by any enymies aland, you maie have some helpe by her by the sea.

As my trust is in you, assist the marchauntes and give them all helpe, for I have placed you in the 4th place with them. In this pointe be verie carefull, as I hope you will be. And hereby I doe acknowledge to have consorted with you from the I of February 1602 [1603], for as longe as you shall be in the marchauntes service, for 8 li. the monneth.

Thus God send His blessinge upon you in all your affaires. In Bantam, this 12 of February 1602 [1603].

2. A Remembraunce for Master Starkie, Thomas Morgan and Master Scott

As sone as our shipps be dispatched from hence, with as much convenient speede as may be made I would have you toi dispatch the pinnace for the Moloccos to the iland of Banda; and lade in her of all sortes of comodities as you can learne to' be vented there. Onelie keepe your narrowe and Mallacoe fardeles to furnish you here, as your most staple comodities to trust unto. You may lade In her some 60 fardells; the most of blewes and checkered stuffes; some fine pinthadoes and some store of corse; some of your Sian rowles, but not many; and some white cloth and some browne, and some of your stuffes that be checkered. In all theis thinges use your good judgmentes; onelie lett them be well furnished.

Alsoe lade in her 500 r[ials] of 8 att the least; for yt may chaunce they maie have neede to use some money.

The next busines that most importeth is your dispatch of your howse. Yf you could sett forward the one in dispatching the other, yt would doe very well. Onelie have this reguard in the building thies yt be as free from fire as chardge will make yt.

For the sales of your comodities, you must use your owne discretions; alwaies holdinge this in mynde, the tyme of the comeing of our shipps; and procure 20,000 bagges of pepper (as neere as you cann) to be in readynes agay[n]st their comeing. And as much money as will dispatch them here of chardges for this next accompte I will not have willinglie to be mingled with any other. If yt please God to send me home, I will wryte to you att lardge about this pointe, for yt will importe us that are ymployed in this busines. Myne opinion is to putt yourselves out of comodities as soone as you cann and putt yourselves into peppers, for in soe doinge you may chaunce to benefitt the Company in the defraying your chardges, for they shall be at above 850 li. the yeare chardge in theis partes.

When you have bought any store of pepper, yf the Holland shipps come and the prise ryse, you may take the benefit and sell to the Companies most proffitt; onelie, have a reguard not to be unfurnished at the expectation of our shipping. You have the benefitt of 2 harvestes; I doubt not but you shall furnish the next shipps in good sorte.

Alsoe, I doe appointe you, Master William Starkey, to be Head and cheefe commander over all in this place; but to take the councell and advise of Thomas Morgan and Master Scott in all matters, that the Companie may be the better assured of all thinges that passeth. And yf yt please God [to lay His hand] upon you, Master Starkey, and to take you out of this world, I would have you to give over your chardge and accomptes to Thomas Morgan. And yf you, Thomas Morgan, die, then to Master Scott. And yf you, Master Scott, then to whom you shall thinke moste meete; alwaies leaveing your thinges in the best manner you cann, and the playnest.

For such wages as shall be due to men that be here, you may allowe yt by the yeare or halfe yeare, as you see mens necessities. Allwaies have reguard that you be not necessited for want of money; lett not to have 1000 rials of 8 at the least att all tymes by you.

And for the boyes, lett them not waunt apparrell and necessaries that apperteyne unto them, for soe they shall doe you better service. Lett the cookes boye be bound for 7 yeares; and to have the freedome of London in his. tyme, accompte the 2 yeares that he hath served in our shippe.

Thus I end, desiering you to meete together in the morninges and eveninges in prayer. God, whom yee serve, shall the better blesse you in all your affaires. Thus I wish His blessing to be alwaies upon you, to preserve and keepe you, and to putt His feare in your hartes. Amen.

Forget not to husband your comodities, that there be nothinge spoyled nor come to decaye under your handes.

3. A Remembraunce for Thomas Tudd, Gabriell Towerson, William Chasse, and Thomas Dobson

As soon as the pynnace is laden by the marchauntes resident here in Bantam, of such and soe many fardells of cloothes and pyntados as they shall appointe, you shall imbarke yourselves in her and, by the helpe of Master Ketch and his company, saile directlie with your said goodes for Banda, unlesses you touch in some place necessarie for your refreshing. And make no longe staye, and have espetiall care of your saffetie and how you putt any man aland in any place, for the people in those partes, their whole bodyes and mindes be all treason; and therefore open your eyes in this behalfe.

And when God shall send you to Banda, take a howse or howses for your business, as you shall thinke most fitt for the Companies best profit, and make sale of your commodities, always advauncing the price the best you may.

In your provision you shall make in nutmegges and maces have a greate care to receive such as be good, for the smallest and rotten nutmegges be worth nothing at home; so that their fraight and principall will be lost. Of maces the fayrest and the best will be soonest sould, and to best rekoninges.

Also, be carefull to get together all the cloves you can, and use all diligence to procure some 60 or 80 tonnes att the least, and the rest of nutmegges and maces. All theis thinges must be carefullie husbanded; which you must have a spetiall reguard unto.

I make accompte the Companie will fraight some 2 shipps for that place of the burthen of 600 tonnes, more or lesse; and therefore have a care to get their ladinge in tyme and aforehand, that it may be redie by such tyme as the shipps be with you (which I hope will be Michaellmas come twelvemonneth or before). Yt doth greatlie ymporte you to be careful and procure ladinge. For this is your whole business there, and therefore ar you sent.

Alsoe, I would have you to agree together loveinglie, like sober men; for your owne discordes, yf you suppress them not, will be to the marchauntes greate losse and hindrance and to your owne undoing. Therefore governe yourselves soe that there be noe brabbles amonge you for any cause.

I have appointed Master Ketch to be an assistant to you in your business; and use him as one of yourselves, ymploying him in your business as you shall have most neede. If you send him to any place, lett yt not be farr off, and without daunger of enymies; for I would not have him farr from you, whatsoever shall befall; neither will I have that he putt himselfe in any daunger.

Alsoe, I doe appoint Thomas Tudd to be chief factor and principall, and the rest to be at his comaund in this busines. Next him I appoint Gabriell Towerson, and next Gabriell Towerson William Chasse, and next William Chasse Thomas Dobson. And you, Thomas Tudd, I would have you to take the councell of the rest in all this business, that every mans advise may be geven, to the benefitt of the voyadge.

Alsoe, my will is that, yf yt please God to call you, Thomas Tudd, out of this world, then comitt the business and your place to Master Towerson. And yf you, Gabriell Towerson, die comitt your place to William Chasse. And yf yt fortune you, William Chasse, to die, comitt the factory to Master Ketch, master of the pinnace. And yf he doe chaunce to die, lett him comitt yt to Thomas Dobson.

Alsoe, I have geven orders to the factours heare to supplie you with 500 royalls of 8, because we knowe not what neede you may have.

And have a care to your money, and dispose yt not till greate occasion serve.

And for the paying of your companie their wages, doe yt sparinglie, and remitt soe much as you can till their retourne. But when necessitie requireth, rather doe yt in comoditie then money, yf you in your discretions see such occasion.

I would have you to paie noe wages to Thomas the barber, and fitt him with clothes meete, not to exceed in any thinge, for he is another man's prentise, and seeketh onelie to wast his masters.

Alsoe, I would have you, Thomas Tudd, to keepe the accomptes of all such business as shall passe.

Per me, Thomas Tudd
Per me, Gabriell Towerson
Per me, William Chasse

Appendix VIII
Lancaster's letter from The Red Dragon 1603

Right Worshipfull, what has passed in this Voyage, and what Trades I have settled for this companie, and what other events have befallen us, you shall understand by the bearers hereof, to whom (as occasion has fallen) I must referre you. I will strive with all diligence to save my ship, and her goods, as you may perceive, by the course I take in venturing my owne life, and those that are with mee. I cannot tell where you should looke for mee, if you send out any Pinnace to seeke mee: because I live at the devotion of the wind and seas. And thus fare you well, desiring God, to send us a merrie meeting in this world, if it be his good will and pleasure.

The Passage to the East India lieth in 62 ½ degrees, by the North-west on the America side.

Your very loving friend,
JAMES LANCASTER

Appendix IX
Lancaster's 'Hints' for the EIC Third Voyage in 1607

(From the EIC Court minutes for 13th. February 1607.)

Firste, yf it please God to send your shippes to the Cape Bona Speranza in time, that is by the first of June, little more or lesse, and your people standing in health, myne opinion is that you stay not att Saldania to water or refresh, but rather hould on your course directlie for St. Lawrence,[Madagascar] and touch att the river of St. Augustine;[SW Madagascar near the Tropic of Capricorn]for theare (as I have beene crediblie informed) is as good meanes of refreshing as is att Saldania. This course will advantage you much in your navigation to the coaste of the India; beside the avoyding of fowle whether, that in that monneth commonlie is in Saldania.

Haveing thear refreshed, have a greate care of the flattes of the ilandes of Judea,[1] for many shipps have been lost thear; for the currant setteth from the coast of St. Lawrence right upon them, soe that, yf you be not very carefull to looke out night and daye, you shall feele them before you see them. Therefore, have a diligent care of this pointe; for I myselfe (having twoe very sufficient masters in my ship) was by this said currant much deceived; but that was in the monneth of September.

If by any misfortune you have further neede of refreshing, you shall fynde the ilandes of Comora. But looke to yourselves; for after their tournes are served of such things as they need, they will imploye all their wittes to betraye you in what they cann. Therefore truste no man aland; for the Flemish have lost men thrice in theis ilaunds, and I myself once.[2]

If the tyme so serve you that you cann get into Indea by the 5th. of Julie, you may (as you see cause) first touche in the mouth of the Redd Sea; for although you make your staye there till the middest of October, yet you shall have wyndes to bring you to Indea; but not longe after. But yf yt soe fall out that you see yt will be the midst of August or thereabouts ere you shall get into the Redd Sea, then I would take my course directlie for Cambaia and follow my business there; for by the 20th. December, or prime of Januarie att the furthest, yf you settle not your trade theare, the winds growe fayre to go for the Redd Sea; whither at that time yf you take your course, you shall have 3 monneths to staye, to see what you cann doe in sellinge your trades. And about April the west and norwest wyndes begynning to blowe, so that you may retourne agayne for the coast of Indea. But thinke not to touch upon the coast, for yt is exceedingly daungerous at that tyme of the yeare, and from thence till August, and therefore come not neare yt, for till August yt is fowle weather and verrie thicke and stormye upon the coaste of Indea, and the wyndes sett right upon the coaste, May, June and Julie. But theis wyndes will carrie you to Bantam; but take not too high or sowtherlie a course, for then you will hem [out] of the way of the westerne monsond, that should helpe you in this navigation. But coming to Bantam before September, you cannot go for the Molloccos, for the western monsonde reacheth but to Bantam. Therefore, as you see cause, you may touch att Pryamon, where is good pepper reasonable good cheepe, and a good ayre.

Note that, yf you touch not on the coaste of Indea before 5th. November, you cannot doe yt till August or September com twelve monneth.

Appendix X
Letter concerning the Basingstoke Lectureship, dated 17th. February 1609

From Samuel Crooke to Samuel Ward
Reproduced with corrections from B & M p. 404-5. Original is in the Bodleian Library, Tanner MSS vol 75, fol. 318

Immanuel[1]
There is a lecture lately created at Basingstoke in Hampshire by means of Sir James Lancaster[2] in Christian love and compassion to the place of his nativity (having been till this time blind with ignorance and superstition) and in zeal for the propagation of the Gospell which one Mr. Mason of Oxford[3] undertaking for a while, hath given over again and the plough now standeth still. It is a place requiring a man not only learned (even in controversies to encounter the spirit of Popery which there haunteth) but also of gravity and integrity to avoid all occasions of offence and exception; and also of meekness and affability to draw on and cherish these babes in Christ whom we shall find, or rather beget there. The maintenance assured is £50 per annum; no great bait to you I

am sure, who are not unprovided of as beneficial a place, or if you were, would not long be; but I may say with the poet, *Ajax armis non Ajaci arma petuntur*.[4] And yet I should as soon accept such a portion (upon the experience I have) as a benefice of £80. I pray you consider of this motion, and direct your answer to my brother Egerton's house in the Blackfriars; you may send your letter open to him if you will, for he entreated me to nominate some one of my acquaintance in Cambridge, to Sir James and him; and thinking you the fittest (though I have no great likelihood to prevail with you to remove) I resolved to refer it to your consideration and to the direction of God. If you incline not to accept of it yourself, yet I pray you conceal it, because I have advised my brother Egerton (in case of your refusal) to a second party. Remember to help us at your leisure with some instructions against the wicked family;[5] and write whether I may not directly send to you in Cambridge or in London. Commend me kindly to all of our Society as if I named them. The Lord be with your spirit.

    Immanuel Wrington Somerset 17th. February 1608-9
    Your very loving friend and brother in the Lord
    Samuel Crooke

Appendix XI
Some Notes on Scurvy

The disease is caused by lack of Vitamin C and it can be prevented, and cured, by feeding suitable food containing the vitamin. It appears about six weeks after the supply of suitable food has been cut off; so scurvy at sea became a serious threat as longer voyages were undertaken for discovery or trade.

The first symptoms are swelling of the gums and teeth falling out, followed by blotches on the skin, leading to lethargy and total exhaustion, and finally death.

The scientific basis for scurvy was established only in the 20th. century but practical men, and some doctors, had discovered the link between diet and the disease by trial and error many years before. It is a tragedy, and something of a mystery, that it took so long for these practical steps (both for prevention and cure) to be generally adopted. A possible explanation is that scurvy was regarded as a 'lower deck problem', (officers ate separately with their own cook and stores, and it is rare to hear of an officer contracting scurvy) and as sailors were regarded as a 'commodity', it was acceptable and less trouble simply to over-man to allow for wastage, and if scurvy broke out a stop for refreshment would be arranged. The two early commanders who took serious preventive measures against scurvy were Lancaster and Captain James Cook, both of whom had risen by merit and were well-known for their concern for the health and well-being of their entire ships' companies, officers and men.

The Chinese appear to have understood scurvy and they made appropriate arrangements to prevent it in the global 'Treasure Ship' voyages made in the early 15th. century.[1] Large stocks of citrus fruit were embarked, sufficient to supply all hands for three months. In addition the staple diet included soya beans, which were grown on board all the year round in tubs. When the beans were soaked in water, they sprouted and this process increased the content of ascorbic acid, riboflavin and nicotinic acid – the basis of vitamin C. These enlightened practices seem not to have become known to Europeans.

Longer voyages undertaken by Europeans from the late 15th. century were devastated by scurvy (as well as other epidemics like dysentery and typhoid). This was due to the victuals carried on board being based mainly on salted meat and fish, ships' biscuit and no fresh vegetables or fruit.[2] The only remedy was to make stops ashore 'to refresh' the crew with fresh provisions, and the initial manning of the ships was set at a level which would accommodate the expected deaths from scurvy.[3] Voyages badly affected by scurvy included the circumnavigation of Magellan in 1519-22; the Spanish Armada on its long voyage home; Lancaster's 1591 expedition to the East Indies;[4] Houtman's first voyage to the East in 1598, and the EIC First Fleet in 1601.[5]

The practice of refreshing crews ashore after scurvy had broken out led, by trial and error, to the discovery of what foods might effect a cure, and indeed prevent the disease:-

(i) The earliest English example described seems to be the disastrous voyage of Edward Fenton in 1582, when lemons bought in West Africa and fed to scurvy sufferers 'scoured their mouths, fastened their teeth and purified their blood'. [See Madox p. 175, 305]

(ii) A similar experience was noted at St. Helena in the course of Lancaster's 1591 Voyage. [See Foster pp. 16-17].

(iii) Sir Richard Hawkins in 1593, after stating that 'In twentie yeeres (since I have used the Sea) I dare take upon me, to give account of ten thousand men consumed with this disease' went on 'That which I have seene most fruitfull for this sicknesse, is sowre Oranges and Lemmons, and a water called Doctor Stevens water . . . '.

(iv) In the course of Cavendish's circumnavigation, in 1592, an effective cure was found to be eating a type of scurvy grass, gathered on Penguin Island in Magellan's Strait, fried with eggs. [See HV XI. 411].

(v) In November 1601, on the EIC First Fleet voyage, as scurvy was recurring (and Lancaster's original supply of lemon juice was exhausted) he and the other commanders decided to make for the Bay of Antongil (in NE Madagascar) to refresh the men with the oranges and lemons available there. These, it was recognized, would 'cleere ourselves of this disease': the description in the Apsley pamphlet was even more specific 'which is the best remedy against the scurvy'.

(vi) By 1616 on the Bylot/Baffin voyage towards the NW Passage the importance of fresh vegetables was well understood. In Cockayne's Sound (at 65 degrees N) a visit to an island produced 'scurvie-grasse, with sorrill and orpen'. The scurvy grass was taken in beer (see next paragraph) and the other two 'eaten as sallads'. The scurvy sufferers were restored to health. [See NW Voyages p. 143]

Some contribution, too, may have been made by doctors working ashore – in London in the 16th. century scurvy grass (cochlearia officinalis) was prescribed, taken in a glass of ale, and Simon Forman (1552-1611), the notorious astrologer and supposedly quack doctor, advised four spoonfuls of lemon juice twice a day.[6]

The effectiveness of citrus fruit was systematically applied by Lancaster in the Red Dragon in the EIC First Fleet voyage. His provision of lemon juice, accompanied by refraining from food in the forenoon, kept his men virtually scurvy-free and the contrast with the other ships in the fleet (all receiving basically the same victuals – apart from the lemon juice) provided a convincing scientific proof, with a much larger 'sample', than that involved in Dr. Lind's experiment 150 years later.

It is puzzling that Lancaster appears not to have followed up this demonstration on his return to England – a contrast with his ongoing advice to the subsequent EIC voyages on navigation, organization of factories and so on. It is possible, however, that he did pass on this valuable knowledge to his specialist colleague. The first surgeon-general to the

EIC was John Woodall (1556-1643), appointed in 1612.[7] Woodhall published 'The Surgeon's Mate' (First edition 1617, third edition in 1639) He describes 'the scurvy called in Latine Scorbutum', and states 'We have in our owne country here many excellent remedies generally knowne, as namely, Scurvy-grasse, Horse-Reddish roots, Nasturtia Aquatica, Wormwood, Sorrell, and many other good meanes . . . to the cure of those which live at home . . . they also helpe some Sea-men returned from afarre who by the only natural disposition of the fresh aire and amendment of diet, nature herselfe in effect doth the Cure without other helps', and goes on to say that experience at sea shows that ' the Lemmons, Limes, Tamarinds, Oranges, and other choice of good helps in the Indies . . . do farre exceed any that can be carried thither from England.'[8]

The accounts of the voyages mentioned above (of Fenton, Lancaster, Cavendish and Hawkins) were in due course available to a wider audience through the published works of Hakluyt and Purchas.

Without this experience being put to good use, the circumnavigation of Anson in 1740-4 was devastated by scurvy. As a result Dr James Lind, the Scottish surgeon in HMS Salisbury, conducted an experiment in 1747. Twelve sailors suffering from scurvy were divided into teams of two. All six teams had the same basic food but they also received supplements – one team had two oranges and one lemon daily, while the other five had apple juice, vinegar, herbs and spice, sea-water &c. The citrus team recovered completely in six days; the apple juice team showed some improvement – but not enough to resume duties, and the others showed no improvement at all. Dr Lind therefore then gave citrus fruit to the other sufferers and they all recovered.

It took the Royal Navy 48 years after Dr. Lind's experiment to introduce a compulsory lemon juice issue. in 1795. Later limes were substituted for lemons, and their use was made compulsory in all British ships.[9]

In the meantime Captain James Cook had established his own effective control of scurvy. His first voyage (1768-71) suffered severely, over 40% of the crew being lost to disease, mainly scurvy. His regime was based on diet, cleanliness (both ship and crew), ventilation below decks (portable braziers were carried round to shift foul air) and airing of bedding.[10] On diet Cook collaborated with the Admiralty Sick and Hurt Board, which supplied novel foods like sauerkraut, concentrated orange and lemon juice, meat soup extract, wort, and saloops (a hot drink). In addition he experimented with fresh plants and vegetables collected ashore in the course of the voyages, like 'wild sellerie' and scurvy grass. The natural reluctance of sailors to try unfamiliar victuals was patiently overcome by serving them to the officers. , whose example encouraged the men.[11] As a result of the new regime scurvy was practically eliminated in Cook's second and third voyages.

Appendix XII
Personal Legacies in Lancaster's Will 1618

A. Cousins[1]

1. 'To my cousin Johan Jefford £40 and to her son £50'. Jefford seems to have been a West Country name, and a number of Jeffords have been found quite close to Wrington in Somerset where the Rev. Samuel Crooke was rector. It is thought that Lancaster may have had some relationship by marriage with the Crooke family: see A 3 below.

2. 'To my cousin Amy Barker, wife of Mr. William Barker of London, Merchant £400'. This Amy may have been Lancaster's niece nee Weekes.

3. 'To my cousin Richard Crookes £30' (The spelling is not certain: it might be 'Cookes'). Richard is probably connected with Lancaster's Puritan friends Thomas and Samuel Crooke – he may have been linked to them by marriage.

4. 'To the children of my cousin Richard Yeates, late of London, deceased, £400 equally between them to be delivered to their mother to bring them up'. This Richard Yates (of a well known Basingstoke family) was the eldest son of Lancaster's sister Agnes and her husband Richard Yates.

5. 'All my household stuff to my cousin Amy Barker and my cousin Elizabeth Yeats equally', For Amy Barker see above, A2. Elizabeth was probably of the same Yates family mentioned in the previous paragraph, but the exact relationship is not known.

B. Other Legacies

1. 'To the two daughters of the son of my brother John, one married to Tho. Taylor £50, one unmarried, £66. 13s. 4d'. In the codicil to Lancaster's will the husband of James' great niece is described as 'married

to the Tailor': it seems surprising that Lancaster did not know his name – perhaps the lawyer who drew the will got confused.

2. 'To the daughter of John Lancaster married to Nicholl, a stockingman, and her children £150'

3. 'To another daughter of John Lancaster married to Crosse £80'. The Crosses were a well-known Basingstoke family.

4. 'To another daughter of John Lancaster (sometime wife of Richard Massam) and to her children £100 equally between them'. The Massams were also a well-known Basingstoke family.

5. 'To Phyllis Stringer, wife of Goodman Stringer £50'

6. 'To the two daughters of my brother-in-law Hopgood the bond of their father of £100 as yet unpaid'. It appears that Hopgood married James' sister Alice.

7. 'To my brother Peter £200 and the lease of land in ?'. Peter appears never to have married.

8. 'To Mrs. Judith Crooke, wife of Samuel Crooke of Wrington, Somerset, Clerk £50'. She was the daughter of the Rev. M. Walsh of Suffolk and she married Samuel Crooke c. 1602. James also left her his library (see below B 33). Since James seems to have known the Crookes, father and son, for some years, it seems likely that he met Judith in Suffolk before she was married.

9. 'To Mary Walsh, daughter of Mary Walsh of Wrington £30'. It seems likely that the two Marys were related to Judith Crooke nee Walsh and the Rev. M. Walsh – but it has not proved possible to work out the relationship.

10. 'To the children of my uncle William Lancaster, deceased, £30 to be divided equally'. William had three sons and two daughters but they may not all have survived until 1618 when Lancaster died.

11. 'To Widow Holland £4'

12. 'To Stephen Egerton, Clerke £4'. Egerton (?1555-1622) was a Puritan divine: he assisted Lancaster in seeking a candidate for the Basingstoke Lectureship established by Lancaster's cousin Sir James Deane in 1608.

13. 'To Widow Frog of Waldingfield £5'. Waldringfield is in Suffolk where Thomas Crooke (father of Samuel) was Rector. This legacy suggests that James may have visited Waldingfield frequently, and thus got to know other residents of the parish. The same might apply to the next four legacies, though we do not know whether they too were resident at Waldingfield.

14. 'To Goodman Trow £8'

15. 'To the daughter of Widow Allen £6'

16. 'To Goodman Heritage £3'

17. 'To Widow Hall £3'

18. 'To the five children of my aunt Izzard £100 equally between them'. She was one of the sisters of Lancaster's mother.

19. 'To Mrs. Thomasine Owlfeild of London, widow, £450 to be distributed amongst poor householders at her complete discretion'. Mrs. Owlfeild appears to have been part of Lancaster's household in London.[2] Lancaster also left her valuable chattels and the lease of his London house (see below B 31 and B 32).

20. 'To Barbara Boyle £5 for Thomasine Owlfeild'

21. 'To my servant Samuel Reynolds £30 in money and all my gowns, cloaks and other apparel'

22. 'To my servant Thomas £4'

23. 'To my other servant Nicholas £4'

24 . 'To my servant Agnes £25'

25. 'To my other maidservant Thomasine How £5'

26. 'To John Taylor, Mrs. Owlfeild's servant £26. 13s. 4d. ' .

27. 'To Mr. Samuel Crooke of Wrington £5 for a ring'. See B8 and B13 above.

28. 'To Mr. Leonard Parker £5 for a ring'. See next two paragraphs.

20. 'To. Mr. Leonard Parker for his pains as executor £120'

30. 'To Mr. Joseph Jackson for his pains as an executor £120 and £5 for a ring'

31. 'The lease of my dwelling house near St. Mary Acks and the tenement at my back gate to Mrs. Thomasine Owlfeild of London, widow' See B 19 above.

32. 'The tapestry hanging of my chamber, a china table gilt, a basin and ewer of glass and half my china dishes to Mrs. Thomasine Owlfeild'

33. 'To Mrs. Judith Crooke of Wrington, Somerset all my library or books which heretofore I have promised her'. She was the wife of Samuel Crooke, rector of Wrington

Abbreviations and Sources

BFC	*Bath Field Club Proceedings*
B & K	Brooke, C and Keir, G, *London, The Shaping of a City*, 1975
B & M	Baigent, F J and Millard, J E, *History of Basingstoke*, 1889
Beavan	Beaven, A B, *The Aldermen of London*, 1913
Bindoff	Bindoff, S T, *Tudor England*, Penguin 1950
Boxer	Boxer, C R, *The Portuguese Seaborne Empire*, Penguin 1969
CSP	Calendar of State Papers
Cook	Villiers, A, *Captain Cook, The Seamen's Seaman*, Penguin 1967
Corbett	Corbett, J S, *Drake and the Tudor Navy*, 1898
Court Minutes	Minutes of the Court of the Skinners' Company
DNB	*Dictionary of National Biography*
Davis	Markham, Clements R, *A Life of John Davis*, 1889
EEIC	Chaudhuri, K N, *The English East India Company*, 1965
EFT	Veale, E M, *The English Fur Trade*, 2nd edn. 2003
EIC	The East India Company
EL	Picard, L, *Elizabeth's London*, 2003
EPV	Andrews, K R (ed.), *English Privateering Voyages*, Hakluyt Society 1959
Epstein	Epstein, M, *Early History of the Levant Company*, 1908
FLB	Birdwood, G C M, and Foster, W (eds.), *First Letter Book of the EIC*, 1893
Forman	Cook, J, Dr. *Simon Forman*, 2001
Foster	*Voyages of Sir James Lancaster*, Hakluyt Society 1940
Fraternity	Millard, J E (ed.), *Accounts of the Wardens of the Fraternity of the Holy Ghost 1557-1654*, 1882
Frobisher	MacDermott, J, *Martin Frobisher*, 2001
GL	Guildhall Library, London
HCA	High Court of Admiralty
HECC	Bendall, S, *et al*, *History of Emmanuel College, Cambridge*, 1999
HRO	Hampshire Record Office
HV	Maclehose, J, *The Principal Navigations etc, Richard Hakluyt*, 1904
Harborne	Skilliter, S A, *Wm Harborne and the Trade with Turkey*, British Academy 1977
Hints	Lancaster's Hints for a Voyage to the East

Keay	Keay, J, *The Honourable Company*, Harper Collins, 1991
Lambert	Lambert, J J, *Records of the Skinners Company*, 1933
Laughton	Laughton, J K, *The Defeat of the Spanish Armada*,Navy Records Society 1895
Lenge	Lenge, R, *The True Description of the Last Voyage of Sir Francis Drake*, Camden Society (*Camden Miscellany* 5, 1864)
London 1568	*The Visitation of London 1568*. Harleian Society 1963
MP	*The Travels of Marco Polo*, Penguin, 1958
Madox	Donno, E S, *An Elizabethan in 1582*. Hakluyt Society, 1976
Markham	*Voyages of Sir James Lancaster*, Hakluyt Society 1877
Mattingly	Mattingly, G, *The Defeat of the Spanish Armada*, Reprint Soc. 1959
Middleton	Corney, B (ed.), *The Voyage of Sir Henry Middleton to Bantam and the Moluccas*, Hakluyt Society 1855
Milton	Milton, G, *Nathaniels's Nutmeg*, Sceptre, 1999
Monson	Monson's Naval Tracts
NW Voyages	Rundall, T, *Narratives of Voyages to the N-W*, Hakluyt Society 1849
OC	Kemp, P, *Oxford Companion to Ships and the Sea*, 1979
PCC	Prerogative Court of Canterbury
Pension Book	Pension Book of Gray's Inn
Porter	Porter, R, *London, A Social History*, Penguin 1994
Pritchard	Pritchard, R E, *Shakespeare's England*, Sutton 1991
Purveyance	Money, W (ed.), P*urveyance of the Royall Household, A Perfect Book* 1575
Raleigh	Trevelyan, R, *Sir Walter Raleigh*, Penguin 2002
RV	Quinn, D B (ed.), *The Roanoke Voyages*, Hakluyt Society 1955
S & C	Shillington, V M, and Chapman, A B W, *Commercial Relations of England and Portugal*, 1907
SPLA	List & Analysis of State Papers, Foreign Series
Scott	Scott, W R, *Joint Stock Companies to 1720*, 1912
Shaw	Shaw, W A, *The Knights of England*, 1906
Southey	Southey, R, *History of Brazil*, 1810
Stowe	Stow, J (Kingsford, C L, ed.) *Survey of London*, OUP 1908
Thomas	Thomas, D A, *The Illustrated Armada Handbook*, Harrap 1988
Thoyts	Thoyts, F W, *History of Ashe*, 1888
Tuck	Tuck, G, *Seabirds on the Ocean Routes*, 1980
VCH	*Victoria County History*
VOC	Vereenigde Oostindische Compagnie
Wadmore	Wadmore, J F, *Some Account of the Skinners' Company*, 1902
Williamson	Williamson, G C, *George, Third Earl of Cumberland*, 1920
Wood	Wood, A C, *History of the Levant Company*, 1935
1421	Menzies, G, *1421 – The Year China discovered the World*, Bantam, 2002

Notes

Introduction

1   Sometimes described as Admiral, sometimes as General.

2   The fact that he left no family in the City may itself have led to Lancaster being overlooked or forgotten.

3   2004 Edition. The previous article, written by the famous naval historian John Knox Laughton, contained a serious error, reporting that Lancaster's ship in the 1591 Voyage to the East Indies returned to England with a rich cargo, when, in fact, she was lost in the West Indies and captured by the Spanish. The new article includes the 1596 portrait of Lancaster, now in the National Maritime Museum, but it is unfortunately reversed, so that his sword is shown on his right hip and the South Atlantic on the globe has Africa to the west and Brazil to the east.

4   Foster makes several intriguing statements about Lancaster for which he provides no source, for example, he identifies his London house as the Papeye, built on the site of the redundant St. Augustine Papeye church and he states that Lancaster did not lead the second EIC voyage in 1604 because of ill health. John Keay in his *The Honourable Company, A History of the East India Company* in 1991 follows Foster's account of Lancaster's life but he makes the prescient suggestion that James may have seen further service under Drake than the literature then available was indicating.

5   e. g. family wills in the HRO; the archives of the Skinners' Company.

6   e. g. Baigent & Millard's *History of Basingstoke*, the Accounts of the Fraternity of the Holy Ghost at Basingstoke; and the literature on the North West Passage expeditions.

7   See notes 5 and 6 above. Writing in 1939-40 Sir Wiliam Foster was unable to get access to the archives of the Skinners' Company owing to WWII.

8   Analysed more fully in Appendix I.

Chapter 1

1   See Appendix I, and, for an overview of the family, the 'family trees' in Appendix II.

2   For the Crookes, see chapter 13 below, and for Mrs Owfield pp. 156-7 below.

3   His depositions in 1586 to the Admiralty Court give his age as 'around 32' and 'around 33': see HCA 13/26 3rd.June, 7th July, and there is other corroborating evidence.

4   Advice from Mrs Anne Hawker, the local historian and authority on Basingstoke land ownership.

5 Lancaster's cousin Sir James Deane also left money to it so that by 1609 it had become a 'free school'.

6 See p. 142.

7 And been published: see Fraternity.

8 See B & M p. 140.

9 As a result literacy levels in London were high, reaching 70% by the end of the 16th century.

Chapter 2

1 This section has drawn on Porter 'Tudor London' and EL.

2 See below p. 131ff.

3 See Pritchard p. 86.

4 See Porter p. 68.

5 Hence the expression 'all at sixes and sevens' to describe a muddled situation.

6 Though their monopolistic position has been criticized as restricting trade and thus as tending to inflate prices.

7 This was the only way to obtain this freedom.

8 See chart of Selected Merchants in Appendix IV.

9 Within this management group, the 'merchants' were always regarded as the 'senior branch', since it was their efforts which determined whether or not the business returned a profit.

10 While suggesting secrecy or confidentiality 'mystery' in this context is a shortened version of the latin word 'ministerium', simply meaning job or trade.

11 See EL p.205.

12 See GL Ms 31719/1 fol.148.It is possible that Freeman came from Northamptonshire.

13 See Ibid.fol.179.

14 EFT p.149.

15 EFT p.187.

16 The original portrait was for many years in the hands of the Christie-Miller family: it is discussed further below at p. 95ff.

17 See EFT p.216.

18 EFT p.25.

19 Lancaster's seond master, Robert Walkeden – see below – was living in 1582 in the parish of St.Martin Pomeroy (Ironmongers' Lane) just off Cheapside: see the 1582 Subsidy Roll, London Record Society p.191.

20 See Court Minutes for 12th July 1582.

21 See HV XI.31.

22 Searches in the Portuguese national and the Lisbon municipal records were unsuccessful.

23 See chapter 13 below.

24 He had previously been rector of Waldingfield in Suffolk – Cambridge and East Anglia were the Puritan 'heartland'.

25 When writing to Gray's Inn to recommend Thomas Crooke to be their chaplain, Lord Burghley described the Inn (his own alma mater) as 'one of the seminaries of the nobilitie and gentlemen of this realme'; See Pension Book 23rd.January 1581.

26 See GL Ms 30719/1 fol.167v}

27 See GL 30719/1 fol.233v.

28 See Court Minutes 2nd.September 1605.The Yeomanry was the general body of the members, who had not been elected to join the livery.

29 See Court Minutes 11th December 1605.

Chapter 3

1 A useful global account of the Spice Trade is provided by The American Spice Trade Association on www.astaspice. org/history.

2 Indeed the Spice Trade was the driver for most international trade throughout the 16th and 17th centuries.

3 See an interesting lecture, delivered

in its revised form in 1988, printed at www. economics. otoronto. ca/munro5/SPICES1.

4 For the Holy Ghost Guild see further p. 6ff above.

5 Guilds augmented their income by brewing ale and selling it to their members: see p. 7 above.

6 See MP p. 237.

7 Not necessarily so; see Monson I. 150, where it is argued that a merchant, like Lancaster, buying oriental spices at Lisbon for England would have made better profits that those realized by the EIC in the early days of the Company.

8 See 1421 p. 85.

9 The Bull actually drew the line 100 leagues west of the Cape Verde Islands but this was modified at Tordesillas to accommodate Brazil for Portugal.

10 These included maps from the Dieppe School and the Jean Rotz map. When Cook escaped from the Endeavour Reef he sailed directly to the only harbour, Cooktown, commenting 'it is not as large as I had been told': see 1421 p. 388.

11 The search for the Northern Passages is considered further below in chapter 14.

12 See below p. 64ff.

13 Linschoten's guide was published in the Netherlands in 1596 and translated into English in 1598: it was widely used.

Chapter 4

1 See p. 77ff below.

2 A few years earlier many English expatriate merchants married local girls, particularly in the Cadiz/Seville area.

3 The suggestion that Lancaster appeared to the Portuguese to have some connection with their Royal Family is strengthened by the facts (i) that the title 'duque de Lencastre' has been in use in Portugal down to modern times; (ii) Lencastre was (and still is) an established surname in Portugal and Brazil ('Lancastre' and 'Alancastre' are also found): I am indebted for this information to Mr Denis Paravicini who knows both countries well. The basis on which members of the Royal House of Avis have adopted the Lancaster name (and perhaps the ducal title) as a result of the marriage of Joao I to Philippa Lancaster is not altogether clear, but for present purposes this is not important. It does seem likely that Lancaster was, in Portuguese eyes, credited with 'rank' because of his surname, thus justifying the statement that, 'I have lived among them as a gentleman'.

4 Though Lancaster was trading in cloth at Seville in 1581 and in April 1582: this is hardly consistent with being persona non grata with the Spanish: see pp. 41-2 below.

5 This section draws on S & C.

6 They were settled in the districts of Cadiz, San Lucar and Seville.

7 Or even earlier. In the course of searches in the Portuguese records for traces of Lancaster, the Torre do Tombo (the National Archive) produced a pardon, granted by King Sebastian in 1578, for a young Englisman, also named James, who had been sent to Porto to learn the language and the trade at the the age of 12. His 'offence' had been wearing clothes 'above his station': see Chancelaria Filipe I. Perdoes liv. 16 fl. 18v.

8 The author of the DNB article replaced in 2004: the new article omits the point.

9 Foster identifies 'his bitter dislike of the Portuguese and his abiding sense of grievance against that nation': see Foster p. xiv.

10 Lancaster's general attitude towards

foreigners is discussed more fully below pp. 167ff.

11 'Frames' are carefully shaped following the design of the hull. They are set vertically every three or four feet along the keel, and, together, form the skeleton of the vessel to which the planks are fastened.

12 H. C. A. 13/26 7th July.

13 See above p. 39.

Chapter 5

1 See the List of Selected Merchants in Appendix IV.

2 The genesis of the Company is described below at p. 45.

3 Further discussed below at p. 45.

4 Further discussed below at p. 51.

5 Further discussed below at p. 52.

6 For the employment of these ships see the List of Selected Ships in Appendix V.

7 The Company switched to acting as a 'regulator' rather than as a principal – with trading being undertaken by individual members – around 1589: see below p. 48.

8 It was indeed a matter of a formal contract between e. g. Drake, authorized by the Queen, and the individuals acting on behalf of the merchant syndicate.

9 This is confirmed by the observations of Sir William Monson: see Monson I. 182n. 'Owners took advantage of any urgency in the demand for armed merchantmen to insist upon nominating their own officers, with the object of keeping their ships out of any serious mischief'.

10 One authority suggests that Thomas Cordell, another prominent London merchant, should share the credit with Osborne and Staper, on the ground that Hakluyt, in his 'Principal Navigations', for some reason played down Cordell's role.

11 The Charter is printed in H. V. V. 202 ff.

12 In addition he was retained as an English intelligence agent by Sir Francis Walsingham.

13 The charter is printed in H. V. VI. 73 ff.

14 See H. V. V. 465.

15 Below p. 64ff.

16 See the model illustrated above. This was built using drawings prepared by the famous shipwright Matthew Baker and measurements taken from several actual vessels: it represents a typical Royal Navy ship of the time, embodying the characteristics, described above. The 'tall ship' pattern was carried on into the East India Company ships: they were often mistaken at a distance for Royal Navy ships on account of the high aspect ratio of the sails.

17 In this context 'race' should really be 'rase' or 'raze' from the French raser – to cut or shave, indicating that the upper decks of foc's'le and poop were reduced: later, in the 18th century a 'razee' was a warship whose upper decks had been cut down.

18 He commanded her in the Armada campaign in 1588, in the 1590 privateering expedition and in his first voyage to the Indies in 1591-4 in the course of which she was wrecked in the West Indies on the way home and captured by the Spanish.

19 Most of them ended up installed in the defences of Santo Domingo: see EPV p. 285.

20 See List of Selected Merchants in Appendix IV.

21 Including the Saloman, Ascension and Centurion: see the List of Selected Ships in Appendix V.

22 See HV. VII. 31.

23 See HV. VII. 35.

24 See Foster p. xiv.

25 This is supported by the 'testimon-

ium' at the end of Hakluyt's account of Lancaster's 1591 voyage to the East 'Witnesse, Master James Lancaster' suggesting that Hakluyt had asked Lancaster to check the accuracy of the narrative.

26 See above p. 41 and n.12.

27 See H. C. A. 13/26 3rd. June.

28 See HV IX 360 ff.

29 See p. 51 above.

30 Below pp. 129-30.

31 see Lenge, Appendix, p. 26ff.

32 See below p. 57: the value of the booty is usually reckoned at £114,000 though Lenge's account gives a slightly lower figure.

Chapter 6

1 The Raid, with the movements of the ships, is illustrated by a chart drawn on the spot by William Boroughs, the Controller of the Navy: it is reproduced on p. but really needs to be studied in its full size: see HV. VI. 448. Burroughs was a capable but prickly officer 'of the old school' who criticized Drake and was court martialled at sea: the matter was, however, subsequently allowed to drop.

2 Particularly barrel staves, essential for storing victuals at sea.

3 See Corbett II. 107n.

4 See HV. VI. 438.

5 See Laughton II. 326.

6 See Monson I. 182 ff.

7 See Laughton II. 324,338. The Elizabeth Bonaventure attacked a great galleon 'most worthily'.

8 He had taken command of the 1591 Voyage to the Indies following the loss of the Admiral, and had sole command of the Recife Raid in 1594-5.

Chapter 7

1 To-day 'to purchase' means to acquire by paying an appropriate price.

In Lancaster's time, in the context of seafaring, 'purchase' meant seizing by force, so 'to make up one's voyage by purchase' meant to realize a profitable voyage by taking forcibly the ships and goods of other seafarers.

2 See EPV p.7.

3 The Lord High Admiral was personally entitled to 10% of the value of prizes.

4 See, for example, Scott II.p.84 ff.

5 For example, Sir William Monson, the Admiral and writer on Naval matters: see his remarks on the 1591 Voyage, below pp. 66-7, and on the EIC first voyage at p. 211 note 8; Robert Southey, the man of letters, criticized the Recife Raid and privateering generally: see below pp. 93-4.

6 See Henry Roberts' pamphlet, printed in Foster at p.57.

7 A similar approach may be suggested for other new/unorthodox weapons/tactics like submarines, mines, tanks, Q ships, using snipers, employing mercenaries, camouflage, deception &c. which have often been denounced as 'underhand', 'ungentlemanly', 'unsporting', 'immoral' and so on.

8 See p. 65.

9 Who was the main owner of both ships.

10 See RV p.620-2.

11 See HCA 14/27 8 October, 15 November and 5 December 1590 and 28 January 1590-1.

12 See SPLA IV.para 146.

13 An abridged account of the voyage is given below at pp. 69ff.

14 Foster suggests that Samuel Foxcroft, Lancaster's partner in privateering in the previous year, was the original captain of the Merchant Royal, but died early in the voyage: see Foster xii.

15 Only a couple of months after the

Admiralty Court hearing arising from the 1590 privateering venture.

16 See List of Merchant Ships in Appendix V.

17 See Monson IV. 182.

18 See above p. 48-9: Monson echoes Hakluyt's description of the ships 'three prime ships at that time both in greatness and goodness': see IV.182.

19 See EPV p. 156.

20 See Laughton 333.

21 See above p. 49: the Merchant Royal was also of the galleon type, but larger displacing 400 tons v. the Edward's 250/300 and carrying proportionally more crew and cannon.

22 The usual rationale was to increase the crew to (i) to have more fighting men (ii) to allow for losses from action and disease, and (iii) to have sufficient spare seamen to man the prizes taken.

23 We do not know under what instructions the disastrous expedition of Captain Benjamin Wood was dispatched in 1596, though it looks as though the aim was to trade with China: see below p. 203.

24 For a discussion of the nature of privateering see above pp. 62-3.

25 See EPV 18.

26 See Monson IV.182.

27 Foster xiii.

28 The 'Hints' are reproduced in full in Appendix IX.

29 These are treacherous shallows in the middle of the channel between Madagascar and Africa.

30 The most notable example was his refusal to abandon the rudderless Red Dragon in desperate weather conditions off the Cape in 1602.

31 Subsequently named Table Bay: the name Saldanha Bay is now attached to an enclosed bay further north up the coast of the Western Cape.

32 In the EIC first voyage in 1601 Lancaster issued rations of lemon juice,

which was effective in preventing scurvy: see below p. and Notes on Scurvy in Appendix XI.

33 The abridgement of this voyage, and that of Lancaster's other two main voyages (see below) are arranged in the form of a ship's log: this form was, incidentally, invented by John Davis, the famous navigator, who served as Fleet Pilot to Lancaster in the EIC First Fleet: see below p. 106. Explanatory notes are in square brackets. For charts illustrating the voyage (copies from facsimiles of Linschoten's charts) see pp. 70, 72, 73 and 75.

34 This was Table Bay, so named by the Dutch commander van Speilbergen in 1601, but the Portuguese name continued to be used: see Foster p. xv.

35 The 1596 Voyage by Captain Benjamin Wood, targetted at China, rather than the Spice islands, ended disastrously when all three ships were lost without trace, probably off Malaya.

36 See the Notes on Scurvy in Appendix XI.

37 In addition to Hakluyt's account of the Recife Raid there is a pamphlet by one Henry Roberts, published in London on Lancaster's return: it is discussed further below at p. 92.

38 'Pre-eminent among the commanders of the great London merchantmen': see EPV p. 284n.

39 For the attractions and use of this timber, see note 50 below.

40 See List of Selected Merchants in Appendix IV.

41 See EPV p.41.

42 It will be recalled that Lancaster commanded this ship in the 1589 Expedition to Coruna and Lisbon.

43 See EPV p.210.

44 Refer to note on p. 41 above.

45 See List of Merchant Ships in Appendix V.

46 See above p. 50.

47 It was customary to describe both the senior commander and his ship as 'Admiral'.

48 The Portuguese called the town Olinda.

49 See chart at p. 84.

50 Brazil wood (Caesalpina echinata) is supposed to have given Brazil its name. When the country was discovered in 1500 by Cabral – see above p. 30 – it was originally named Vera Cruz. Cabral sent home samples of this useful wood, and it was found to be similar to a tree already found in the East Indies (Caesalpina sappan) which, because of its colour, had been named 'bresel wood'. It provided red dye and high quality timber for cabinet making.

51 Perhaps the son was in the deputation which waited on Lancaster: see below p. 87.

52 See p. 84.

53 This may have been due to the current which flows continuously at up to two knots west from the Cape Verde Islands, and then splits with one part turning SW towards NE Brazil. Without the means of calculating longitude the fleet would have had no idea of this additional speed over the land: see 1421 p. 109.

54 Robert's pamphlet reckons 1000.

55 According to the pamplet, 'beat their watchouse about their ears'.

56 Henry Roberts has Lancaster using more heroic language 'Saint George, brave gallants, this is our owne': see Foster p. 62.

57 Once again Lancaster demonstrated his ability to turn events to advantage, strengthening his overall force and employing the Dutch and the French to station their boats in the river at night to protect the fleet against attack, particularly by fire-ships. The lessons of Cadiz and Calais had been well learned.

58 See above pp. 35ff.

59 A similar accident occurred on the first EIC voyage at Antongil in December 1601: see below p. 111.

60 See reference to James' letter to the Exchequer, arranging payment of the pension while he was away on the EIC First Fleet Voyage below at p. 107.

61 See CSP Domestic 1610 4th May. An annuity of the same amount was immediately awarded to one Martin Basill.

62 At Lisbon by 20th April 1595 and confirmed by a caravel from Pernambuco on 13th May: see SPLA V.para 274.

63 See CSP Venice 1592-1603 para 355.

64 See CSP Domestic 1595-97 p. 75.

65 See Foster pp. 52n. Roberts apparently specialized in laudatory pamphlets: he celebrated the exploits of Drake and Cavendish as well.

66 See Foster p. xxiii.

67 For example, the names of two additional backers; the recruitment of Captain Cotton; how the Dutch ships came to be at Recife.

68 Compare the attitude of the EIC promoters to the attempt to foist courtiers upon them, below p. 105.

69 See above p. 4.

70 See above p. 51.

71 See below pp. 95ff.

72 See Vol. I.364ff.

73 He was appointed Poet Laureate in 1813.

74 It seems surprising that Southey was not aware of James' later services to the EIC.

75 Compare the criticisms of privateering by Sir William Monson, noted above at p. 206 note 5.

Chapter 8

1 We have suggested – see p. 91 above – that this may indeed have been

awarded to him in recognition of his Recife exploits.

2 The National Portrait Gallery has expressed the view (in a private communication dated 9th March 2004) that Lancaster's dress is ' a little old-fashioned' relative to 1596: this would be consistent with his having then been over 20 years abroad or at sea.

3 See Appendix VI.

4 In a private communication dated 9th March 2004 the National Portrait Gallery suggested that a Flemish artist working in England would be 'very likely'.

5 In 1902 Mrs Christie Miller of Britwell Court, Burnham, Berkshire permitted J. F. Wadmore to reproduce the portrait in his History of the Skinners' Company.

6 See Foster p. xxxvi.

7 The portrait is discussed further below in relation to Lancaster's character and personality: see p. 164.

8 See below p. 158.

9 Professor J. P. Carley of York University, Toronto in a private communication to the author on 12th February 2004

10 There is no reference to it in Lancaster's will which disposes of several valuable-sounding chattels, but it appears that pictures at that time were not commonly mentioned in wills.

11 His association with the EIC commenced only four years later, when it was incorporated at the end of 1600.

12 At p. 97, probbaly recorded about 1680, some 60 years after Lancaster's death.

13 A note in The Mariners' Mirror in 1927 drew attention to Pepys' memorndum.

14 The Chancery Court also transferred the real property to Basingstoke: a fuller account is at pp. 135-6.

15 This idea was put to the Company by the present writer in December 2005 in the hope that there might be some oral tradition about the matter, but nothing has emerged.

16 The family could throw no direct light on their acquisition of the portrait in the mid-19th century (private communication from Mr Andrew Christie-Miller on 23rd. Jamuary 2004), though there is some suggestion, in the notes made by the National Maritime Museum in 1971 when they acquired it, that Lancaster's connection with the EIC had something to do with the Christie-Miller purchase. At least two members of the family had served with the EIC: see the article 'Christie Miller of Clarendon Park formerly of Britwell' in Burke's Landed Gentry.

17 Private communication from the College of Heralds 6th June 2002.

18 See Appendix I.

19 A 'mullet' is the toothed metal wheel attached to a spur: see Wadmore p. 210 reproduced on p. 155: this book was published in 1902 and on the subject of Lancaster's arms may have followed the account in B & M.

20 The church was re-built in the 1760s.

21 See B & M p. 223-4.

22 B & M p. 91.

23 B & M also reports that notes made on 20th June 1702 show a variation in the description of James' arms – ' . . . a mullet of six points pierced or'.

24 B & M p. 90.

25 The text is not clear in meaning: it appears that the four 'corner shields' were mounted on the corbels supporting the roof beams between the pillars which divide the Nave and the Aisles.

26 There is, however, on the west wall

of the church a board on which James' charitable bequests to Basingstoke (and some others) are summarized – it appears to be 18th century or perhaps older.

27 See Foster p. xxxiv. The history of the Papeye is set out by Stow (see Stow I. 146, 160) and is discussed more fully below at pp. 131-2. One of the previous occupants was the Secretary of State Sir Thomas Walsingham. For a bird's eye view see the map reproduced on p. 134.

28 The Guildhall Library has been unable to provide any corroboration.

29 See HV X 205.

30 See above p. 61.

31 See further Williamson, on which this account is based.

32 In view of his rank he did not seek letters of reprisal from the Admiralty Court but was authorised by a special patent from the Queen.

33 See Monson II. 215.

34 Though initially they had thought her too large: see Monson Ibid.

Chapter 9

1 See HV II. 288. Since the destination was China the voyage was presumably not perceived as provocative towards Spain.

2 The house had been built by his father 'Customer' Smythe, nicknamed because he was a farmer of the Customs.

3 See Scott I. 103.

4 See above pp. 31ff.

5 Some £30,000 was committed by a heavyweight civic and commercial group headed by the Lord Mayor: see NW Voyages p. 250.

6 Later the number was increased to 24.

7 See Foster p. 134n,.

8 'The merchants of London. joined together . . . a stocke of £72,000, to be employed in ships and merchandizes, for the discovery of a trade in the East-India, to bring into this realme spices and other commodities' says Purchas; but it did not escape the critical eye of Sir William Monson: 'And, moreover, his employment was as well to take by violence as to trade by sufferance, and unworthy the name of an honest design. For the hands of merchants should not be stained or polluted with theft; for in such case all people would have liberty to do the like upon them': see Monson II. 293-4. This lofty attitude seems remote from the accounts of the war at sea which have come down to us.

9 See above p. 48.

10 See above pp. 100-2.

11 He was subsequently expelled.

12 £72,000 according to Purchas.

13 See above pp. 48-9: and the List of Merchant Ships in Appendix V. The Red Dragon, as we have noted (see above p. 101), was built and equipped to Royal Navy standards.

14 See FLB p. 430.

15 Based on Purchas His Pilgrimes III. ch 3 and the Apsley pamphlet published in 1603 and written by a member of the crew of Ascension, probably a merchant: both sources are printed in Foster.

16 See above p. 91.

17 See further the Notes on Scurvy in Appendix IX.

18 See further next note below.

19 While very useful to James – who acted as his godfather when he converted to Christianity in October 1601 at the Cape – the Jewish interpreter evidently had another side to his character, since he changed religions and 'married' on a number of occasions and stole money from James in Bantam and absconded: see Foster p. 97n and p. 125.

20 Davis was a famous and competent navigator and pilot and had recently returned from a voyage to the East Indies in a Dutch ship: see further below pp.148-9. While James' worries over the cargo were obviously genuine, this gripe about Davis – which is the only reference to him in the account of the voyage – is out of character and hard to understand: one explanation which has been advanced is that the account of the voyage was written by a merchant, and merchants traditionally looked down on the seamen. It has been suggested that Davis was dissatisfied with his treatment on the First EIC voyage, and that this is why he went as pilot in 1604 with Sir Edward Michelborne 'the interloper'; see below p. 146.

21 This incident illustrates the high risk/high reward nature of privateering and provides support for Lancaster's preoccupation, in the 1591 Voyage – when he was reduced to a single ship, the Edward Bonaventure – with seeking prizes and abandoning attempts to trade.

22 She had an uneventful voyage – apart from sighting two mermaids on 13th January 1603 – called at St. Helena to refresh, and arrived in England in mid-June 1603.

23 This may have resulted from the experience in the 1591 Voyage: Lancaster was then often accompanied ashore by his faithful lieutenant Edmund Barker, and on the final occasion when they were both ashore, the crew of the Edward Bonaventure cut the cable and sailed away.

24 For the text of this historic letter see Appendix VIII.

25 The lesson was learned, and future EIC fleets received precise instruction about what to buy: see below p. 128.

26 See Appendix VII and, for another example of Lancaster's low key but masterly style, see Appendix IX where the 'Hints' – navigational guidance for ships making for India after rounding the Cape – prepared for the EIC Third Voyage, are set out.

27 There was a famous occasion in Banda in 1605 when the English – in order to emphasise the distinction – mounted a parade to celebrate the Queen's coronation (not knowing that she had died), with much display of the red and white colours of St. George: see Keay p. 31.

28 See further the Notes on Scurvy in Appendix XI.

29 On a famous occasion, when a privateering venture returned 100% in quite a short time, Raleigh commented to Lord Burghley that he could have earned more by sending his ships fishing: see Raleigh p. 157 and Ralegh's Letters p. 57.

Chapter 10

1   On 16th June 1603 the Court of the EIC noted that the Ascension had 'nowe come in to the Ryver' i. e the Thames, and they ordered 'six seates of cavass dublett and hose without pockets for six porters to be employed in the filling of the pepper'.

2   Probably from the capture of a Portuguese carrack: see Foster p. xxxiii.

3   Keay explains the make-up of the shareholders and their differing interests – some seeking a straightforward return on capital and others being more interested in supplying the fleet or re-exporting the spices brought home: see Keay p. 25ff. A modern parallel could be seen at Lloyds of London a few years ago, prior to the near collapse, between 'working names' and 'outside names'.

4   Foster p. xxxiii.

5   See Milton p. 104.

6 See Middleton, Appendix II.

7 See CSP Colonial 1513-1616 para 336.

8 'Notwithstanding any grant or charter to the contrary'.

9 See above p. 211 note 2.

10 See W. A. Shaw, *The Knights of England.*

Chapter 11

1 In elections of directors held in July 1607, 1608, 1609 and 1614 Lancaster was not included: see CSP Ibid, paras 374, 417, 448, 742.

2 See CSP Ibid para 426.

3 This is the high spot of the Skinners' year when the Master and other officers for the ensuing year were and are elected with considerable ceremony. For the invitations and the list of guests, see Court Minutes for 10th May 1605 and 10th May 1606.

4 The only deal which he failed to pull off was to exchange the Susan for a cargo of pepper with the King of Achen in June 1602: see Foster p. 132, but even this turned out for the best since pepper was acquired at better prices at Priaman and Bantam.

5 Lancaster's two executors were described as merchants and it seems possible that they were his partners in this ongoing business: see below, p. 155.

6 It was re-chartered in 1584.

7 Though they seem to have achieved the national objective of enhancing English mining and metalworking skills.

8 See below p . 153.

9 See BL Loan No. 16.

10 See discussion above pp. 99-100.

11 Mrs. Owfield was a widow at the time of Lancaster's death in 1618 and seems to have been part of his London household: her identity and relationship with Lancaster are further

considered below pp. 156ff.

12 See Stow I. 146, 160; VCH, London p. 550.

13 Sometimes 'St. Augustine on the Wall' or 'St. Augustine Pavia' – the latter being derived from Padua, indicating that it was Augustine of Hippo, not the saint of Canterbury, who was being honoured: see B & K p. 141.

14 See p. 134.

15 The actual 'Hospital' – the building housing the decayed priests – appears to have been across the street, in the angle between St. Mary Axe and Bevis Marks.

16 See Stow *op. cit.*

17 His will describes 'a tenement at my back gate'.

18 Walsingham apparently settled at Barns Elm, Surrey (the Ranelagh Club) in 1579 and died in 1590. Stow's first edition was published in 1598, so this provides some support for our suggestion that Lancaster did not acquire the Papeye in the 1590s.

19 See Appendix X.

20 See Court Minutes 15th October 1604.

21 See the Court Minutes for 10th May 1605.

22 See above p. 19.

23 See Court Minutes for 10th May 1606.

24 See CSP Colonial 1513-1616 para 356.

25 They seem to have met at least once a month, judging by the years for which the minutes have survived.

26 Which are reproduced in Appendix IX.

27 See further above pp. 129-30.

28 See CSP Ibid para 362.

29 Ibid.

30 See Middleton p. 7.

31 The Union did sail in the Fourth Voyage in 1608.

32 Ibid para 386: Rowles did command

the Union in the Fourth Voyage.
33 Ibid para 388.

Chapter 12

1 Some eight miles north of Basingstoke.
2 According to a 1771 map belonging to Basingstoke Corporation (see HRO 28 M 98/1) half the the original nucleus of the estate i. e. about 150 acres, was a rabbit and hare warren, with the rubric 'The number of young heirs growing on this estate amounts to 515'. In modern times the estate has supported a partridge shoot.
3 A small part, Abie Wood, had been sold in 1875.
4 It has not proved possible to trace the exact extent of Lancaster's original Maidenwell estate: it looks as though it was the middle one-third of the area shown on the map on p. 135.
5 In around 1720, when the Chancery Court was considering the matter, the total income from the properties was £238. 13s. 4d. and the total legacies payable £286. 13s. 4d. – a deficit of £48. However, the Skinners received an annual legacy from the estate for acting as trustee of £35, so if that is deducted the actual cash shortfall comes down to £13.
6 By 1976 the annual rent from all Lancaster's properties, after two disposals, was £18,280 while the total cost of the legacies was still £251. 13s. 4d.
7 See an interesting historical account of the estate (of which a copy is held in the Willis Museum, Basingstoke 1961. 82) produced by A. J. Stevenson, a partner in the firm of John Taylor, Stevenson & Sowerby of Louth which for many years prior to 1977 acted as Land Agent to Basingstoke Corporation: the account was printed in the *Hants & Berks Gazette* (now *The Basingstoke Gazette*).
8 There were three more fields each exceeding 100 acres.
9 Deane's will is at PCC 52 Windebank, and its provisions are conveniently transcribed in B & M p. 588 and Thoyts p. 43 (An account of an Inquisition held on Deane's will).
10 CSP Colonial 1513-1616 para 415.

Chapter 13

1 This pleasing description of the Puritans is taken from HECC.
2 See Appendix XII.
3 Quoted Bindoff pp. 227-8.
4 Burghley was also Chancellor of Cambridge University and in that capacity supported the weeding out of extreme Puritans from the colleges.
5 Court Records 20th October 1586.
6 'A singular college which, in full accordance with its founder's wishes, sent out into the nation cohorts of godly preachers, men like Samuel Crooke . . . ': HECC p. 187: the Dixie scholarships had been endowed by the will of Sir Wolstan Dixie, Master of the Skinners' Company and Lord Mayor of London.
7 'a time when the desire to die Rector of Wrington might well be strong upon him' BFC III. i. 6: resistance would have meant deprivation and perhaps imprisonment.
8 See Appendix XII.
9 See below p. 171.
10 See below p. 7.
11 See Appendix X.
12 His character is discussed more fully, below pp. 164-5.
13 By his own will in 1618 Lancaster augmented the lecturer's stipend, and directed that the lecturers should be approved by Sir Henry Wallop during his life (he died in 1624) and thereafter by Basingstoke Corporation.

14 See HEEC p. 21ff.

15 HEEC p. 185-6.

16 1572-1643: a Fellow of Emmanuel College, and subsequently of Sidney Sussex College at Cambridge (of which he became Master) he went on to become Lady Margaret Professor of Divinity at Cambridge and to hold several cathedral appointments.

17 The relevant part of the letter is in Appendix VII, reproduced, with corrections, from B & M p. 404: the original may be read at Bodleian Tanner MSS. Vol. 75 fol. 318.

18 We may doubt whether Samuel had any knowledge of Basingstoke, and it would be totally out of character for Lancaster to have described his relations and the other inhabitants of his home town in this way: we noted (see above p. 7) that the Fraternity of the Holy Ghost at Basingstoke, judging from its accounts, abandoned expenditure on Catholic images and ornaments around the end of Mary's reign, some 50 years earlier, in 1558.

19 Although it is possible that John Mason, Master of the Holy Ghost School at Basingstoke, was the first lecturer for a few months in 1608-9: see Appendix X.

Chapter 14

1 See above chapter 9.

2 See CSP Colonial March-April 1614.

3 See above pp. 31ff.

4 See 1421 p. 301ff.

5 In this instance by some 500 years.

6 And some sketches of the native inhabitants.

7 See 1421 p. 305-6. A mini Ice Age commenced about 1450, and, in the middle of the previous century 20 disastrous summers had wiped out the Viking 'Western Settlement' in Greenland.

8 See Tracts IV. 378, 382.

9 See BL Lansdowne MSS 100/4. While never printed Grenville's manuscript was annotated by Lord Burghley, so it may have been circulated amongst the influential. MacDermott who quotes Grenville (see Frobisher p. 100) suggests that he may have been emphasising the problems in order to discourage attempts from the east end of the Passage, since he himself was trying to mount an approach from the western end.

10 See Frobisher p. 153ff.

11 There is a brief, inconclusive, reference at the end of Hakluyt's account of the 1591 Voyage: 'Certaine Portugales, which we tooke' stated that they had 'discovered the coast of China to the latitude of nine and fiftie degrees, finding the sea still open to the northward; giving great hope of the north-east or north-west passage'.

12 See Davis.

13 Sanderson (1538-1638) was married to a niece of Sir Walter Ralegh and had a long and eventful career, acting as banker and backer to Ralegh – with whom he had a violent quarrel – and also backing the first English globe-maker Emery Molyneux.

14 Which he named for his constant patron, William Sanderson.

15 Davis was an expert on English Channel navigation: it was probably this service under Lord Howard of Effingham which caused Davis later to dedicate to him his classic navigation handbook 'The Seaman's Secrets'.

16 A leading privateer and a favourite of Queen Elizabeth: see above pp. 100-2.

17 It is in 65 degrees N.

18 See above pp. 63-4.

19 His circumnavigation had taken place in 1586-8.

20 Thomas Harriot, the polymath in

Sir Walter Raleigh's household, appears to have conceived the idea some years earlier, but, as with many of his outstanding innovations, Harriot failed to gain recognition because he did not 'publish'.

21 See above pp. 33-4.

22 See above pp. 117-18.

23 For the full text, see Appendix VIII. The letter starts with 'Worshipful'. This mode of address was appropriate either for an individual or for a body corporate like the EIC, but since Lancaster signs off with 'Your very loving friend, James Lancaster' it seems that this was a personal message to Sir Thomas Smythe with whom he had been working for some time. Unbeknown to Lancaster, Sir Thomas had stepped down as Governor of the EIC after Lancaster's fleet had left England, after becoming implicated in the treasonable activity of the Earl of Essex: he was eventually cleared of any offence and resumed the Governorship in July 1603.

24 See the chart on p. 147.

25 Hudson was set adrift in an open boat with his son, aged 18, the sick crewmen, the carpenter, who said that 'he would rather die with true men than live as the associate of cowards', and two other loyal sailors.

26 He was to be one of the witnesses of Lancaster's will.

27 see NW Voyages p. vi. On the chart can be found Smith Strait, Lancaster Sound, Cape Digges and Digges Island, Cockin Sound, Jones Sound, Wolstenholme Sound and Wyche's Sound (in Spitzbergen).

28 The mutineers who survived and reached England – several were killed by the Inuit – escaped punishment, their prosecution being abandoned.

29 See CSP Colonial 26th July 1612.

30 These instructions have been admired – see NW Voyages p. 81 – so it may be that Lancaster, as the only naval commander among the backers, had a hand in their preparation, particularly as they lay down how the expedition should conduct itself when it reached the 'South Sea'.

31 He in fact commanded the voyages in 1615 and 1616, which are usually named for William Baffin: see below.

32 For his voyages with Robert Bylot, see below.

33 NW Voyages p. 93.

34 See NW Voyages p. 96. Sir Thomas stated in 1614 that the EIC had contributed £300 p. a. in the last three years towards North West Passage expeditions and recommended that £200 be granted to the venture under consideration 'so that there may bee no expectation of any further supplie'.

35 NW Voyages p. 95.

36 Ironically, despite Baffin's doubts, Lancaster Sound does in fact open to a NW Passage – a fitting memorial to the subject of this book: see the photograph on the back cover.

37 We have already noted – see p. 145 above – the very long odds against the commercial viability of a North West Passage, if one was ever discovered.

38 See above p. 145.

Chapter 15

1 See CSP Domestic 4th May 1610.

2 See Beavan p. 116.

3 See Beavan p. xliv.

4 It is difficult to make precise comparisons, since dates of birth for most aldermen in the 1600-20 period are not available, but it looks as though the majority were first elected around the age of 50.

5 See above pp. 100-2.

6 We do not discover whether in fact he had retained it: a copy is printed in Foster p. 159.

7 CSP Colonial 1513-1616 paras 706, 709.

8 CSP Colonial 1617-21 para 198.

9 CSR Ibid. paras 176, 194, 208, 216.

Chapter 16

1 PCC. 65 Meade: there is a codicil dated 4th June 1618 increasing some of the legacies. Most of the provisions are conveniently transcribed in Wadmore p. 211ff.

2 That is the Maidenwell estate, the Pamber farm and the Kent rentcharge.

3 At that time it was still the practice not to rely on a will alone to dispose of real property on death. Later the three transferred the property to the Skinners' Company which was appointed trustee of the will. All three trustees were Masters of the Skinners' Company: Wyche and Bateman were also original members of the EIC.

4 As mentioned above Wyche was also appointed one of the trustees of Lancaster's real property.

5 See further below.

6 See Beavan I. 37. He may have been the same man as a Roger Afield who was an original member of the Barbary Company in 1585.

7 See minutes for 21st. November 1608; 26th June and 25th September 1609.

8 See CSP Colonial 4th November 1614.

9 This ceased when the Court of Chancery removed the Skinners' Company and substituted Basingstoke Corporation in 1713.

10 These have already been included in the figures mentioned above.

Chapter 17

1 The National Portrait Gallery commented that, in relation to the 1596 date of the portrait, his dress is 'a little old-fashioned': private communication 9th March 2004 This would tie in with the facts that Lancaster had been abroad or at sea almost continuously for the previous 22 years and that, by character, he was modest and 'understated'.

2 Globes were a common feature of portraits at that time, but the clear delineation here of the South Atlantic and Brazil suggests a specific reference to Recife rather than symbolizing world domination.

3 An interesting comparison may be made with the only surviving portrait of Martin Frobisher: see Frobisher, facing p. 272. We see the 16th century equivalent of a Wild West gunman, with his hands on or near his weapons, about to attack.

4 See above p. 128.

5 See above p. 141 in connection with the Puritans.

6 Referring to the Recife Raid 'God be thanked, who was always with us, and our best defense in this voyage; by whose assistance we performed this so great an attempt with so small forces'.

7 Sharif strictly describes a descendant of the Prophet, but the title may simply indicate a religious leader .

8 See Foster p. 96. It seems that he was the 'siddy' or sayyid – strictly speaking, again, a descendant of the Prophet, but perhaps merely a title indicating respect.

9 So Foster p. 122n.

10 October 1601: Apsley's account: see Foster p. 124. The interpreter turned out, incidentally, to be a serial proselyte and bigamist, who eventually stole money from Lancaster and absconded: see Foster p. 97n., but in the meantime he seems to have been very useful.

11 See Markham p. ix.

12 See above pp. 114-15.

13 See Appendix VII; Foster p 161ff.

14 e. g. Saldania (Cape) and Antongil in the EIC First Voyage.

15 See above pp. 35-6.

16 The force, as it eventually developed, engaged in the Recife Raid, was a model of multi-national cooperation. It was a tragedy that the initial friendly relations between English and Dutch in Indonesia, under pressure of commercial rivalry and driven by the militaristic policy laid down by the VOC, descended into hostility and, eventually, into extreme brutality.

17 He undoubtedly set the tone, and, in so doing, was following the official EIC policy, in formulating which he no doubt had a hand.

18 It has to be admitted that not all Englishmen were as open-minded, and the Dutch were inclined to be aggressive and heavy handed with the native people they encountered: cf. Houtman's first voyage, considered above at pp. 148-9. The ferocity of the Dutch tended to rub off onto the English to the latter's disadvantage, since no doubt all northern Europeans looked the same to native Indonesians.

19 See Hints, Appendix IX.

20 See 1591 Voyage, above p. 71. James had 32 men killed by them.

21 1591 Voyage.

22 See above pp. 35-6.

23 See Appendix VII.

24 This might have been more difficult for an Englishman 'of rank'.

25 For which there seem to be special explanations: see above p. 68.

26 Lancaster's principal servant Samuel Reynolds received '£30 in money and all my gowns, cloaks and other apparel'. Of the others Thomas received £4, Nicholas £4, Thomasine How £5, but Agnes received £25: see Appendix X.

27 See Appendix XII paras. B 8, B33.

28 A more prosaic explanation of Lancaster's generosity on this occasion may be a link through marriage between his family and the Walsh family.

Chapter 18

1 See Frobisher, passim.

2 For the present writer his North Hampshire origins and connections are an additional interest.

Appendix I

1 ODNB, Foster (His introduction has valuable biographical material), Keay and Wadmore.

2 One of the three or four 'open fields' which were farmed collectively by the men of Basingstoke.

3 See map inside front cover.

4 Referred to in this book as 'B & M'.

5 As we will discover these two Lancasters were brothers. From other sources there are suggestions of one or two other contemporary Lancasters, either brothers or cousins, who might be assigned to The First Generation. These additional Lancasters are associated with communities close to Basingstoke, namely Odiham, Kingsclere and Overton: see the map inside front cover.

6 Doubt arises only because Richard did not refer to John in his will: there might have been a quarrel, since in 1539 a relief was paid to John for certain lands alienated by Richard: see B & M 329: by 1541 John was paying rent for 'Skydmore's' – which looks very much like the land that Richard had held – perhaps John had come to some arrangements with his siblings.

7 In the 1504 mention Hugh Lancaster was stabbed by one John Justice: see B & M 310 – perhaps a

quarrel between a local man and a newcomer to the area.

8 These are the wills (and inventories) for Elizabeth Lancaster (nee Seagrave or Seagrove), James Lancaster's mother 1581 BO68; Thomas Seagrove, his father-in-law 1562A49; Hugh Lancaster, his paternal grandfather 1525 B09; Richard Lancaster, his great uncle 1522 B14; William Lancaster, probably his uncle 1583 B51; John Lancaster of Overton (possibly his first cousin, once removed) 1562 P4 and Richard Yate, whose second son (also Richard) married one of James Lancaster's sisters 1559U/227/1.

9 The modern meaning of 'draper'– a retailer of cloth articles – came later. The Lancaster brothers were, with other drapers, fined 4d. each in 1516, presumably for producing sub-standard cloth; see B & M 319.

10 In 1523 Hugh paid a 'subsidy' (tax) of £1 on his goods: see B & M 396.

11 In identifying and locating the properties referred to in this Appendix I have had considerable help from the Basingstoke local historian, Mrs. Anne Hawker: for ease of reference, see the town plan on p. 5.

12 See B & M 312.

13 In 1521: see B & M 325.

14 See the picture on the next page.

15 Information from Mrs. Anne Hawker.

16 Sec above p. 178 and note 6.

17 B & M 383: in 1509-10 it comprised a messuage, garden adjoinging and 3 acres of land.

18 This is deduced by Mrs Hawker from the sale of part of the property in 1803 to the Navigation Company for constructing the dock of the Basingstoke Canal – it was subsequently converted into the Bus Station.

19 B & M 385.

20 The chapel was associated with the Guild of the Holy Ghost – further considered at pp. 6ff – which organized the boys' school in Basingstoke.

21 Probably Donte's and Heyron's.

22 The traditional meaning for a mercer is a dealer in superior textile fabrics i. e. not woollen cloth, but this may not apply here: he is also described as mercator (merchant) and salsamentarius (fishmonger), and seems also to have had some connection with baking; see B & M 333, 341 and Thomas Seagrove's inventory, which includes a 'fishboard': see the reference in note 8 above.

23 B & M 385.

24 See B & M 210. This was one of the three or four 'open fields' farmed on a co-operative basis by the men of Basingstoke.

25 See p. 7: on the same occasion, William, probably James' uncle, contributed 12d.

26 Peter seems to have been about five years junior to James, since he was apprenticed that much later.

27 See pp. 18ff.

28 See p. 178 and note 6 above.

29 See B & M 331: this means that he was responsible for ten families in the local government system.

30 See B & M 385: as the amount of the rent suggests, Skydmore's was a large holding, comprising three houses and several parcels of land in Basingstoke: it also looks to be part of the land held by his father, Richard, suggesting that John had made some arrangement with his siblings to vary their father's will.

31 See B & M 206: this was another of the Basingstoke 'open fields'.

32 See B & M 341.

33 Information from Mrs. Anne Hawker; and see picture on p. 179.

34 See his will and inventory and also

B & M 333. He paid 'subsidies' (taxes) of £20 in 1559, a substantial sum: see B & M 398.,

35 A Christopher Lancaster died at Kingsclere in 1628 i. e. 10 years after James' death – perhaps a son of the elusive William(s) – and there may well have been other Lancasters there.

36 To benefit if there were no children or further issue of the testator surviving.

37 In the 16th century 'cousin' did not mean 'first cousin': it was vaguer, perhaps equivalent to 'kinsman', and might extend to a relation by marriage.

38 See Purveyance p. 74.

39 See MS. Harleian 1544 Folios 78-9 & 173.

40 In 1559-60 the subsidies (taxes) were, for James' father 40/- in respect of land, and, for William Lancaster £5 in respect of his goods: see B & M 398.

41 Though he did buy a farm near Pamber and Little London, five miles to the north of the town, in 1608, perhaps to install a kinsman.,

42 Though John Lancaster, probably a son of Richard, was elected a 'tithingman', as mentioned above

43 Although both James' father and his uncle William contributed in 1557 to the costs of re-establishing the Guild after it had been 'dissolved' under Reformation legislation: see p. 7.

44 see B & M 461.

Appendix IX

1   Baixos da Judia was the Portuguese name: 'Judia' seems to have become 'India' on English charts, so they are often called Bassas da India. They are midway between Madagascar and Africa in about 21½ degrees S.

2   In the 1591 Voyage: see p. 71. The Comoros Islands are between Madagascar and Africa in about 12 degrees S.

Appendix X

1   The opening lines deal with a number of matters – the difficulty in finding the Rev. Ward's address, he seems to have been abroad, his resignation from his fellowship at Emmanuel College, the Rev. Samuel Crooke and his wife send their best wishes, as does Mr. Chetwynd &c.

2   Actually by the will of Sir James Deane, though Lancaster was charged, during his life, with the selection of the lecturers.

3   B & M suggest that this may refer to John Mason who was master of the Holy Ghost School 1608-39. He could not have acted for very long, as Sir James Deane only died in May 1608.

4   The quotation is from Ovid: B & M translate and explain 'An Ajax is sought for the armour, not armour for Ajax' i.e. What we want is a man for the place, not a place for the man: see B & M p. 405n.

5   B & M comment, We are unable to explain this reference.

Appendix XI

1   See 1421 p. 65.

2   It seems that, even in those days, the French, Spanish, Portuguese, Italians and Dutch sometimes managed to improve diet at sea, for example, with freshly baked bread, preserved sardines and anchovies, dried codfish, rice, powdered tomatoes, olive oil, garlic, raw and preserved herring and eels, cheese and sausages; but the English seem not to have tried: see Cook p. 122.

3   And from other illnesses and from battle.

4   Leading to the sending home from

the Cape of the Merchant Royal; see above p. 69.

5   At least in the ships which did not follow Lancaster's provision of lemon juice: see above pp. 107-8.

6   See EL p. 94. It seems that Forman's poor reputation – probably generated by jealous fellow physicians – is overdue for revision: see Forman, *passim*.

7   He had started as a military surgeon.

8   See www. mc. vanderbilt. edu.

9   Hence 'limeys' as a description by Americans of English sailors and, eventually, of all Englishmen. Limes, incidentally, turned out to be only half as effective as lemons.

10 See Cook p. 125.

11 And on one occasion only he had to resort to the lash, when a sailor and a marine refused the novel diet: see Cook p. 126.

Appendix XII

1   See discussion above on pp. 4-5.

2   See discussion above on pp. 156-7.

Index

Page references in **bold type** indicate the main treatment of the topic. Page references in *italic type* indicate an illustration or map.

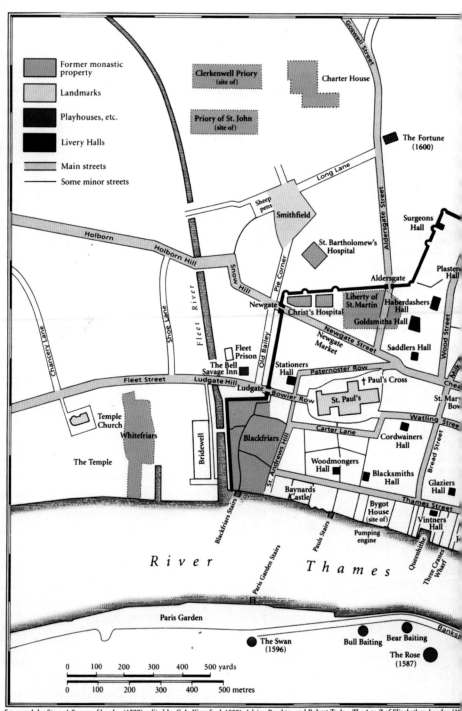

Former monastic property

Landmarks

Playhouses, etc.

Livery Halls

Main streets

Some minor streets

Clerkenwell Priory
(site of)

Charter House

Priory of St. John
(site of)

Goswell Street

The Fortune
(1600)

Long Lane

Sheep Pens

Smithfield

Surgeons Hall

Aldersgate Street

Holborn

Holborn Hill

Snow Hill

St. Bartholomew's Hospital

Plaster Hall

Aldersgate

Shoe Lane

Pie Corner

Newgate

Liberty of St. Martin

Haberdashers Hall

Chancery Lane

Fleet River

Christ's Hospital

Goldsmiths Hall

Wood Street

Fleet Prison

Old Bailey

Newgate Street
Newgate Market

Saddlers Hall

The Bell Savage Inn

Stationers Hall

Paternoster Row

Ches

Fleet Street

Ludgate Hill

Ludgate

† Paul's Cross

St. Mary Bow

Temple Church

Bowier Row

St. Paul's

Whitefriars

Bridewell

Blackfriars

St. Andrew's Hill

Carter Lane

Watling Street

Cordwainers Hall

Bread Street

The Temple

Woodmongers Hall

Blacksmiths Hall

Glaziers Hall

Baynards Castle

Bygot House
(site of)

Thames Street

Blackfriars Stairs

Pumping engine

Vintners Hall

Queenhithe

Three Cranes Wharf

Pauls Stairs

River

Thames

Paris Garden Stairs

Banks

Paris Garden

The Swan
(1596)

Bull Baiting

Bear Baiting

The Rose
(1587)

| 0 | 100 | 200 | 300 | 400 | 500 yards |

| 0 | 100 | 200 | 300 | 400 | 500 metres |

Sources: John Stow, *A Survey of London* (1598); edited by C. L. Kingsford, 1908), Adrian Prockter and Robert Taylor, *The A to Z of Elizabethan London* (19 and Andrew Gurr, *The Shakespearian Stage, 1574-1642* (1980). John Gilkes delineavit 2003.

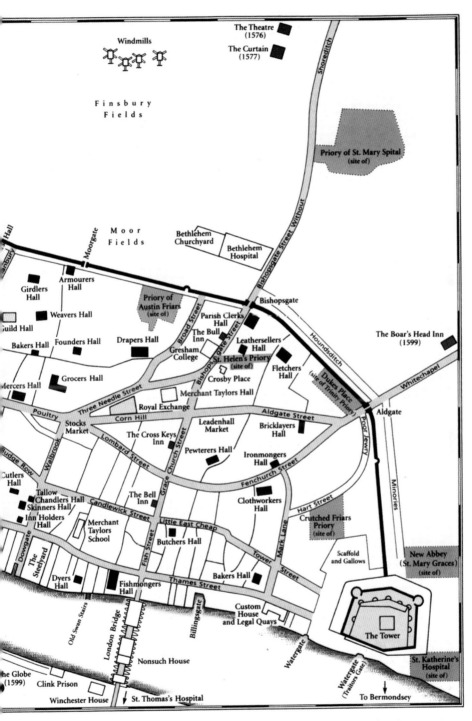

Map of London from Elizabeth's London, *by L. Picard, 2003, reproduced with permission*